Developing Educators for The Digital Age: A Framework for Capturing Knowledge in Action

Paul Breen

University of Westminster Press
www.uwestminsterpress.co.uk

Competing interests

The author declares that he has no competing interests in publishing this book.

Published by
University of Westminster Press
115 New Cavendish Street
London W1W 6XH
www.uwestminsterpress.co.uk

First published 2018

Cover design: Diana Jarvis

Printed and bound by CPI Group (UK) Ltd, Croydon, CR0 4YY
Print and digital versions typeset by Siliconchips Services Ltd.

ISBN (Paperback) 978-1-911534-68-6
ISBN (PDF): 978-1-911534-69-3
ISBN (EPUB): 978-1-911534-66-2
ISBN (Kindle): 978-1-911534-67-9

DOI: https://doi.org/10.16997/book13

The full text of this book has been peer-reviewed to ensure high academic
standards. For full review policies, see: http://www.uwestminsterpress.co.uk/
site/publish/

Suggested citation:
Breen, P. 2018. *Developing Educators for the Digital Age: A Framework for
Capturing Knowledge in Action*. London: University of Westminster Press.
DOI: https://doi.org/10.16997/book13
License: CC-BY-NC-ND 4.0

To read the free, open access version of this book
online, visit https://doi.org/10.16997/book13 or
scan this QR code with your mobile device: 

Contents

List of Figures and Appendices

Thanks and Acknowledgements

'To know fully even one field or one land is a lifetime's experience. In the world of poetic experience it is depth that counts, not width.'
— **Patrick Kavanagh, 'The Parish and the Universe'**

I would like to firstly thank the friends (now) and colleagues (then) who participated in the teacher education workshops, and freely gave their time for focus group sessions, interviews, and observations. You have all been given pseudonyms for the purposes of completing a PhD and writing this book so forgive me, if in the future, I call you Harry, Kelly, Matthew, Rosemary, Emily, Derek, Frank, James and Patricia back in the world outside of research. Your contribution to knowledge in the field of EAP and teacher development is one that will hopefully be recognised and appreciated for many years to come.

I would also like to thank those in the broader language centre of INTO UEA London, and the organisation as a whole for providing the opportunity to conduct a study such as this. Similar thanks to all at the University of Manchester and to my parents for the use of their holiday home in Bundoran as a writing retreat. Additionally, I express gratitude to my wife Sarah, my PhD supervisors Gary and Diane, and then Magdalena and Achilleas, my fellow graduates of the University of Manchester with whom I have established lasting friendships and an international community of practice.

In more recent times I have cause to be thankful for the tireless efforts of my editorial team at University of Westminster Press, particularly Andrew Lockett for his sharp advice, Dr Terry Lamb for his mastery at feedback, and those who reviewed the work anonymously. I also thank Dr Alex Ding for his advice along the way, both formally and informally. Further to this, I thank my colleagues in the Westminster Professional Language Centre, particularly Doctor Julio Gimenez, head of department, and Jayne Pearson whose assistance has been invaluable in helping me to manage courses and facilitating time for research. Finally, I give mention to Paul Anderson, a friend of mine who would never have expected a dedication in a work such as this, preferring comedy, fiction or football, but who sadly passed away unexpectedly in the week in which this book was being finalised.

CHAPTER I

Building Knowledge: Foundations

1.1 – Contextualisation

EAP – The chameleon discipline

English for Academic Purposes (EAP) practitioners occupy a unique space within higher education that is sometimes perceived as 'operating at the margins of academia' (Ding & Bruce, 2017, p. 204). Partially, this is to do with the socio-political contexts within which EAP occurs and the historical tendency to frame the subject as part of a service to other departments rather than a discipline in its own right. Thus, within higher education, EAP tends to be framed in terms of its economic rather than academic contribution. Other academics sometimes view the primary purpose as being remedial language work. Within university language centres I have experienced colleagues in other departments refer to Academic English as 'the teaching of apostrophes' and 'the boring stuff we don't have time to do.' Such views are generally shaped by a lack of knowledge not just of what happens in our classrooms, but also of the growing body of work, in the form of books, research articles, and monographs, that has attempted to define and theorise EAP as a discipline. Above all, though, there seems to be a lack of understanding about the major contribution that both EAP practice and EAP practitioners can make to pedagogic knowledge and approaches in contemporary higher education.

For decades, EAP practitioners have played a critical part in the life of universities while standing apart from what are considered more mainstream disciplines. This is partly due to the nature of the subject, which Liz Hamp-Lyons (2011, p. 89) describes as an 'eclectic and pragmatic discipline', often needing to adapt to circumstances in order to survive. This latter scenario has given EAP some of the characteristics of an academic chameleon. However, this is not simply related to the fact of so frequently having to change its colour according

---

How to cite this book chapter:
Breen, P. 2018. *Developing Educators for The Digital Age: A Framework for Capturing Knowledge in Action.* Pp. 1–20. London: University of Westminster Press.
DOI: https://doi.org/10.16997/book13.a. License: CC-BY-NC-ND 4.0

to needs and background context. Despite being most commonly associated with camouflage, the chameleon's name actually translates from the Greek term for '*lion of the ground*.'

Perhaps this meaning, a calque from the now-extinct Akkadian language, encapsulates what it is that makes English for Academic Purposes, and the teaching of it, unique. As a subject, EAP is very much grounded in real, everyday practice shaped around the needs of students and their particular disciplines as well as the broader socio-political and economic contexts in which today's universities operate. The comparison with a chameleon is appropriate because there is much more to this subject than might first of all meet the eye, and far more than the teaching of apostrophes. EAP is a relatively young subject 'emerging as an entity distinct from English Language Teaching (ELT) in the 1960s' with the first usage of the name occurring in the 1970s (Alexander, 2010, p. 2). Originally EAP was a branch of English for Specific Purposes (Jordan, 2002, p. 73) but it has gradually evolved to become a subject in its own right, due to the numbers of international students now coming to English-speaking countries to study within higher education. Hamp-Lyons (2011, p. 92) claims that this is a consequence of 'the gradual growth of English as the leading language for the dissemination of academic knowledge.' Today, in the United Kingdom and other native English-speaking countries, thousands of international students undertake courses in EAP, either as foundational programmes before their degree studies or concurrently with content study (Gilbert, 2013, p. 119).

Alongside the growth of EAP as a subject, there has been a parallel drive towards professionalism in the conceptualisation and delivery of the subject, especially through the work of such groups as BALEAP in the United Kingdom, and other professional networks of EAP practitioners based overseas. The organisation known as BALEAP began life in 1972 as SELMOUS, a network of practitioners developing Special English Language Materials for Overseas University Students (Jordan, 2002, pp. 69–71). This group at the outset mainly concerned itself with 'pre-sessional courses, research projects, and English tests' (ibid, p. 70) and sought to establish a community of practice based on the principle that 'small is beautiful' and that 'a small group could get to know each other well' (ibid, p. 71). Over time, though, the network expanded and in 1989 changed its name to BALEAP as an acronym for British Association of Lecturers in English for Academic Purposes, as part of 'an increase in professionalism' which was attained through the formalisation of a Code of Practice and introduction of an Accreditation Scheme (ibid, p. 73). These documents are still recognised as providing critical guidance for EAP practice in the UK and further afield, with BALEAP now recognised as a title in its own right rather than an acronym.

The origins of EAP instruction generally had 'a dual focus of helping students to develop both the language competency and study skills which will help them to succeed' in the two main broad types of EAP teaching scenario (Gilbert,

2013, p. 120). These are labelled as EGAP *(English for General Academic Purposes)* and ESAP *(English for Specific Academic Purposes)*, and are primarily differentiated by increased emphasis on subject-specific tasks in the latter compared to general skills work in the former (Blue, 1998, p. 41). However, contemporary monographs have charted the radical developments within the subject in the present century, as in the work of Douglas Bell (2016, p. 3) who speaks of EAP as a contested field that now stands at a 'crossroads' in terms of assuming its rightful position as a recognised academic discipline whilst facing a number of existential challenges. One of the key challenges that he details is the lack of teacher development at the same time as the subject is reaching maturity in terms of its knowledge base.

Increasingly, the methodology and theory of teaching EAP has taken precedence over micro-techniques in the classroom (Watson-Todd, 2003, p. 149; Alexander, 2010, p. 5), but not to the detriment of an emphasis on developing better pedagogic approaches inside and outside the classroom. The increasing emphasis on theory and methodology has simultaneously sparked discussions about criticality, as in the seminal work of Sarah Benesch (2001), and the role of EAP in helping students navigate their way to the formation of a social identity that is not pre-determined or shaped exclusively by the environment in which they are studying (Bhatia, 2004).

Hamp-Lyons (2011, p. 89) argues that the subject has shifted towards incorporating 'the linguistic, sociolinguistic, and psycholinguistic description of English as it occurs in the contexts of academic study and scholarly exchange'. Greater attention has also been paid to the Teaching of English for Academic Purposes from both practical and theoretical perspectives (Watson-Todd, 2003; Alexander, 2010). This has been defined as a 'leap into TEAP' by Kirk (2012), who contends that for this to become consolidated, there has to be a shift in EAP teaching philosophy as well as teaching practice. Contemporary research also calls for deeper understanding of transformative and ideological roles that EAP practitioners play within both the individual classroom and the wider higher educational context (Ding & Bruce, 2017, p. 120). Furthermore, a contemporary strain of thought within EAP is that there is a need for increased awareness of social and political contexts in today's global-facing, sometimes neoliberal UK universities (Jenkins, 2013; Hadley, 2014; Pennycook, 2017).

However, despite the increasing theoretical depth to the field and the struggle of its practitioners to find a settled identity within the academy, those outside of EAP do not always view our chameleon subject's colours in the same light as we see ourselves. Sometimes our community of practice can seem 'hermetically sealed' off from the rest of the academy, as argued by Ding & Bruce (2017, p. 10). This suggestion echoes Lincoln & Denzin's (2003, p. 6) reference to higher education as the place of 'an intellectual priesthood' (Knorr-Cetina, 1981) trading knowledge 'principally among themselves.' Hamp-Lyons (2011, p. 91) has also spoken of EAP as being the 'poor relation' of more 'specific' subjects in higher education, whilst Macallister & Kirk (2013) lament the subject's lack of a consistent home within British universities. One means of ameliorating this situation has been a greater demand amongst EAP theorists to incorporate a disciplinary focus, which entails 'grounding instruction in an understanding of the cognitive, social and linguistic demands of specific academic disciplines' (Hyland & Hamp-Lyons, 2002, p. 2). These range from 'hard' to 'soft' disciplines as described by Borg (2006, p. 4) wherein 'hard disciplines such as Physics and Engineering emphasise cognitive goals such as learning facts while soft areas such as Humanities and Education focus more on general knowledge, character development, and effective thinking skills.'

In most British universities, within the past decade, there has been increased acceptance of the role that English for Academic Purposes can play in preparing students for specific disciplinary study. There is now almost universal acceptance of the need for in-sessional Academic English provision that specifically addresses the particular subject requirements of students. Ideally, though, this has to be conceived in a way that raises course provision above the level of what Raimes (1991, p. 243) defined as 'a butler stance' in which language courses are 'in service of the larger academic community.' In practice, this means that if the EAP teacher were to be tasked with helping Media students to write essays on a TV series such as *Game of Thrones*, their contribution would be limited to remedying structure and language. Ding & Bruce (2017, p. 9) describe this as providing 'technical support' for other subjects rather than allowing EAP to operate as a subject in its own right.

In a conceptualisation of EAP that goes beyond Raimes' 'butler stance' (1991), the EAP practitioner uses their linguistic and pedagogic expertise to help students critically unpack the discourse and practices of other disciplines, as envisioned by Hyland & Hamp-Lyons (2002) and Hyland (2003; 2006) with their demand for a shift towards academic literacies. Here, the students are not served by the EAP teacher helping to polish up their work in the manner of shoeshine attendants at airports. Rather, in this model of disciplinary partnership and attainment of academic literacy, the EAP practitioner is helping to steer students not just towards language competence but also the criticality, creativity, and questioning that is needed to find their own academic voice. Drawing on their personal and communal experience of moving in from the margins, EAP teachers can scaffold students towards membership of the academic community, and the broader society of which that is a part. Hyland's (2003) position then is that student writers need to understand much more than a decontexualised sense of 'how' texts are written and to have an awareness of broader social practices in their field, so that they are active in not just replicating ideas but also creating their own.

This would mean that in the *Game of Thrones* example, a student with an interest in post-structural feminism might get assistance from the EAP teacher in unpacking 'substantive and syntactic structures' giving shape to this theoretical perspective (Shulman, 1986, p. 9). Then they would be given guidance in applying knowledge from this to the practical act of writing an essay in their specific discipline of Media Studies, using language, sources of information and ideas appropriate for the task. In the *Game of Thrones* situation, they might use their guided learning to challenge concepts of strong female characters as being those who exhibit traditionally male characteristics, and then relate the fictional context to a real issue such as the ways that women in politics are portrayed in the contemporary media. The practice and pedagogy behind the activation of this type of learning is certainly far from being merely 'a few hours of fixing up grammar in the language centre' (Hyland & Hamp-Lyons, 2002, p. 9). Furthermore, a considerable amount of linguistic and critical expertise is needed in EAP teaching and this is why so many leading thinkers within the profession place such emphasis upon the need for teacher development (Bell, 2016).

Despite this, stereotypical views of EAP are embedded and maybe even fossilised within the context of higher education, and often openly voiced in staff rooms or encounters with disciplinary colleagues at photocopiers. My belief is that such perceptions will only disappear at a point where the pedagogy of what we do as EAP practitioners is prioritised over technical aspects, including the one that lies at the very heart of our practice. So long as the label of English teacher is used to define us by our colleagues in the wider university, we will never earn the respect accorded to those who are seen as experts in a more specific subject. Even though EAP has 'come of age as an independent academic field' (Hamp-Lyons, 2011, p. 100) there remains a lack of a single, formal qualification in the subject (BALEAP, 2008). This adds to the difficulties for those within the wider domain of higher education understanding who we are and what we do as practitioners. Even our route into higher education is often very different to those around us who generally get into university teaching courtesy of holding a PhD or coming from a research background.

The professional habitat of EAP

Most of those who end up in the chameleon world of EAP teaching have found their way there through studying Education or Linguistics at university, navigating an escape from private language schools, or making return journeys from places sometimes as remote as the forests of Madagascar. There are, though, several dangerous myths spawned by the last of these scenarios. Firstly and categorically, not everyone who teaches EAP spent hedonistic years in Asia picking up girls and getting drunk on the basis of qualifications earned along Bangkok's notorious Khao San Road. Secondly, this is not a fallback option for failed authors, actors, and amateur musicians. Thirdly, the profession entails far more knowledge, skills, and qualifications than it takes to simply teach somebody how to speak in your own native language. And lastly it bears little resemblance to the classrooms of such shows as the 1970s ITV sitcom *Mind Your Language*, which again peddles stereotypes of simplistic lessons in broken

English, albeit acted out for the purposes of comedy rather than social commentary. For the majority of long-term EAP teachers, the job is as much of a vocation as the practice of any other craft or the teaching of any more traditional subject in universities.

Persistently, EAP suffers from the perception that it is a subject which requires little more than a teaching certificate, a few years' experience abroad, and the good fortune of knowing somebody in a university. For some teachers, generally those with minimal to zero professional development along the way, that is the reality created by the economic and employment practices of today's universities. However, key figures within the profession recognise that there is a need to pay greater attention to staff development, as exemplified by Olwyn Alexander's (2010, p. 6) call for a 'shared understanding of what is involved in teaching EAP and a more rigorous approach to teacher recruitment, induction and professional development, especially for novice teachers and teacher educators.'

Of course, reaching a shared level of understanding is a monumental task since the very issue of qualification could become agenda-laden, and end up as nothing more than another revenue stream in a profession already certified to the tail-bone. The qualifications required to be an English Language teacher are as specific as those expected of any other vocational path. However, unlike in professional fields such as Accountancy, Medicine, and Law, many people do not enter the world of ELT with the intention of being a permanent member of its community. Some people become English teachers out of a desire to travel and see the world or as a means of paying the bills whilst they study, or decide what they really wish to do with their lives. Many of these people work in the private language school industry *(where there are minimal employment rights)*, on the basis of having a Bachelor degree and a *Certificate of English Language Teaching to Adults* (CELTA). These are the minimum requirements accepted by the British Council for teaching English. The CELTA is generally seen as a TEFL-initiation course (Alwright & Hanks, 2009) and lasts a mere four weeks, which contributes to and consolidates some of the stereotypes and stigma attached to English teaching, particularly in environments where doctoral qualifications dictate employment possibilities. Generally, then, since the CELTA is not recognised beyond the world of ELT, it serves as a stepping stone to working in private language institutes, but these offer few long-term career prospects.

Over time though, teachers who are serious about their profession tend to become more heavily involved in professional bodies, development programmes, conferences, workshops, and so on. They may also progress to gaining more recognised professional qualifications later in life and continue to build on these qualifications over the duration of their career. Many will go on to undertake studies at Masters degree level or the equivalent *Diploma in English Language Teaching to Adults* (DELTA). This DELTA qualification, in the UK context, is considered one of the highest qualifications in ELT, through being 'the only teaching diploma placed at Level 7 of the UK's Qualification and Credit Framework (QCF)' (Sokol, 2011). Candidates must have completed two years of teaching before embarking upon the DELTA, since they have to acquire both 'received' and 'experiential' knowledge so as to be able to incorporate reflective and theoretical elements into their practice. This brings the course in line with changing principles of teacher education as described in such works as Strevens (1974), Schön (1983), Kolb (1984), Ellis (1986), and Wallace (1991). Furthermore, the reflective aspect helps foster 'a philosophy of (EFL) teaching as profession' as advocated in Pennington (1990, p. 134), and echoed in the EAP context through the work of Alexander (2010). Despite these strengths, this is also a qualification that is not easily understood in an environment where a PhD serves as the standard currency of trade in employment prospects. Yet, for language teachers, the completion of such courses serves as a stamp of identity, a tattoo of realisation that English Language Teaching has become the staple of their professional life. That consciousness, for many people such as myself, serves as a significant point in the continuum of our professional journeys as teachers.

Back in 2013, in writing a research paper on the professional development of two DELTA trainees at the outset of their careers, I drew a comparison between English Language teachers and characters from a seminal movie of the 1970s (Breen, 2013). This was the classic film *Taxi Driver*, directed by Martin Scorsese, in which there is a sub-theme of identity formation (Mortimer, 1997, p. 28). One occasion where this theme manifests itself is in a conversation between two of the leading characters. The central character, a directionless Vietnam war veteran named Travis Bickle, takes on a job as a cab driver in New York, having found it difficult to sleep at night, and after working some of the worst areas of the city becomes increasingly angry against the society he sees through the window of his cab. At this point he decides to purchase a weapon and has a conversation with one of his colleagues, a cab driver called Wizard, who states the following:

'Look at it this way. A man takes a job, you know? And that job – I mean, like that – That becomes who he is. You know, like – You do a thing and that's what you are. Like I've been a cabbie for years. Ten years at night. I still don't own my own cab. You know why? Because I don't want to. That must be what I want. To be on the night shift drivin' somebody else's cab. You understand? I mean, you become – You get a job, you become the job' (*Taxi Driver*, 1976).

Though such dialogue from a screenplay may seem out of place in the world of teaching, one of the DELTA trainees in my 2013 study mirrored the sentiments of Wizard's speech with a description of her progression from a language school in Spain to the British EAP classroom. This young teacher named Caroline exemplified the journey of many fellow professionals when she spoke of starting out with a plan to spend a few summers teaching conversation classes, after her university degree had finished, so as to see the world. She suggested that 'many English Language teachers sort of fall accidentally into it as a method of being abroad and just supporting yourself.' But gradually she found herself drawn towards a more professional sense of being a language teacher and ended up making a career out of something that had begun as a short-term overseas adventure. Language teaching started out as a job and became her profession. A sense of this is captured in her conclusion that 'the pyramid narrows as you get into a smaller community of very focused English Language teachers who see it more as a calling than a job' and she could now 'see where people get forty, fifty years' worth of a career out of it rather than two or three summers' (Breen, 2013).

Becoming an EAP teaching professional

My journey into the EAP 'ecosystem' (Fenwick & Edwards, 2010, p. 9) is one which mirrors that of many in the 'broader TESOL[1] community' (Edge, 2005, p. 186). I have been an English Language teacher for about 15 years, having originally worked at the base level of old media employment, in newspapers and television, back in Ireland, my home country. Growing tired of the limited opportunities and closed doors encountered in the Irish media industries, I travelled across the water, to undertake a postgraduate teaching degree in Huddersfield, where I chose Media Studies and English Literature as my main subjects. This was an exciting time to be studying Media, and one of my professors would often describe it as a 'sexy' subject with practices that seemed more exciting than for fellow students in the EFL/ESL context.

During teaching practice in a sixth form college, I had the opportunity to take my students out on the streets to make short films, produce a radio show, or go to the recording studio to simulate news broadcasts. This was a world away from the evening classes of my EFL/ESL colleagues, often going into prisons and sixth form colleges equipped with dictionaries and textbooks that seemed dull in comparison to discussions about cinema and soap operas. Amongst those of us teaching 'specific' disciplines, there was a misguided view of EFL/ESL teaching as belonging to those without a vocation for a 'real' subject. That was until the second semester when I chose to do EFL as an elective module, which was taught by a very inspirational woman. Over the course of a few months, we learned of exciting travel opportunities provided by the teaching of English, and several classmates applied for jobs in places as diverse as Barcelona and South Korea. Along the way, I decided to do the same – just for a couple of years overseas before coming back to the British Isles to settle down to 'proper' teaching again in the Media classroom.

My travels would last two years, taking in the high-tech atmosphere of Tokyo, and language schools on the edge of Australia's rainforests. Upon coming back, I sought out work in regular teaching but none was forthcoming. My two years of travel seemed to have burned a mark of Cain through my CV, and my only route back into work came about through language schools. Wanting to escape these dreadful places (in terms of prospects), I embarked on a part-time Masters degree in Education with the University of Manchester, focusing on a combination of English Language Teaching and Educational Technology.

At this stage I was becoming more entrenched in the profession of ELT and seeing technology as an escape from, and supplement to, generic textbooks. Often, these seemed mundane and disconnected from 'sociological realities of learners' lives' (Tomlinson, 2003a; 2003b). Seeking to make lessons fun, I arranged frequent trips to the few computer labs available, or brought authentic video and audio materials into the classroom at every opportunity. Then, through a combination of circumstances, I ended up moving from ELT to EAP, via two years in a South Korean university of technology, and a summer pre-sessional course in the University of Greenwich.

Here, I found what seemed a natural home for my teaching. Having experienced formal teacher education, I had always felt that something was lacking, in terms of content, at the heart of ELT. Suddenly, there was specific material giving lessons a depth of substance, and new ways of engaging students with subject matter. I found new purpose and satisfaction in marrying together elements of language and discipline-specific work in an environment commensurate with my motivation for becoming a teacher in the first place, which was to share knowledge with others, and help them progress in their education and their lives. Teaching EAP then had given me a professional identity that I could be proud of, a craft that I could hone and develop. To do so might necessitate further knowledge, I felt, so I undertook doctoral studies – once again at the University of Manchester. At the same time, I found a 'permanent' role at a point when sessional work seemed in danger of drying up as a consequence of the mood of austerity that was sweeping the country in the aftermath of the global banking and financial crisis of 2007–2009. That permanent role was one that gave my work and research a new direction, influencing the orientation of my PhD studies and giving me the opportunity to synthesise my interests in new technologies and teacher education.

Half a decade later, there was a certain irony in how I finished the thesis, which has served as the groundwork for this publication. Equipped with a MacBook, I retreated to my parents' holiday home in a town called Bundoran on the west coast of Ireland. There, without the distraction of the Internet, at the intersection of sea, cliffs, and shore, I wrote and reflected for several weeks, setting out on a research journey that Robert Yin (2009, p. 29) has likened to Christopher Columbus embarking on a search for the new world. There too, less than fifty miles from where I first encountered chalkboards, colour televisions, sandpits, and arithmetic, I reflected on the words of T. S. Eliot, in that 'the end of all our exploring will be to arrive where we started and know the place for the first time' (1943, pp. 143–144), as I returned to the origins of the study, and traced out the journey from the very beginning.

The context and shaping of a new EAP ecosystem

On Monday the 4th of January 2010, I started out on a journey, catching a train to a place that would shape and change my life over the four years that followed. Liverpool Street Station was to be my destination, a great sprawling glass mountain of a place first built in 1874 and famed, amongst many other things, for its role in the *Kindertransport* rescue mission of the late 1930s. Today, the station serves commuters to the financial district of Bishopsgate with its many sparkling towers that house the headquarters of banks and insurance firms.

In more recent times, the area has attracted higher educational providers too, particularly business schools. However, in that cold winter of 2010, the University of East Anglia became the first regional university to open a satellite campus right in the heart of London's financial district. Based in the city of Norwich, about 100 miles north east of its satellite campus, the University of East Anglia can be described as one of the 'plate glass' universities established in the United Kingdom in the 1960s (Beloff, 1970). Originally it was a provider of English Studies and Biological Sciences, before its rapid expansion in the 1970s to include an esteemed Centre for Climatic Research, a school of Computing, and the UK's first Creative Writing course. Since then, graduates of the university have included writers Ian McEwan, Owen Sheers, and Kazuo Ishiguro, alongside several past and current Members of Parliament in Britain and overseas, renowned international diplomats, distinguished scientists, and university vice chancellors.

However, the marketing of Norwich as a destination for international students remained a challenge, despite the attractiveness of the city's ambience, facilities, and history. Thus the University of East Anglia, so often at the forefront of innovation, embarked upon a business venture with private educational provider INTO University Partnerships in 2008. This was intended to be a 'unique partnership model' which developed an on-campus college to 'prepare international students for success at higher education worldwide' (INTO, 2010). This preparation was based on the twin cornerstones of providing state of the art educational and accommodational spaces (ibid), alongside an emphasis upon increasing the amount of EAP jobs available within higher education (Butler, 2007).

Within the universities that had partnered with INTO, particularly the University of East Anglia, there was a general acceptance that greater numbers of international students were now coming onto degree studies through Foundation Programmes provided by the partnership. This then created a series of jobs for teachers who might not otherwise have taught EAP in their home countries or cities, whether in Norwich, Newcastle, Belfast, Exeter or elsewhere. Yet, despite the company's rapid rise since its formation in 2005, INTO and other private educational providers such as Kaplan and Study Group have attracted criticisms, particularly from the teaching unions and those who ask whether such companies should be seen as 'prophet' or 'profiteer' (Butler,

2007). Others such as Bell (2016) see this type of privatisation as being the cause of 'much tension and heated debate' (p. 90). This is because there is a perception of private enterprises contributing to a 'further weakening of EAP's position and status within the academy as a whole' (ibid, p. 91) since they tend to sit outside the university mainstream, and are seen to offer significantly worse working conditions to teachers than those found in standard academic contracts in the UK.

However, there has also been a large amount of unfair criticism levelled at private providers such as a lack of development opportunities on offer and 'systematic downgrading and de-professionalisation' of English for Academic Purposes as a discipline (Bell, 2016, p. 91). The qualifications and experience of the participants within this research study prove the latter criticisms to be overly harsh. In my experience, there are plenty of teachers working for private providers who are as well qualified as those working for more established universities. Often, they can be more motivated too, since they have sought permanent employment in their field rather than sessional work. Furthermore, as this study testifies, there is just as much scope for teacher development when working for private providers, even if questions remain about their possible long-term impact on EAP as a profession.

The task within this book though is not to investigate such issues, but to look at the setting that this organisation provided, and to relate that to the theory and practice of developing educators for the digital age. In my own case, INTO's partnership with the University of East Anglia allowed me to move from contractual work to full-time employment, after I applied to become Programme Manager of English Language provision and was accepted for the position, with a starting date on the very day the centre opened. That happened to be on a very frosty morning, in one of the coldest winters of the decade, when I arrived to find the building almost empty of furniture and still undergoing the final stages of construction. That, though, was to serve as a metaphor for the building work that was still to be done, in terms of creating a team from scratch in a place without a prior history.

It was my responsibility as Programme Manager to take care of the recruitment and induction of a teaching team to provide a suite of pathway courses over the coming year. Martin (2014, p. 5) describes INTO UEA's educational provision as entailing Foundation courses onto which students enrol with the aim of matriculation to 'target' or partner universities. These courses involve a combination of subject-specific work (Business, Law, Economics etc.) and EAP, in order for students to cross the bridge between pre-degree and actual degree studies. Because of the nature of these courses, particularly those focusing primarily on language for students with lower levels of English language competency, it was going to be possible to recruit some less experienced teachers, and subsequently offer some form of professional development. That, though, was not going to come without its challenges because teachers were expected to do up to 800 hours of teaching per year, which worked out at around 20 hours per week: a workload more comparable with private language schools than public universities. However, this was balanced out by offering staff full-time or fractional contracts, rather than adopting the zero-hours or sessional approach that has become an endemic feature of EAP teacher employment in universities.

For me, the cornerstone of creating an effective teaching environment was the construction of a solid team of teaching professionals. Therefore I drew more heavily on ideas from actual management practice than from the type of decontextualised guidance offered in HR manuals. As a hobby, I also write articles on sport and have published two works of fiction set against the world of English football. Whilst researching the first of these, entitled *The Charlton Men* (Breen, 2014) I came across the autobiography of a football manager named Jimmy Seed, published in 1958. Though not intended to serve as any kind of guideline for management outside of the football context, I found parts of this work highly relevant to my own context of trying to build up a team. Seed (1958) notes that he built up his teams not necessarily by looking at the skills of individuals but by considering how they fitted in and worked alongside their fellow players; slotting them into positions according to the collective good of the team. Having a focus on the whole rather than the individual brings this approach into line with such theorists as Etienne Wenger (1998) whose work on Communities of Practice theory is discussed at a later stage.

Over a period of nine months, fourteen English Language teachers would arrive in the centre, with a further four arriving by Christmas. This was staged according to needs and student numbers, which had an impact on the standard of teacher that we could hire, particularly at short notice. By the end, the gender split was precisely equal, nine male, nine female, with an age range from early twenties to upper fifties. Regarding countries of origin, we had twelve English, two American, one Scottish, one Welsh, one Irish, and one Singaporean. Of the teachers who were English, one was of Chinese ethnicity, whilst the rest were from different regions of England, particularly the south, close to 'home' and in line with INTO's goal of creating localised EAP jobs.

Echoing my own career path, most of these teachers had undertaken professional journeys which included a considerable amount of certification. Most had Masters or DELTA qualifications, though one or two fell into the category of 'novice' teachers (Alexander, 2010, p. 4), holding no more than a Bachelor degree and a *Certificate of English Language Teaching to Adults* (CELTA), which is the British Council's minimum requirement for teaching EAP/ELT. Those teachers who possessed DELTA or Masters qualifications had mostly followed a career path which involved prior work in either British or overseas universities, in a diverse range of places that included China, Indonesia, Japan, Poland, Saudi Arabia, Spain, and Turkey. On the other hand, the 'novice' teachers tended to come from a private language school background within the UK, where they had minimal opportunities for training, development, and use of technology. Teaching in private language schools also offered fewer opportunities to develop awareness of the core criteria and competencies detailed by BALEAP (2008), which can be found in Appendix 1. These competencies essentially characterise EAP teaching and the expectations of professionals within this environment, placing a primary emphasis upon understanding of academic context. Usually, such knowledge is acquired through practice and this was why it was important that novice teachers had a passion for their profession and a willingness to learn.

1.2 – Theoretical foundations

Building knowledge as a team

The structure of this book is such that the second section of each chapter is based on theoretical input. However, in this opening chapter, there has to be an element of crossover between theory and practical examples in order to provide a solid foundation of context. That is why the parts that follow retain elements of contextualisation, so as to provide the 'thick description' (Lincoln & Guba, 1985, pp. 359–360) of the setting, as required in the underlying qualitative research study from which this work has evolved. At the time of taking up this position, my prior managerial experience had been in the running of courses and looking after small groups of teachers in a public university context. It was a considerable culture shock to see the differences in the private sector's rules of operation. Although INTO is an educational organisation, it must be remembered that it has many corporate features in its upper echelons which in turn have an impact on its structure. Though such organisations may operate on the margins of academia, they are often detached from values historically embedded within higher education, where success is measured in terms of academic output rather than hours physically spent in the workplace, as happens in the private sector. There was a culture of being managed rather than managing the self in terms of time and workload, as is common in public universities, and strangely for me an expectation amongst staff of being overtly managed, particularly amongst those novice teachers from language school backgrounds. Such teachers constituted a minority within the language centre but were the ones in most immediate need of assistance in the form of professional development. There were other pressing issues that had to be dealt with, again possibly due to the influence of the private sector, or perhaps the newness of the situation.

Certain points in the opening months of running the language centre felt like walking into a storm straight off the pages of Bruce Tuckman's (1965) '*Forming, Storming, Norming, Performing team-development model.*' Within this framework people are seen to form relationships over time, within teams, moving from states of conflict to cohesiveness as boundaries and roles become established. One means of addressing or negotiating contextual and sociocultural challenges, such as those referred to in earlier parts of this chapter, is through the establishment of friendships and communities in the workplace (Hargreaves & Tucker, 1991). Darling-Hammond & Richardson (2009, p. 47) suggest that research on 'effective professional development' highlights 'the importance of collaborative and collegial learning environments.' Schlager & Fusco (2003, p. 211) write that 'a strong community can wield the power to enact policies or subvert them, foster change or resist it, spread innovation or impede it.'

There is a limit, though, to what personal relationships on their own can create within the context of continuing professional development and ways of facilitating this outside of the 'busy classroom lives' which teachers inevitably lead (Burns, 1999, p. 214). However, the creation of 'collaborative and collegial learning environments' can 'help develop communities of practice able to promote school change beyond individual classrooms' (Darling-Hammond & Richardson, 2009, p.47). The extent or nature of such developments or changes is also inextricably linked to broader systems of activity within the workplace and its particular set of values.

Situating Communities of Practice theory in EAP contexts

Etienne Wenger (1998, p.6) has stated that we all belong to Communities of Practice (COP) in both our personal and professional lives. In the earlier stages of his work, Wenger (2000) sought to define Communities of Practice in straightforward terms as being 'groups of people informally bound together by shared expertise and passion for a joint enterprise'. Similarly, they 'share a concern, a set of problems, or a passion about a topic' and 'deepen their knowledge and expertise by interacting on an ongoing basis' (Wenger et al, 2002, p. 4). It is this reference to 'passion' in particular that offers insight into the force that often germinates and grows the community of practice. Sometimes, as voiced in Wenger's later work, this shaping of communities does not have to be organic, but can be 'cultivated' (Wenger & Snyder, 2000) as a 'practical way to manage knowledge' (Wenger et al, 2002, p. 6). That takes on significance in this context where the research study was based around a series of workshops, where the goal was to cultivate knowledge rather than to have it grow organically (Wenger & Snyder, 2000).

Essentially, in the words of Rogers (2000, p. 385), the core feature of such a group is that the actual 'practice serves to bring coherence in a community.' This sense of practice being at the heart of a community is nothing new, as admitted in Wenger & Snyder (2000, p. 40), in which the authors outline how such groups have existed since ancient times up to the present day. They use artisans of Ancient Greece and guilds of the Middle Ages as examples of communities that had both a business and social function, as well as an element of apprenticeship and what is defined as situated learning. The main difference between such groups and those that we see in contemporary times is that today's COP groups often exist within large organisations (ibid). INTO, having centres in various cities and countries, fits the definition of such an organisation, and is also one that lends itself to its members belonging to overlapping communities working on common enterprises.

EAP teachers fit the definition of a Community of Practice by virtue of the fact that they share 'a unique perspective on their topic as well as a body of common knowledge, practices and approaches' (Wenger, 2000, p. 5). Furthermore, the COP literature is particularly salient to the EAP context, which has historically encouraged collegiality, as detailed in Hyland & Hamp-Lyons (2002), and Hamp-Lyons (2011). It must also be stressed that BALEAP itself is a collegial organisation and the Competency Framework (2008) was born out of collaboration across institutions and contexts. Added to this, EAP practitioners have long strived to create such types of collegial environments, detailed throughout the literature from Johns (1981), through to Jordan (2002), up to the present-day workings of BALEAP.

Communities of Practice in teacher education

Richards (2008, pp. 7–8) argues that Communities of Practice theory can play a considerable part in contemporary teacher education because 'Lave and Wenger's (1991) concept for learning' is one that similarly 'takes place within organizational settings, which is socially constituted and which involves participants with a common interest collaborating to develop new knowledge and skills.' Without some form of community, EAP teaching could simply become the 'patchwork' profession described by Hamp-Lyons (2011, p. 92). Indeed it was a perceived need for shared practice that was central to the development of EAP as a distinct profession, particularly in the evolution of BALEAP. Jordan (2002) explains how this group emerged from its earlier incarnation as a group that assumed the rather long-winded title of Special English Language Materials for Overseas Students (SELMOUS). This group was originally conceived as a means of sharing ideas and resources, to end the relative isolation of EAP practitioners. Over several decades, BALEAP has grown into a community of practice that connects together other communities of practice working across a range of contexts.

Furthermore, Richards (2008, p. 3) suggests that being an English Language teacher often entails membership of a community wherein participants have shared discourse and practices, shared histories, and sets of experiences that are particular to the profession. Marland (1993, p. 131) states that the practice of teachers does not always come solely from what they have been taught on teacher education programmes and that their classroom actions 'are guided by internal frames of reference which are deeply rooted in personal experiences, especially in-school ones.' Richards (2008, p. 3) adds to this by discussing the self-critical and transformative drive at the heart of teacher development. Teaching is a context-rich environment in which communities of practice can flourish, as has been demonstrated by the depth of literature since Lave & Wenger's (1991) joint publication in this field, including Wenger's seminal 1998 work, commonly recognised as COP theory's definitive text. This work, which details the lives of claims processors, again has echoes of the earlier *Taxi Driver* comparison, where people's roles come to define not just their everyday tasks, but their place in the world as a whole. Here, in the language centre, a group of strangers could become a community of practice.

1.3 – Practical considerations

Identifying needs and expectations of teachers

Liz Hamp-Lyons (2011, p. 100) suggests that 'the provision of professional education and training for EAP teachers lags behind the vast expansion in the need for teachers.' It has long been recognised that the practice of EAP teaching requires a highly specialised skill set and knowledge base, just as with other areas of teaching. For example, when I started out on my teaching degree, I had several months of pre-service induction and 'training'[2] before going into a classroom situation. For EAP teachers this is very rarely the case. Most are thrown in at the deep end, with initial training generally of an 'informal nature', as evidenced by Olwyn Alexander's (2010) survey of EAP teachers, and their preparation in teaching the subject. Interestingly, in this study, the author raises a point of particular relevance to Communities of Practice Theory (Wenger, 1998). She points out that there is less scope for apprenticeship in today's EAP teaching context than in the past (2010, p. 4). Partially this is due to today's teachers often entering the profession through Pre-sessional courses, which provide 'little scope to develop EAP expertise' (p. 5). Rather, development appears to come about through 'sharing ideas with colleagues, using EAP coursebooks, reading books or journals, and attending meetings' (ibid). Perhaps the informal nature of professional development occurs for different reasons, according to context, but one major reason is EAP's heavy workload (ibid, p. 4) and the fact of teachers having 'busy classroom lives' (Burns, 1999, p. 214).

Added to this, a great deal of work remains sessional, especially in university language centres where much of the employment is seasonal and weighted around summer pre-sessional courses for international students. Many teachers enter the pre-sessional circuit to fill a few summers but find themselves repeatedly going back years or even decades afterwards. As such, they often become a loose collective of 'lone ranger' semi-professionals, to borrow a term used by Samaras & Gismondi (1998, p. 716). I was determined to ensure that this did not happen in our context, and to provide a communal focus for development based on addressing actual needs and wants of teachers. From the outset, I placed emphasis upon developing a team. The fact of everyone being new at almost the same time created a sense of egalitarianism. I also identified a need to run development sessions in areas that would have direct relevance to teachers' classroom lives. To do so, I had to find a system of needs analysis that would help teachers to investigate 'their own practice' and develop 'the reflective and analytic skills necessary to integrate this into a process of informed professional growth' (Garton & Richards, 2007, p. 8).

In this instance, I opted for a semi-formal approach of direct experience and observation. This was done through discussions with staff in group meetings, and by reviewing work samples gathered, by consent, during and outside of lesson observations. Technology, time management, familiarisation with a new environment, and understanding of courses and learning objectives emerged as recurring themes and issues in this identification process. The depth of teachers' knowledge was apparent, not just in terms of pedagogy, language and academic practice, but also cross-disciplinary knowledge gained from previous studies, work, or teaching in this field. Pedagogy and content appeared to be areas where experienced teachers felt comfortable. Less experienced colleagues, novice teachers, had acquired the rudiments of pedagogy through a combination of CELTA training, and subsequent teaching experience, but lacked content knowledge, and perhaps an overarching sense of their own identity as teachers.

Technology's emergence as developmental focus

Technology, being an area in which I had some expertise as a consequence of experience and study in the University of Manchester, appeared to have the potential to provide the bedrock of development. Through focusing on this area, I could draw on teachers' existing knowledge to develop awareness of using technological resources to assist in the areas of time management, familiarisation, and understanding. Virtual Learning Environments, for example, could be used as a means of structuring, organising, and mapping out courses. Underpinning this was a philosophy of 'EFL teaching as profession' (Pennington, 1990, p. 134), and an aspiration to forms of 'cognitive self-direction' espoused by Vygotsky (Manning & Payne, 1993, p. 369) and supported by empirical experience of teacher development.

Rubin (1978, p. 136) states that 'teachers need to be involved in the articulation of their own training needs whenever possible.' Thus, I conducted further discussions, on an individual and communal basis, to understand my teaching colleagues' perception of their placement on the professional continuum, where they wanted to be, where they needed to be, and how they could reach such a point. Within these discussions, references to technology's ubiquitous presence again featured strongly, and a desire for 'training'[3] in how to best utilise the institution's resources. As a consequence of this demand, I decided to run developmental workshops with direct relevance to teachers' classroom lives, and the technological tools at their disposal, particularly the Hitachi Cambridge Smart Boards with which each classroom was equipped, and the shared learning platform of a Moodle Virtual Learning Environment. However, in taking this approach I paid heed to the suggestion of Laurillard (2002), cited by Motteram (2004, p. 1), that 'academic conversations' must take primacy over the 'technologies that service' institutions.

Creating an opportunity for action research

As I began to plan the development project, I realised that the affordances of this situation were such that it also presented a tremendous opportunity to conduct an instance of action research. Burns (1999, p. 24) speaks of action research often being prompted by 'concrete and practical' issues of 'immediate concern' in the workplace, echoing Kurt Lewin's original conceptualisation of 'research which will help the practitioner' (1946, p. 34). In this instance, alongside benefits for myself as researcher, there were advantages for the EAP practitioners at the heart of this study. As such, this resonates with Zuber-Skerritt's (1991) essential processes and outcomes of action research. These are listed as 'empowerment of participants, collaboration and participation, acquisition of knowledge, and social change' (ibid). Further to this, there could be benefits to the field of EAP as a whole, and its growing research tradition. Coghlan & Brannick (2009, p. xi) support this initial conceptualisation of the study as an action research project through the emphasis on outcomes which are both action and research oriented, as the name suggests. Additionally, this approach is 'appropriate when the research topic is an unfolding series of actions over time' in a specific context wherein participants undergo a process of investigation, experiential learning, and reflective practice (ibid, p. x). This is particularly compatible with the tradition of ELT research, as outlined by Freeman (2002, p. 8), in which there has been a consistent emphasis on reflective practice as advocated by Schön (1983). Lastly, it is important to stress that this was very much intended to be 'research *in* action, rather than research *about* action' (Coghlan & Brannick, 2009, p. 4), with a strong emphasis on collaboration with participants.

Decision to run teacher education workshops

Having established a workplace community and identified an opportunity to combine teacher development with a form of action research, the next step was to decide on practical approaches, the 'planning' element of a three-stage research cycle (Lewin, 1946; Coghlan & Brannick, 2009, p. 7). Workshops have served as a platform of development within teacher education since the 1930s (Richards & Farrell, 2005, p. 23). These are commonly recognised as 'an intensive, short-term learning activity' which facilitates longer-term developmental impetus (ibid). However, good workshops are more than just 'cookbooks for effective teaching' (Crandall, 2000, p. 37) delivered by means of a 'traditional episodic, fragmented approach' (Darling-Hammond & Richardson, 2009, p. 3). The age of the 'drive-by' workshop model has evolved into more sustained approaches to development (ibid, p. 46), which are more experiential and reflective than 'one-shot' formulas of the past (Meltzer, 2010; McGrath et al, 2011).

Thus, these workshops could not be limited to the 'training sessions' teachers themselves had requested. I wanted to avoid the 'technocentric' approach first referred to by Papert (1987), which is one that emphasises a study of individual technologies or tools and how they work, even if this may have been what some teachers felt that they needed. Rather than a focus on individual tools, I placed an emphasis upon a contextualised and ecological process of learning linked to practice, offering opportunities for experience, reflection, and construction of knowledge, through time. However, it was also important to provide teachers with their requests for learning about individual tools such as interactive whiteboards. This, though, would be done in such a manner as to educate them in ways of teaching with technology, and then an application of those ways of teaching to specific tools.

From the start, I had a sense of the types of workshops that were needed, from discussions with the teachers, and the technological resources at our disposal. Interactive whiteboards and Moodle would play a central role, and from these other areas would take shape, according to needs, demands, and contemporary developments. I also had to provide a theoretical base for the workshops in terms of providing contemporary theory in teacher education as a means of supporting the approach that I was taking. At this stage, I had the rudiments of the study in place, but had not yet found a framework for developing teacher knowledge. That would come at a later stage when I discovered the TPACK model, to be explained in subsequent chapters.

1.4 – Lessons learned at this stage

The practice of EAP often appears to be undervalued in universities, where it sometimes exists in the margins of academia (Ding & Bruce, 2017, p. 204) and risks even greater marginalisation from higher education's mainstream, with EAP courses increasingly farmed out to private providers. However, within such organisations, there does tend to be a drive towards professional development of teachers, albeit as much for the good of the company as for the individuals themselves. There is also a clear ambition on the part of EAP teachers to experience forms of professional development that make them better practitioners, not just for their own sakes but also for those of their students. Yet, in order for the EAP profession to develop as a whole and gain greater recognition within academia, there is probably a need for a sea change in practices of employment and qualification.

There is a proven need to professionalise EAP and to create collegial environments not just in the immediate work context but across the profession as a whole (Hyland & Hamp-Lyons, 2002; Hamp-Lyons, 2011; Bell, 2016). This will help to solidify EAP as a subject or even discipline in its own right, and groups such as BALEAP have laid the groundwork for this to happen. However, there are still challenges with how the teaching of English (albeit for Academic Purposes) is perceived within the university. Perhaps it is even the word *English* that conjures up images of classroom ball-games such as those described in CELTA course textbooks and literature, or remedial work that features little more than 'a few hours of fixing up grammar in the language centre' (Hyland & Hamp-Lyons, 2002, p. 6). Teachers need to challenge stereotypes of their field, and illustrate to others the power of the EAP practitioner's knowledge base in contributing to the academy as a whole.

If EAP wants to be taken seriously as a discipline, then its practitioners have to acquire a reputation as serious professionals, strengthened rather than inhibited by the importance of classroom teaching to their work. The 'lone ranger' mentality is largely the fault of university employment practices, but partially also the fact of such practices attracting a certain type of individual. Within this study, in finding individuals who firstly sought full-time employment and then 'training', as they described it, there is evidence that EAP teachers want to situate their work in professional and academic communities. Educating such teachers in their practice is a vital first step towards cultivating the sea change needed throughout the profession as a whole. The opening chapter of this study has thus hopefully offered suggestions and insights into how the foundations for building EAP teacher knowledge can be laid.

CHAPTER 2

Technology, Knowledge, and Workshops

2.1 – Contextualisation

Technologies in the language centre

Increasingly, teacher knowledge needs to incorporate an understanding of integrating technological resource into course content and pedagogy. This, of course, is not new because technology has been a part of classroom life since long before the coming of the digital age (McGrath et al, 2011). However, in recent decades, new conversations and circumstances have evolved around the position of technologies within the higher educational domain. Going back two decades, Diana Laurillard proposed 'rethinking university teaching in the digital age' (1993). In her book of that precise title, she advocated greater integration of technology into the higher educational curriculum, and designed a practical framework for such integration, so as to move the discussion beyond theory and resource, to meaningful usage of technologies.

The aspiration for meaningful use of technologies was one that the language centre held from the outset. There had been considerable investment in two resources intended to serve as a staple of cutting edge educational provision to students. The first of these came in the form of Hitachi Cambridge Starboards, with which each classroom was equipped, and the second was the shared learning platform of a Moodle Virtual Learning Environment (VLE). Although VLEs have become an established feature of higher educational provision, the Star Boards, also known as interactive whiteboards, are more generally associated with 'school' teaching. However, they also provide a suite of functions that make them highly suitable for use in Higher Education. Branzburg (2008) describes these boards as 'being connected to a computer and LCD projector' which can be used for the purposes of display, input, annotation, projection, and recording. He goes on to say that these offer classrooms 'the next

How to cite this book chapter:
Breen, P. 2018. *Developing Educators for The Digital Age: A Framework for Capturing Knowledge in Action.* Pp. 21–37. London: University of Westminster Press.
DOI: https://doi.org/10.16997/book13.b. License: CC-BY-NC-ND 4.0

generation interactive whiteboard' through multi-touch gestures similar to those of an iPhone (ibid, p. 3). However, he does note that this brand originates in the corporate world, unlike such tools as Promethean's Activboard designed 'by teachers for teachers' (ibid, p. 7).

In the beginning, many of the teachers found these whiteboards quite clunky and awkward, inhibiting their favoured classroom practices. Some teachers used the boards for simple projection of PowerPoint or internet images onto the screen, thereby using technology for technology's sake and defeating the purpose of investing in such high-tech equipment. The boards also seemed best suited to the teaching paradigm of presentation, production and practice, commonly known by its acronym PPP and now seen as outdated, as outlined in Richards & Rodgers (2014). This is a model of teaching used more commonly in yesterday's language schools than today's universities. The Moodle Virtual Learning Environment, on the other hand, created scope for pedagogic approaches that were not necessarily as teacher-centred. Thus, right from the outset, Moodle seemed to have greater potential to become as natural a part of teachers' everyday life as their morning arsenal of board markers or Friday evening socialising in the pub.

Moodle is an acronym for Modular Object Oriented Dynamic Learning Environment and also 'a verb that describes the process of lazily meandering through something, doing things as it occurs to you to do them, an enjoyable tinkering that often leads to insight and creativity' (Cole & Foster, 2008, p. ix). This was very much a feature of the early months of Moodle's usage in INTO UEA London. Such a sense of 'tinkering' (Cole & Foster, 2008, p. ix) and stumbling upon a sense of identity and better practice, almost by accident rather than design, fits in with Etienne Wenger's earlier work with Jean Lave on organic communities of practice (1991). Significantly too, according to Robb (2004), the learning platform itself had been born out of such a mood of experimentation, created by Martin Dougiamas 'while working on his PhD. at Curtin University of Technology, Perth, Australia.'

Out of frustration with the university's existing course management system and his role as Web CT administrator, Dougiamas 'developed it as a tool for his dissertation which was on a Socio-constructivist approach to learning' and incorporated 'features which supported this approach to education' (Robb, 2004). Part of the design included an emphasis upon 'community building', which was very much in line with my stated aspiration to draw upon Communities of Practice theory and help teachers develop as a team (ibid). Moodle is thus a system that is designed to be built by educators rather than engineers (Cole & Foster, 2008, p. ix). However, as Hung & Chen point out, the fact of simply 'creating these environments does not ensure that these facilities are well used by participants' (2001, p. 3). It was my responsibility as manager and teacher educator to facilitate everyday usage of Moodle, and also the interactive whiteboards, but I decided to start with the former.

Contextualising technologies in ELT, EAP, and beyond

Technology has thoroughly permeated the lecture theatres of contemporary institutions within higher education, according to Liz Hamp-Lyons, a leading theorist in English for Academic Purposes (2011, p. 96). This is as true of the EAP context as in all other subjects and disciplines within academia. However, when it comes to Computer Assisted Language Learning (CALL), English Language Teaching has often been ahead of the game in many respects. There has long been a tradition of incorporating technology into English Language classes (Warschaeur, 1996; Bax, 2003; Beatty, 2003; Motteram & Sharma, 2009; Chapelle, 2010; Motteram, 2013), and thus EAP teachers can draw on pre-existing strategies for doing so. Traditional phases of CALL (behavioural, communicative, and interactive) also broadly relate to a combination of language teaching methodologies and software available (Warschauer & Healey, 1998; Warschauer, 2000/2003; Motteram, 2013).

Bax (2003) further amended the categories of CALL development to 'Restricted, Open, and Integrated', and spoke of a normalisation of technology's usage in the classroom to a point where it would be as natural and 'unremarked' as 'the coursebook or the whiteboard' (Motteram, 2013, p. 182). Gary Motteram (ibid, p. 5) adds that 'in this early part of the 21st century the range of technologies available for use in language learning and teaching has become very diverse and the ways that they are being used in classrooms all over the world [...] have become central to language practice.' Some of these technologies are listed as blogs, wikis, Second Life, Skype, Songify, teacher feedback videos, Windows Movie Maker, learners' own mobile devices, and audio blog software (p. 8). Julie Watson provides further examples such as content curation tools, data capture tools, screencasting facilities, social networks and referencing resources amongst others listed in a BALEAP keynote speech in November 2012 on the subject of '*An A to Z of Technologies*'. Jarvis and Achilleos (2013) update this landscape with mobile devices such as smartphones, MP3 players, podcasts, iPads, eBook readers and other resources which facilitate Mobile Assisted Language Learning (MALL). Four years down the line, the list keeps on growing, such is the speed of advancement in the use of technologies in teaching.

There is much more, though, to this relationship between ELT and technologies than just a practical element defined by the tools that people are using at a particular point in time. There has long been a substantial research component attached to the usage of technologies and their intersection with such areas as pedagogy and second language acquisition. Research has been conducted too within the domains of EAP and ESP. As far back as 1997, Huw Jarvis 'conducted a survey amongst BALEAP members to discover the extent to which Information Technology (IT) formed a part of pre-sessional EAP studies', according to Jordan (2002, p. 76), who adds that this research fits into studies on the role of IT in academic culture as much as purely EAP teaching. Watson-Todd (2003, p. 151) echoes this in his claim that technology has become a strong driver in the teaching of EAP possibly because of the 'innovative' methodologies used in the subject (p. 149) and the fact of approaches based on sound teaching and learning principles, rather than methods and techniques, guiding its pedagogical ethos (p. 148).

Setting the right context for workshops to take place

My goal, then, was to further build upon ELT's relationship between research, teacher education and classroom practice, by combining my PhD studies with a practical project in teacher development. Such a project would not just benefit myself but also the institution that I worked in, the broader field of EAP, and possibly other subjects and disciplines within higher education. Much like the evolution of Moodle, my PhD studies up to that point had involved a great deal of tinkering and exploration. It was important to move beyond these tentative steps and create something more solid from this platform of opportunity. BALEAP, after all, has long held aspirations for more research into EAP practice, going back to the creation of their Research Register in 1995 (Jordan, 2002). Furthermore, by researching topics of such contemporary importance as pedagogy and technology, EAP research could assume a less marginal role. The potential existed to set in motion a shared exploration with a group of teachers in the hope of generating findings of relevance beyond EAP. However, there was a lot of work to be done before such a point could be reached. To paraphrase the Irish poet Patrick Kavanagh, it was important to understand the local context – 'the parish' - before trying to understand the wider 'universe' of higher education (1967).

2.2 – Theoretical foundations

TPACK's evolution as a framework for knowledge

TPACK serves as an acronym for Technological Pedagogical Content Knowledge. Essentially, this is a framework for teacher knowledge and technology integration, which was originally known as TPCK, or technology, pedagogy, and content knowledge (Koehler & Mishra, 2009, p. 60). It is intended as 'a professional knowledge construct' designed to create 'expert' teaching in the classroom (ibid, p. 66). This adaptation of Shulman's (1986) PCK framework has been variously described in the literature as a teaching model for the twenty first century (Pierson & Borthwick, 2010; McGrath et al, 2011) and an extension of PCK for the digital age (Kirk, 2012). Drawing on this sense of TPACK being an extension of an earlier model, it is important to firstly define PCK in order to get to grips with its later incarnations.

Back in the 1980s, Professor Lee Shulman lamented the absence of a recognised knowledge base for teaching. This, he argued, has an impact upon teacher education, and that is especially true in higher education where traditionally lecturers have been trained separately in their subject knowledge (Law, Bioscience, Criminology) and their pedagogic strategies for delivering this. If teachers could find an 'intersection and synergy' between these two components then it could engender 'excellence in teaching' (Hofer & Swan, 2008, p. 181). Thus, as a potential solution to this dichotomy of expertise, Shulman advocated the creation of a periodic table of knowledge for teachers (1987, p.4). Such a construct would be designed along the lines of Dmitri Mendeleev's periodic table of chemical elements which, at the outset of its publication in 1869, contained 'distinct gaps for the then unknown elements' (Schwerdtfeger, 2011, p. 93). Shulman, though, provided a 'rudimentary' *(by his own admission)* outline of teacher knowledge (Ball et al, 2008, p. 397) with his formulation of the PCK (Pedagogical Content Knowledge) framework.

Although some leading ELT theorists such as Donald Freeman have suggested that PCK is 'a messy and possibly unworkable concept' (2002, p. 6) within language teaching, others could argue that EAP should be treated the same as any other subject. All forms of teaching can involve ill-structured activity (Spiro & Jehng, 1990; Koehler & Mishra, 2009; McGrath et al, 2011). That does not have to be a negative feature, especially in the EAP context where teachers need to be reactive to the needs of students (BALEAP, 2008). Added to this, the forms of knowledge described by Shulman (1986) are highly transferable across contexts, and can be readily mapped to BALEAP's (2008) competencies, which in themselves can be seen as a type of periodic table of EAP teacher knowledge. The following characteristics of PCK, summarised by Ball et al (2008, p. 391), appear particularly compatible – 'knowledge of educational contexts'; 'knowledge of educational ends, purposes, and values'; 'knowledge of learners and their characteristics'; and 'principles and strategies of classroom management and organisation.' Another significant category within both the PCK and BALEAP models is 'curriculum knowledge' described by Ball et al (ibid) as the 'particular grasp of the materials and programs that serve as tools of the trade for teachers.'

Where Shulman's (1986) PCK framework involved the interaction of two main bodies of knowledge, TPACK involves the interaction of a third: technology working in 'dynamic equilibrium' with the others (Mishra & Koehler, 2006, p. 1029). This then creates a set of sub-domains represented as PCK, TCK (technological content knowledge), and TPK (technological pedagogical knowledge), which together form TPACK (Mishra & Koehler, 2006; Koehler & Mishra, 2009). The overall construct then fits the definition of what Piaget (1970) referred to as a broader 'schema of knowledge.' Through practical and theoretical interaction of these knowledge bodies, there is creation of the flexibility 'needed to successfully integrate technology use into teaching' (Koehler & Mishra, 2009, p. 60), and a description of how understanding of educational

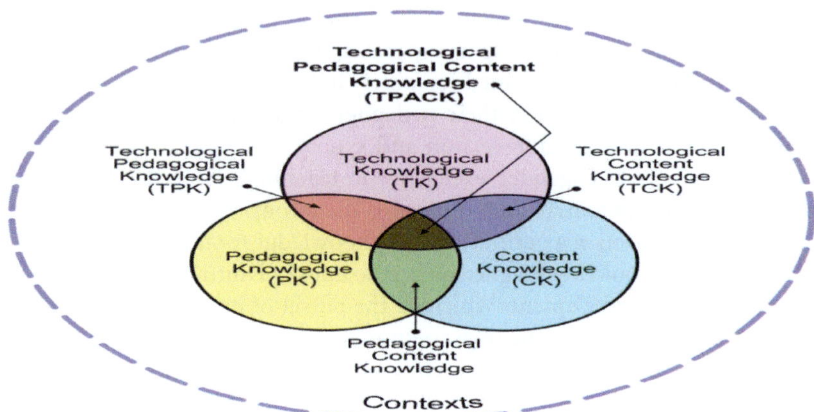

Figure 1: The TPACK framework and its knowledge components.
Reproduced from Koehler & Mishra (2009, p. 63)

technologies and PCK interact to produce 'effective teaching' (ibid, p. 62). The original depiction of the TPACK model, as first published in *Teacher College Record* (2006) is provided in Figure 1.

Knowledge components within TPACK

Within the framework there are six categories of knowledge, which intersect to form Technological Pedagogical Content Knowledge.

Pedagogical knowledge (PK) – This is very much in line with Shulman's (1986) categorisation and represents 'teachers' deep knowledge about the processes and practices or methods of learning and teaching' (Koehler & Mishra, 2009, p. 63). Similar to elements of BALEAP's categories of 'Teaching Practices', 'Assessment Practices', and 'Academic Contexts' (2008), this necessarily entails an understanding of 'overall educational purposes, values, and aims' and 'understanding how students learn, general classroom management skills, lesson planning, and student assessment' (Koehler & Mishra, 2009, p. 63).

Content knowledge (CK) – Again, this draws heavily on Shulman's original definition (1986, pp. 8–9). At its most fundamental it is 'teachers' knowledge about the subject matter to be learned or taught' (Koehler & Mishra, 2009, p. 63). Shulman (1986, p. 9) had previously defined this as 'the amount and organization of knowledge per se in the mind of the teacher' which goes beyond 'knowledge of the facts or concepts of a domain', and requires a deeper understanding of 'both the substantive and the syntactic structures' of a discipline (ibid). Substantive structures are those that give shape to the body of knowledge within a discipline, whilst syntactic structures establish the rules of a discipline, much as grammar establishes the rules of language (ibid). Content knowledge thus needs to include 'knowledge of concepts, theories, ideas, organisational frameworks, knowledge of evidence and proof, as well as established practices and approaches toward developing such knowledge' (Koehler & Mishra, 2009, p. 63). Significantly for EAP, it also involves knowledge of the differences in content across disciplines (ibid).

Pedagogical Content knowledge (PCK) – Koehler & Mishra (2009, p. 64) summarise this as being knowledge of pedagogy applicable to the teaching of specific content and creation of associated materials. This is essentially the same as Shulman's original formulation and goes beyond subject matter per se 'to the dimension of subject knowledge matter *for teaching*' (Shulman, 1986, p. 9), thus allowing both theory and practice to inform teachers' work. Early versions seemed to place greater emphasis on content, but later adaptations appear to have found a stronger equilibrium with pedagogy, and incorporation of student needs (Shulman, 2012).

Technological knowledge (TK) – The integration of technological knowledge is what sets the TPACK framework apart from PCK, and therefore plays a critical role in understanding the overall model. Koehler & Mishra (2009, p. 64) summarise this as being a productive working knowledge of technology, alongside a deeper understanding of how it can be used from a practical perspective. This, though, is not limited to 'the traditional definition of computer literacy' but requires 'a deeper, more essential understanding', 'mastery', and ability for adaptation (ibid).

Technological Content knowledge (TCK) – This entails an understanding of 'the deep historical relationship' between technology and content, plus 'understanding the impact of technology on the practices and knowledge of a given discipline' (Koehler & Mishra, 2009, p. 65).

It is the disciplinary emphasis that separates TCK from TK alone (Ward & Kushner-Benson, 2010). Kirk (2012) adds to this by speaking of how the simple act of setting up 'a Facebook site or a blogging space for EAP learners' is a form of TK. However, this evolves to TCK if teachers understand 'how academic blogging may change relationships with knowledge, readership, dissemination, notions of academic style, and publication' (ibid). In order to fully enact such instances of TCK, Koehler & Mishra (2009, p. 65) argue that teachers not only need to understand how to relate appropriate technologies to specific content but also 'how the content dictates or perhaps even changes the technology – or vice versa'.

Technological Pedagogical knowledge (TPK) – Koehler & Mishra (2009, pp. 65–66) state that this involves 'an understanding of how teaching and learning can change when particular technologies are used in particular ways' according to purpose, and disciplinary 'context'. Unlike TCK, the emphasis in TPK is on how technologies shape teaching and learning, rather than how they shape content, as they are used in specific ways. As with Motteram's (2013) examples of technologies being used for different purposes to those for which they were originally created, Koehler & Mishra (2009, p. 66) go on to cite ways of using popular software programmes not designed for educational purposes.

TPK thus requires an ability to reconfigure tools for 'customized pedagogic purposes', and 'a forward-looking, creative, and open-minded seeking of technology use, not for its own sake, but for the sake of advancing student learning and understanding' (ibid).

Technological Pedagogical Content Knowledge (TPACK) – The six categories of knowledge that I have described intersect to form the core of the TPACK framework. Technological Pedagogical Content Knowledge is defined as 'an emergent form of knowledge that goes beyond all three 'core' components (content, pedagogy, and technology knowledge)' and is based on their purposeful integration (Koehler & Mishra, 2009, p. 66). Serving as the basis for effective teaching, this 'professional knowledge construct' (ibid, p. 66) establishes 'a dynamic equilibrium' (ibid, p. 67) amongst all of its component parts, and they must all be brought into play before an instance of TPACK is enacted. Going back to Kirk's (2012) examples of blogging, as instances of TK and TCK, there is a greater need for 'knowledge in action' (ibid) before something can be defined as TPACK. One possibility that he offers is 'scaffolding a group blogging project that centers around collaborative reflection on and critiquing of a selection of journal papers on a theme of disciplinary relevance to learners' (ibid). Through doing so, teachers enact what Hofer & Swan (2008, p. 181) describe as going beyond a process of design and action, to a form of knowledge in action that involves understanding the specific needs of students, and then facilitating a learning experience around these needs, which is the essence of TPACK.

Potential benefits of relating TPACK to an EAP context

Key terms in the TPACK schema strongly echo those of the core competency statements conceptualised by BALEAP (2008). Terms such as disciplinary context, purpose, knowledge, creation of materials, and integration of ICT resonate across the descriptors of both. Discipline-specific content is of particular salience to the contemporary direction of EAP, as discussed in Hyland (2006), Dudley-Evans & St. John (2009), Sloan & Porter (2010), Alexander et al (2011), Gilbert (2013), and Bell (2016). Furthermore, even though EAP and ELT are not 'subjects' commonly featured in TPACK literature, there are many references to disciplines supported by EAP. These include History and Medicine (Koehler & Mishra, 2009); Physics, Engineering, and Sociology (Harris et al, 2009); and Education (Dickenson, 2014).

In the specific context of EAP, Steve Kirk (2012) talks about using technology in sync with discipline-specific work by getting 'our hands dirty with e-AP tools', which are those electronic tools available for use in the teaching of English for Academic Purposes. He goes on to define TPACK in this context as being 'knowledge that develops to *enhance* EAP practice through technology' which needs to be turned into '*techknowlogy,* before it can be *enrolled* into pedagogical practices' (ibid). This new sense of practice amalgamates EAP and e-AP

(Fenwick & Edwards, 2010) which come together and connect to make technology an essential part of a new 'EAP practice ecosystem' (Kirk, 2012), where new tools are not simply applied to past pedagogy (Koehler & Mishra, 2009).

This new ecosystem can create 'a new learning environment' (Spires et al, 2012, p. 4) where teachers' professional knowledge can make a 'pedagogical shift to accommodate learning that is continuous, changing, and above all exponential' (Spires et al, 2009, p. 10). The emphasis on learning for both students and teachers again links TPACK's underlying values to those of BALEAP (2008). Further to this, and particularly salient to the EAP context, where there has been a historical demand for sharing of ideas and practice (Johns, 1981; Jordan, 2002), Mishra & Koehler argue that TPACK can help connect 'isolated pieces of the puzzle in our separate classrooms and discrete research studies' (2006, p. 1019). However, in making this claim, the door is opened to potential criticisms of TPACK because it assumes a popular knowledge of the framework that does not come across in the broader literature as yet, because of its relative newness.

Addressing a potential drawback of TPACK

Mishra & Koehler, from the outset, have admitted that it is 'extremely difficult' to represent teacher knowledge 'within one overarching framework or theory' and that any such representation of knowledge needs to reflect its 'socially constructed and dynamic nature' (2006, p. 1045). As such, elements of their framework remain as rudimentary as that of Shulman (1986/1987); hence why these constructs are best viewed as evolutionary frameworks of teacher knowledge. McGrath et al (2011, p. 1) support this notion by suggesting that TPACK 'does not appear to be a model that can be used as a single source of conceptual guidelines.' They go on to cite Angeli & Valanides (2008) who question 'whether TPACK is an adequate analytical theoretical framework' if used on its own (McGrath et al, 2011, p. 9). Largely, such concerns had arisen because of the absence of a sociocultural element in the framework.

However, TPACK's creators have tried to address this by more latterly placing their framework within the broader domain of teacher cognition, with direct reference to such works as Jackson (1968) and Clark & Peterson (1986). Through doing this, they aspire to bringing technology integration into play with other forms of knowledge in teaching and the profession's broader sphere of activity (Koehler & Mishra, 2009, p. 67). More recent adaptations of the TPACK model have included sociocultural elements, as in Figure 2's model of *'Context Influence on TPACK Knowledge'* (Mishra & Koehler, 2012). This model takes a new set of variables and interlinks these in an outer ring composed of the labels 'teacher training', 'experiences', 'students', 'resources', 'objectives/aims', and 'attitudes'. This adaptation is shown in Figure 2 and provides a more solid theoretical framework than TPACK in its initial formulation in Figure 1 for the

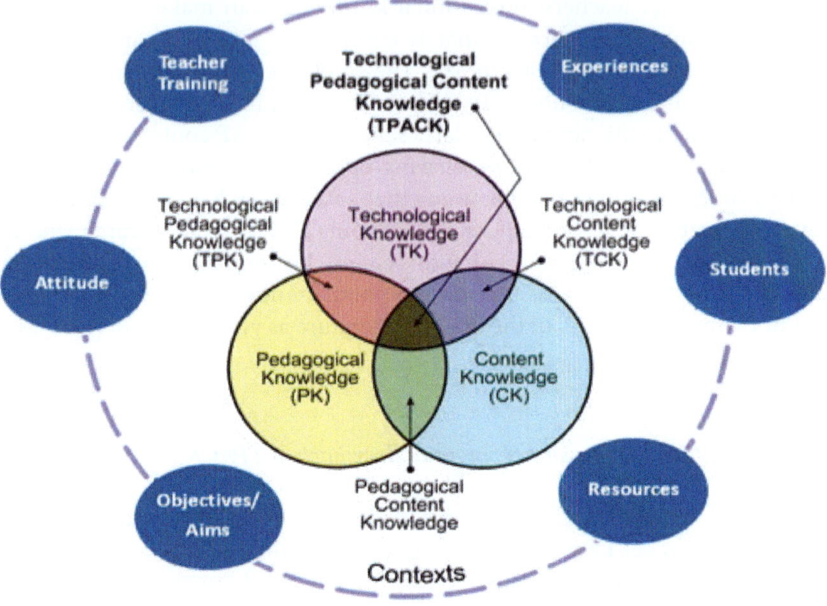

Figure 2: Contextual influences on the TPACK framework. *Reproduced by permission of the publisher, © 2012 by tpack.org*

principles that guided the teacher education programme, around which the research study was sculpted.

2.3 – Practical considerations

Preparation for the teacher education workshops

Preparations for the workshops began in the late summer of 2010, a time of great change and construction beyond the walls of the language centre. Every morning, on my journey to Liverpool Street Station, I passed through Stratford, deep in its last stages of preparation and development for the coming of London's 2012 Olympic games. Before events began, the country's top athletes had to undergo an intensive training programme at Lilleshall National Sports Centre in Shropshire. As a result of such development, many would eventually progress to becoming champions and household names.

Medals are very rarely awarded to those in the teaching profession, but the same standards of excellence are expected of its practitioners. To achieve this, there is a need for education rather than training. After all, Edge (2003, p. 7) states that 'to train is to instil habits or skills, and the word collocates just as happily with dogs and seals as with teachers.' Mann (2005, p. 105) suggests that teacher education is a 'bottom up process' that values the 'insider' view whilst training is 'top down' and places more emphasis on the 'outsider' view. This is again voiced by Diaz-Maggioli (2004) who suggests that too many professional development days have given rise to 'images of coffee breaks, consultants in elegant outfits, and schools barren of kids'.

Bearing this in mind, these workshops had to avoid such pitfalls, and place an emphasis upon 'self-direction' (Mann, 2005, p. 104), where teachers were not 'surreptitiously pushed in pre-determined directions' (Tomlinson, 2003b, p. 2). The way of doing this was to consult the teachers throughout the design process and to plan sessions around an ethos of interactivity and reflection. The fact of this being a research study also served to create a distinction between these sessions and other 'one-shot' (Meltzer, 2010) workshops in areas such as HR training, management training, or Health & Safety. For reasons of both ethics and ethos, participation in workshops was voluntary, with invitations sent by email through a fellow programme manager, as shown in Figure 3's authentic extract from the original contact with potential participants.

Dear all,

You are invited to consider taking part in a research study relating to developments in actions, knowledge, and practice that occur after a teacher education programme on the use of technologies in teaching.

This project is being undertaken by a colleague as part of his PhD research for the University of Manchester. Before you decide whether or not you wish to take part, it is important for you to understand why this research is being done and what it will involve and to this end, I have attached the information sheet alongside the consent forms which you are invited to sign if you decide to take part in the research.

Participation is entirely voluntary in both the workshops or the research. You are free to decide whether you wish to take part or not. If you do decide to take part you will be asked to sign two consent forms, one is for you to keep and the other is for our records. You are free to withdraw from this study at any time and without giving reasons ....

Thank you for your consideration of this request and I look forward to your response.

Dr. _______________________________

Figure 3: Extract from the email sent to all teachers at the outset.

This email from my fellow Programme Manager also offered the proviso that teachers had the freedom to participate in the teacher education workshops, without having to become involved in the research study. He also explained that those who signed up as full participants in the study would be invited to participate in focus group sessions, leading to individual interviews. There would also be teacher observations at various points of the study, which again were for developmental reasons rather than performance management. It was important from the outset to create as much of a distinction as possible between the research study and contractual obligations in the workplace.

To achieve this, I sought to give participants a sense of collaboration in the design of workshops, and perhaps even a form of ownership as envisioned in the work of Anne Burns in the field of collaborative action research (1999) or Wenger's Communities of Practice theory (1998, pp. 200–202). Rather than following the traditional definition of ownership, Wenger defines this as having control over the personal meaning that we attach to our practice and seeing that sense of meaning valued in a shared repertoire (ibid). Schlager & Fusco (2003, p. 209) further suggest that 'when professional development is embedded in a strong community of practice focused on instructional improvement, the community of practice owns a stake in the outcome of the activity.' It was thus important in setting up the teacher education programme that participants felt as if they had not just a stake and share in activities, but also a stake in the objectives and direction of the programme.

Establishing Moodle as a focus at the outset

In order to give teachers a meaningful stake in their own education, it was important to have a concrete focus for the introductory workshops, and the language centre's Virtual Learning Environment served this purpose. The reason for this was that Moodle was the much-publicised platform of use within the organisation; it was something that participants were already familiar with, and there was a demand from participants for greater knowledge in how to use the Moodle site. This was in keeping with a belief expressed by Brooks-Harris & Stock-Ward (1999, pp. 12–15) that the needs and voices of participants must be listened to at the outset of the design process. A workshop was thus designed drawing on ideas from Cole & Foster's (2008) publication *'Using Moodle – Teaching with the Popular Open Source Course Management System'* and Laurie Korte's (2007) training handbook entitled *'Moodle Magic: Make it Happen'*.

There was already a limited use of Moodle within the organisation and a half-formed, almost self-taught awareness of how to use it, but what was now required was for teachers to be shown to use it in a way that married together pedagogy and practice in the 'love match', as defined by Ham (2010), rather than any form of coerced relationship. The goal was to work upwards from what teachers already knew, rather than starting out with the view that the solution to development was to give them new knowledge on its own. This meets Richards & Farrell's (2005, p. 26) suggestion that the topic of teacher education sessions should also 'be one that participants have relevant experience in and ideas that they can draw on, or in cases where participants have little experience of the topic, a strong interest in learning more.' This also fitted in with Wenger's (1998, p. 249) assertion that the 'trainer' (sic) should find a point of leverage to 'build on learning opportunities offered by practice.' The point of leverage in this instance was the pre-existent usage of a Virtual Learning Environment in INTO UEA London. This could be described as what Nidumolu et al (2001, p. 3) have called the 'ground beneath' the management of knowledge, which consists of 'the situated contexts in which the production and exchange of knowledge occur' (ibid).

The ground beneath this context was the increasing usage of technology in the language classroom and the growing realisation of its benefits, and to develop closer 'integration of pedagogy and technology' as referred to in Thorpe (2002, p. 107). However, Thorpe does warn that projects are not 'necessarily collaborative or constructivist purely on the basis of using new technologies' (ibid). Nor should the introduction of these new technologies be uncritical since Njenga and Fuerte (2010, p. 191) and others suggest providing educators with the time and opportunity to explore both 'the dangers and rewards of e-learning on teaching and learning.' On the basis of this, I decided that the initial workshop on Moodle should be an exploratory one, looking mainly at the VLE, and its technological affordances. Through this, discussion might then be generated around its synergy with pedagogy and provide a starting point to initiate conversation in the first set of focus groups that would happen at a later stage.

Physical setting of the workshops

Brooks-Harris & Stock-Ward (1999, p. 46) argue that the physical environment of the workshops is a key area of consideration at the outset. Pacing, timing and ways of imparting knowledge are also crucial aspects of creating the right environment for participants. In this case the location was the London campus which was the 'home turf' (ibid) of the participants, and rich in technological affordances, particularly in terms of visual aids, access to computers, and to a wide range of media applications. Brooks-Harris & Stock-Ward (ibid, p. 58) suggest that 'media and other resources can be used to encourage reflection on experience' but warn against using resources for resources' sake by suggesting that specific resources should be used to match real-life situations (ibid). For example, as in the case of using Moodle, they state that 'if the workshop promotes the use of computers or other technology then it is best to have computers available with which to experiment and practice.' This, of course, would not always be possible at the outset but gradually, as the organisation invested in a greater number of laptops for teacher usage, it became possible for everyone to have access to the technology that was required.

TIME	KEY ACTIVITY	DATA GENERATED
Months 1–3	Needs analysis; planning of research & workshops; publicising workshops; getting ethical approval & consent	Field notes – from analysis of questionnaires, classroom observations, & discussions
Months 4–6	Workshops one & two – Introductory usage of Moodle/ Pedagogic approaches to IWB usage	Data from three focus group sessions, classroom observations, and field notes (diary records); analysis of work on Moodle
Months 7–9	Workshops three & four – Adapting traditional approaches to feedback in the digital age/ Advanced usage of Moodle	Data from three focus group sessions, classroom observations, and field notes (diary records); analysis of work on Moodle
Months 9–11	Workshops five & six – Blogs & wikis on Moodle/Use of technologies as a means of capturing lectures and recording feedback	Data from three focus group sessions, classroom observations, and field notes (diary records); analysis of work on Moodle
Months 12–14	Selecting cases & setting up of interviews, and observations	Individual interviews with four participants and observations of their lessons, & analysis of learning materials
Months 15 on	Data analysis.	Clarification (*if needed*) from participants.

Figure 4: Roadmap of time and activity in the research project.

Proposed sequence of the workshops

The workshops would take place over an eight month period and feature the specific subjects of *Introductory usage of Moodle; Pedagogic approaches to Interactive Whiteboard usage; Adapting traditional approaches to feedback in the electronic age; Advanced usage of Moodle; Blogs & wikis on Moodle;* and *Use of technologies as a means of capturing lectures and recording feedback.* The sequence of these and the details of how they fitted in with other aspects of the data collection process are outlined in Figure 4's Roadmap of Time and Activity in the research project. Further information on the pragmatics of this roadmap are provided in subsequent chapters relating to methodology.

Offering the first workshop to teachers

The first workshop in the sequence outlined in Figure 4 took the form of a demonstration of the affordances of the Moodle VLE and then an open discussion which I led about how this technological resource might assist us in our teaching and provision of content. This worked well because the audience was much more engaged than I had expected. This fits in with Klatt's (1999, p. 16) assertion that workshops should focus on 'opportunity and willingness', with people using their abilities collaboratively to overcome barriers in the workplace. I had identified one potential barrier that limited full usage of the VLE's rich set of affordances. That barrier was double edged: in some instances, there was a lack of understanding about what exactly the VLE entailed, but also a lack of certainty about how much autonomy users were expected to show in exploring the resource. Again, background context is important here because some of the teachers had never experienced workplaces that encouraged the freedom and self-direction found in higher education.

Creating understanding, stimulating discussion and providing information, mainly around technological knowledge, were the intended objectives of this introductory workshop. As Klatt (1999, p. 96) states 'workshops and training programs need direction and design to be successful, but first they need a destination.' The destination in this instance was the point of better usage and awareness of the VLE's affordances. Of course it was unlikely that such an ambitious destination could be reached immediately. This workshop would act as a point of leverage to steer participants towards more self-directed actions. As stressed by Richards & Farrell (2005), there had to be follow-up events, and space was made in the timetable for more explorations with Moodle to be arranged for smaller sub-groups. This was particularly useful for those who were less confident with using technology, and hence the prioritisation of presenting them with information at this stage, rather than creating a situation where they felt under pressure to demonstrate their usage under the scrutiny of public view in front of peers they might not necessarily have known well.

This also seemed the best way of setting the tone for the first of the three focus group sessions detailed in Figure 4 and discussed further throughout this work. These sessions were composed of nine teachers drawn from the broader pool of participants in the teacher education programme, and divided up into random groups of three for each of the focus group sessions. Even though the first workshop had been attended by twenty teachers across a range of subjects and not solely those connected to language, the people who participated in the focus group sessions all came from an EAP background. Further information about the participants is provided in Chapter 3, but the mood in the aftermath of the first workshop was one of growing desire to understand the usage of Moodle, and to work together to harmonise and utilise the energy and enthusiasm building up around its potential benefits. Practical instances of this included teachers beginning to personalise Moodle and use it as a forum for communication and interaction with their students.

As in Wenger's (1998) study of claims processors, teachers began to use the resources within their workplace in ways that these had not specifically been designed for. The EAP teachers and their colleagues from other disciplines such as Business and Economics effectively turned Moodle into an open and social space that was paradoxically private at the same time, almost beyond the walls of institutional interference. The prevailing mood of senior management appeared to be happiness that an expensive resource, which incidentally had never needed to be expensive, was now being used on a regular basis. The reason it was expensive was because of a management decision to host the site on an external server, rather than the language centre's own system. The fact of teachers using it consistently and for the benefit of students made this seem economically viable. Thus, seeing and hearing of developments with the VLE, senior management opted for minimal interference in teachers' affairs and allowed them to get on with the job themselves in a way that was perhaps more typical of traditional higher education than the private sector. Consequently, teachers reacted to this by treating Moodle as belonging to themselves and the students, beyond the radar of management. The VLE became a space for exploration, collaboration and the shared enterprise emphasised by Wenger (ibid).

2.4 – Lessons learned from the first workshop

It has long been established in teacher education that we need to be able to reflect upon our own progress in order to develop professionally (Wallace, 1991; Freeman, 1996; Roberts, 1998). Wenger (1998) suggests that this does not necessarily have to be done individually, but can happen through the emergence of communities. In this case, a community based on mutual engagement and shared repertoire began to emerge in the aftermath of the first workshop. Teachers, informally, more collectively than individually, began to explore new ways of using the Moodle Virtual Learning Environment. As such they seemed to 'deepen their knowledge and expertise by interacting on an ongoing basis' (Wenger et al, 2002, p. 4). These developments had been largely cultivated as a result of the workshops rather than growing organically, and perhaps supported an argument made by Wilson & Berne (1999, p. 194) that 'teacher learning ought not to be bound and *delivered*, but rather *activated*.' They go on to argue that such activation is triggered only when teachers come to an understanding of their own knowledge (ibid).

Developments at this stage remained subtle, though, strengthening and growing in a slow but noticeable manner much like the Olympic Stadium I passed every day on my way to the language centre. There was no great change or a sudden transition to practice informed by TPACK, but the trigger had been pulled on the starting gun of development. Teachers were finding their own voice in terms of the Virtual Learning Environment, making it a greater part of their pedagogy, while possibly at the same time continuing to use it as a repository, rather than teaching tool, for content. They were also working together as a community to a greater extent, which of course had been one of my initial objectives for the language centre.

I had set out to build a team of teachers and improve their practice by cultivating an environment where they would become self-directed to a much greater extent. Brockett & Hiemstra (1991, p. 29) define self-direction as the 'characteristics of an individual that predispose one toward taking primary responsibility for personal learning endeavours.' This often occurs at the juncture of past knowledge and new experience (Vygotsky, 1978; Manning & Payne, 1993). In order for such self-direction to be triggered, reflection plays a crucial part and in this research study, I was fortunate to have access to teachers' voices in the synchronous focus groups, and the teachers too were fortunate to have such a forum for the sharing of ideas, because this is accepted as being a vital part of activating self-direction, regardless of the theoretical lens such developments are viewed through. From the Communities of Practice literature to that of teacher cognition and TPACK, there is a shared acceptance of the fact that individuals at some point need to interact with others in order to become better at what they do. The focus group sessions would serve as a forum for such interaction.

CHAPTER 3

Insider Research and Ethical Issues

3.1 – Contextualisation

Creating space for verbal commentaries

Until now, the story has focused on the teachers as part of a team forming, and a group playing out their professional lives in a new language centre. Yet, like the Olympic Stadium's growing shadow a few miles along the rail tracks in the direction of Stratford, foundations had been laid for the next chapter. The main actors in the process of development and associated research study could now move centre stage. Against the backdrop of workshops, a group of nine teachers had volunteered to participate in focus group sessions held in comfortable, quiet, secluded non-teaching areas of the workplace.

Focus groups seemed more appropriate at this stage than individual interviews because the group met some of the criteria proposed by Arksey & Knight (1999, p. 75). These included the fact of being 'a naturally occurring social group' in the workplace, having information and knowledge that could be shared, corroborated and supplemented, and the counterbalancing effect of having participants offer insights on the same stories from a range of angles (ibid). Furthermore, such groups create 'opportunities for sustained concentration and discussion' (Mann, 2005, p. 111).

However, in arranging focus groups, nothing can be left to random chance. It is not a case of *'if you book them they will come'*; to cite a famous line from the postmodern American comedy *Wayne's World* (Spheeris, 1992), where the central characters arrange a rock concert purely by chance. Focus groups require a systematic approach from conceptualisation through to enactment of the discussion. In this study, other variables had to be taken into account too at this stage, such as the fact that teachers had 'busy classroom lives' (Burns, 1999, p. 14). Thus the sessions had to be both purposeful and productive, alongside Onwuegbuzie et al's (2009, p. 2) suggestion of being 'economical, fast and

How to cite this book chapter:
Breen, P. 2018. *Developing Educators for The Digital Age: A Framework for Capturing Knowledge in Action.* Pp. 39–56. London: University of Westminster Press.
DOI: https://doi.org/10.16997/book13.c. License: CC-BY-NC-ND 4.0

efficient.' Sessions were therefore arranged in conjunction with teacher needs and availability, giving the participants an equal right in making decisions about timing, and allowing them the right of withdrawal at any time. This latter option, though, was never taken up and everyone participated until the close of the focus group sessions.

I recorded the sessions through a sophisticated Olympus Digital Voice Recorder, which eliminated many of the traditional problems with audio-recording, and I also took notes simultaneously. As immediately as possible after sessions, which lasted from as little as 15 minutes to as much as 35, I transcribed the dialogue so as to not only capture 'the whole of the conversation verbatim' (Arksey & Knight, 1999, p. 105), but also to recall the 'emotional dynamics' (Poland, 1995, p. 221), while they were still freshly in mind. Further to this, I added in notes regarding non-verbal utterances and interactions so that when returning to the data, at later stages, I had preserved a sense of the naturally occurring interaction (Silverman, 2005, p. 157), which facilitates the qualitative researcher's requirement to see the world from the subjects' perspectives (Glassner & Loughlin, 1987, p.37).

This ability to see the world from the subjects' perspectives is particularly important in the teaching context because much of the literature highlights a discomforting absence of teachers' voices from the inside (Elbaz, 1991; Hargreaves & Tucker, 1991; Ellis, 1997; Freeman, 2002; Borg, 2006; Darling-Hammond & Richardson, 2009). Freeman (2002, p.11) advocates a need 'to return to teachers the right to speak for and about teaching' and suggests that 'while we might arrive at crudely accurate maps of teaching by studying it from the outside in, we will not grasp what is truly happening until the people who are doing it articulate what they understand about it.' Darling-Hammond & Richardson (2009, p. 5) further state that 'an understanding of the particular ways teachers talk and collaborate can provide insight into the role of professional learning communities in improving teacher practice.'

Travellers on the shared research expedition

In order to understand the voices of teachers in this study, it is important to firstly know who they are, or have as much knowledge as we can gain from the surface detail of a person's biography. These nine participants are detailed below, under pseudonyms, with the first four being the main cases within the later stages of this story (*Kelly, Harry, Matthew, and Rosemary*) and the remaining five participating in focus group sessions, but not the study's final stages. These five are, though, a part of the story, rather than a mere appendix. Justification for this view comes from Seawright & Gerring's (2008) discussion on the role of 'background cases' in small-scale qualitative studies, which 'are not cases per se' but 'are nonetheless integrated into the analysis in an informal manner' (p. 294). I have also heeded the advice of Hitchcock & Hughes (1995,

p. 319), who suggest taking into account other key variables such as participants' functions and roles, and their work responsibilities.

(1) **KELLY** – Teaching for five years, mostly in private-sector English Language schools, Kelly's first degree was in Criminology & Sociology. After completing this, she studied a CELTA course and spent a year working in China, teaching English and organising social activities. Returning to the UK, she assumed a position as a Senior EFL and Business teacher, in which she participated actively in what she terms as 'training' sessions with other staff. During her time there, she completed a Masters degree in Sociology and then moved to her present position as an EAP teacher, where her background in Sociology meant that she was also invited to teach some Humanities-related subjects on Foundation and Graduate Diploma programmes. Kelly, compared to the other main cases under investigation, was unique in having been in the English Language teaching profession all of her working life, since completing her university studies.

(2) **MATTHEW** – Matthew's background featured a combination of language teaching, freelance work in the music industry, and children's workshops facilitation. Having completed BA/MA degrees in Film Studies & Philosophy, and then a CELTA, his earliest work in English Language teaching served as a means of supplementing freelance work in the music industry. After six years of this, he became an Assistant Director of Studies in a language school for four years, before a two-year return to the music industry. Then, after twelve years of dipping in and out of English teaching, Matthew came to work as a General English teacher in the language centre. Seeing the opportunity to make a career of this, and move into EAP, he undertook a DELTA course at the same time as these workshops.

(3) **HARRY** – Having graduated with a BA in Politics and Modern History, Harry spent the first two and a half years of his working life as a charity fundraiser, during which time he completed a CELTA though did not move into English Language teaching immediately. Eventually, however, he found a position as a teacher in an international language school, where he moved into EAP through a Foundation Year programme, and then to a management position three years later. This was a role as University Pathways Manager where he was responsible for the delivery and organisation of a Foundation course, providing international students with access to UK universities. In this role and others, he was a self-professed advocate of using as much technology as possible in the classroom, and when he joined the language centre, five years into his teaching career, he expressed excitement at the prospect of working with a greater supply of technological resource.

(4) **ROSEMARY** – Similarly to Matthew, Rosemary's background involved dipping in and out of English Language teaching. After completing a BA in Business Management, she spent six years working in customer services, before going travelling and completing a Trinity TESOL course in Prague. Following a brief return to customer services, she moved to Japan where she spent eighteen

months as an English Language Instructor and Kids Trainer, before coming back to the UK to work in administration for another year. Having a self-professed love of travelling, and a growing interest in teaching, she spent two years working in language schools in Spain and Portugal, before returning to her home city in the north of England to work on a pre-sessional, thus entering EAP through the route described by Alexander (2010, pp.3–5). Having been considered a very good teacher on this course, she was recommended to the language centre as a prospective employee, and soon after took up a full-time position teaching Foundation EAP.

(5) **Derek** – Teaching for over thirty years, in both the British Isles and Japan, Derek wanted to participate in the workshops and focus group sessions as a means of learning more about the use of technology, particularly in the context of EAP. This was because he had moved into this branch of English teaching later in life. As a self-confessed technophobe, much of his experience was in EFL, initially, and later ESOL, particularly in the context of UK Further Education, to which he would eventually return.

(6) **Emily** – Different to the other members of the group, in the sense of coming from south east Asia rather than 'the west', and being fully bilingual, Emily holds two Masters degrees, one in Education and one in Linguistics, a portfolio of academic publications, and around fifteen years of teaching experience across various educational contexts in Singapore, the United States, Japan, and the United Kingdom. She had joined the language centre at a very early stage and progressed to an ELT/EAP management position, prior to starting the workshops, playing an important role in helping teachers in the use of Moodle, particularly for purposes of course organisation.

(7) **Frank** – One of three non-British teachers, Frank's introduction to teaching was in American elementary schools, after graduating as a certified teacher of ESOL, and foreign language instruction. This was followed by half a decade of English Language teaching, and management positions in China, before moving to the UK for personal reasons, where he first taught IELTS in a private language school, and then found work in the language centre. As with Emily, Frank joined the language centre at an early stage and had assumed a more senior management role (non-EAP) prior to the workshops.

(8) **James** – Having moved into English Language teaching six years after his initial graduation in English Language & Literature, James had over ten years of teaching experience in various contexts. These included spells in Poland (two years), China (seven years), and then London (one year). Again, as with Rosemary, his entrance into EAP, in the UK context, came about through work on a pre-sessional, and then some sessional lecturing in various places, before he took up a full-time position in the language centre six months before the workshops began.

(9) **Patricia** – Another American teacher, Patricia had, like Rosemary, spent the early part of her career in administration before moving into English Language teaching where she worked in the Middle East, completing a Masters

degree in TESOL before settling in the United Kingdom for personal reasons. Until taking up a position in the language centre, she had spent a year doing sessional teaching. One of Patricia's primary interests was in the design of materials not just for EAP but for other courses in the centre.

The role of ethics in research practice

Ethics is the common ground that unites all research from the moment that a project is conceptualised until, and even after, the final story is written or told. That is particularly evident in a study such as this where the goal is to present a narrative shaped by the voices of teachers. Such a narrative could have been further complicated by the fact that I knew these teachers very well, and was not conducting the research as a detached outsider. However, it is important to stress that ultimately the teachers were not writing their own stories. Even if their words and actions laid foundations for the research story, the final authorial voice is mine, as researcher. Working now for a different organisation, I can look back from a distance on people and events, but at the outset of this study, I was a manager within the research setting. This raises a particular set of ethical issues, taken very seriously within the higher educational milieu, as reflected in the abundance of regulatory codes of practice and literature related to these (Cohen et al, 2013, p. 75).

Contemporary literature on ethics covers a broad canvas connecting Nuremberg to the Northern Ireland Police Service, social research to medicine, and the Stanford Prison Experiment (Zimbardo, 1972) to Jean Piaget's (1959) study of his own children. Yet each situation is unique, and this is why there is 'no one framework that can be agreed upon to ensure ethical research' (Richardson & McMullan, 2007, p. 1116). Even within and across institutions, different rules often apply in each unique context. Most contemporary research, though, begins with ethical approval, and I had to seek this from two institutions: firstly, the site of my PhD studies, and then my work setting. This is perhaps one of the reasons why Cohen et al (2013) recommend a situated, context-specific approach (p. 76) and the design of a personal code of ethical practice (pp. 102–103). Such a code of practice would complement Figure 4's Roadmap of Time and Activity in the research project.

Alongside the creation of such a code, there is also a need to accept the pre-eminence of ethics above all else, and to work out how to ensure that the voices of participants 'can be heard in the way they wish them to be heard' (Bird, 2005, p. 228). A person's voice is more than simply 'verbal sound and authentic dialect' and must include 'social context' along with 'embedded and intended meaning' (ibid). To demonstrate this, I will use the example of Rosemary, one of the central participants in this research study. Getting a sense of Rosemary's voice does not simply mean that I describe what she says and then add a basic layer of interpretation to that. Rather, it is more important to understand her perspective on time available for experimentation with technologies than to know she has a North Eastern English dialect.

However, it could be important to make that a part of her story if it relates in some way to our understanding of how she might approach teaching with underlying social conscience and compassion generated by the experience of growing up in a post-industrial region ravaged by unemployment. She values hard work and sets high standards for herself. That, though, is my characterisation of her based on what I have seen as well as heard, which gives rise to another issue highlighted by Roberts (1997, p. 169) regarding 'whose story' is actually the one that is being presented. Yet, surely this knowledge of Rosemary's character and who she is as a person, rather than simply a research participant, adds to the story and gives it a richness that might not be attained through the detached perspective of an outsider.

This use of Rosemary as an example illustrates two of the main ethical issues in this research study, namely the methods of generating data, and the subsequent means of reporting findings from that. Ethical considerations, though, could not just be reduced to these two issues. Although the main goal of my study was to find credible information about teachers' actions and knowledge, such revelations would only be acceptable if I ensured the participants' wellbeing (Teddlie & Tashakkori, 2009, p. 198). Laying the foundations for this involved adherence to guidelines from the Economic & Social Research Council (2005), whose Research Ethics Framework serves as the basis upon which most universities establish their ethical policies.

However, it is also important to stress that reducing people to being no more than subjects, or even no more than their profession, goes against the grain of this study and the values of qualitative research. Support for such a position is found from Hammersley & Traianou (2012, p. 12), who point out that participating in research based around 'ordinary activities that we all engage in every day' (EAP teaching in this context) is a very small part of people's broader lives. Therefore, from my perspective, it would be unethical to report this study without acknowledgement of the broader lives and personalities of the four teachers who make up the final cases in this research study.

Further support for such a decision comes from Susan Malone (2003, p. 800) who draws on the work of Williams (1996) in calling for 'a kind of 'coming-clean' genre' in our research literature. She argues that this can be achieved by encouraging researchers to share honest accounts of how they have faced ethical challenges in their work,. When researchers are being honest, such challenges are presented not as a sanitised and surgically altered appendage but as a story baring its scars in their rawest form. In this instance, that means highlighting the issue of how knowing the participants on a personal level enhanced the final story, rather than detracted from it. Thus, having offered an overview of all nine participants in the focus group sessions, I am now going to provide vignettes from the (inter-)personal lives of the four teachers who would serve as the final cases to be examined in detail. By doing so, I hope to show a more naturalistic context that will lend itself to Miles & Huberman's (1994, p. 21) call for 'well-grounded rich description and explanation of processes occurring in local contexts', which again falls in line with the underlying principles of the qualitative paradigm as a whole.

Vignettes of the teachers' broader lives

i. Harry

Harry, amongst other things in life, is a talented musician, and was embarking on a voyage into England's folk music scene at the start of this research study, making a name for himself as a singer and songwriter. One evening, I made a journey to London Bridge to watch his band performing folk tunes and sea shanties in a replica ship on the edge of the city's financial district. Under the boat's low ceilings there was barely room to move, as Harry's three-piece folk group took to the stage as darkness set in. Tuning up, and setting up, they took several minutes to switch roles from spectators of other acts to main performers themselves. Then, as the show started, Harry, an EAP teacher for most of the day, transformed into a purveyor of folk songs, some traditional, some he'd written, and others cleverly adapted. From a position below in the audience, I watched eagerly, in the company of another colleague.

On stage, Harry's performance had echoes of English Language teaching. He'd stand up, sit down, change positions, and move around the stage according to the resources at his disposal, whether his voice, guitars, or other instruments he would sometimes use. With his adaptation of instruments to the needs of a particular song, or performance piece, tools were being configured around the purposes and objectives of each situation. Comparisons could be drawn with the way that he integrated technologies into his teaching and improvised according to student needs, but this vignette of Harry, the musician outside of the classroom, serves mainly as a snapshot of who he is as a person, and how that too might feed into his practice.

ii. Kelly

After one Christmas break, Kelly decided to undertake a new challenge of running the annual Brighton marathon in the spring. There, she would find herself alone against the elements, relying entirely upon natural resources to get through the race and push across the finishing line. She had set out to raise funds for the charity *Mind*, and collected a considerable amount of money through her promotion of the race, and the cause, on social media. Throughout her preparation, she provided updates on her development, sharing stories with the friends and colleagues who had supported her. From this combination of her own resourcefulness, and the usage of the internet, whether to inform, advertise, or collect money through electronic payments, she raised several hundred pounds for the charity.

On the day of the race, I went to watch. Running, as a spectator sport, holds no great appeal for me, but I decided to lend some moral support. It was also interesting to see how technology had been incorporated, in a normalised, unobtrusive manner (Bax, 2003). In the olden days, there might have been legions of auxiliaries with clipboards, and stewards governing the starting line. Here, the process was simplified by equipping every runner with an electronic device that clicked into action as soon as they crossed the starting line, and recorded timings. Better still, this acted as a tracking device through which it was possible to keep up with a runner's progress on the internet. Therefore, hours later, I would see that Kelly's friends and colleagues in London had been posting social media updates of her progress, and finishing time.

Here, in the digital age, she was not so alone as she might have been a generation ago; running the very same route but equipped with an iPod's wealth of songs to keep her entertained, and the knowledge of being connected to those supporting her from the sidelines, or through cyberspace. She still had to run the 26 miles, though, and did so, before a beer to celebrate, and then a train journey back to London, to teach the following morning.

iii. Matthew

Matthew was one of several teachers who gave me a gift when I finally left the workplace in which I had conducted this research study. His choice of farewell present was something very personal, a CD of his own instrumental music on which was handwritten *'Best of luck and thanks for your help.'* Outside of teaching, Matthew is a composer for theatre and film, creating soundtracks for shows and festivals on the arts scene throughout the country and beyond. His music is experimental, a combination of natural resources and uncommon instruments producing what he describes as 'layers of melody'. Added to this, the accidental and the improvised are integral parts of his music, echoing 1920s jazz, and in the ELT context, Scott Thornbury's advocacy of Dogme (2000), based on the cinematic approach of the Dogme 95 movement (Von Trier & Vinterberg, 2002).

This CD, then, contained a range of sounds such as I might find on the cliffs and by the sea of the Irish coastal town where I had come to write my thesis. The emphasis was on the natural and the atmospheric. This was a form of storytelling without words, or using no more words than necessary to get the meaning across. Listening to these 'songs', studying the ornate artwork of the cover, I recalled Matthew's arrival at the language centre three and a half years previously. Then, he was on his way to Italy to perform in a festival of theatre and music, but seeking work for September when this was done.

After a decade of drifting between language schools to feed the hunger of his avocation, he wanted steady work, though not just yet. He was looking for someone to give him a chance, to explore new areas of teaching, and develop for the future. At the time, we needed a General English teacher, and preferably one who might 'progress' to EAP after some further experience and 'training'.

On that basis, we decided to give Matthew a career opportunity, sensing that he was as passionate about teaching language as he was in composing and producing those songs without words.

iv. Rosemary

Rosemary, at the start of her time in the language centre, had moved down from the north of England. She had grown up in a town with a strong regional identity, and a rich history stretching back to Roman times. From an economic perspective, the town had known riches too in the days after the Industrial Revolution, thanks to shipping and coal mining. But the halcyon days of those industries had started to pass in the decade of Rosemary's birth, and in the early years of her childhood, the last of these businesses closed down. This led to a gap in the economy that has blighted the north of England ever since.

Despite the challenges posed by the break with traditional industries, this part of England has retained a strong community spirit and distinct character. Those who know Rosemary might say she bears the same hallmarks. She enjoys doing things and getting things done effectively, being the organiser, and the motivator. Very often, she acts as the fulcrum for social events and team building, whether in the workplace or outside. Even long after this research study has ended, she still brings former colleagues together to meet up on occasion, as in the brief vignette offered here.

The scene, then, is one of Rosemary and colleagues, including Derek, gathered in a famous vegetarian restaurant in the centre of London. Here, we see her at the core of the group, having scheduled and planned the meeting. When chatting, she switches between tales of work and personal life, perhaps sharing stories of journeys back up north to her close-knit family. Everyone's engaged in the conversation because she likes them to be, and they agree this is a great choice of venue. It was Rosemary who first discovered it, being a long-term vegetarian who had stayed faithful to her convictions even when teaching and travelling in Asia, where such a diet is more challenging. The scene in this restaurant, then, provides a glimpse of Rosemary as a person perhaps not so different from her character as a teaching professional. There too, she played a central role in the formation of a community, based around teachers and the Moodle Virtual Learning Environment. Similarly, in the centre and in the focus groups, she was never shy in voicing her opinions, particularly regarding issues such as having enough time for development.

Ethical minefields that could arise

Research, like teaching, can be a messy business, with various personal or political 'minefields' and 'realities' along the way (Malone, 2003, pp. 797–799). In this study, as might be expected in qualitative research, many of the potential minefields emerged along the way rather than being predetermined. Though there were no major ethical issues in comparison to a medical study, for example, several pitfalls had to be avoided in the course of the journey. Susan Malone warns that, regardless of any 'checklist' at the outset, 'unanticipated ethical dilemmas' are bound to arise (ibid, p. 814). One such dilemma was that of 'casualties among participants' (ibid, p. 797), which is not to be taken in its literal form but as referring to drop-outs in the research study. Such a situation arose towards the end of focus group sessions, where some of the participants withdrew for various reasons, such as finding employment elsewhere. As outlined throughout this work, this situation was not without benefits and actually helped avoid a potential minefield of participants being unhappy about final selection of cases.

Other ethical situations existed from the outset. To begin with, there was a need to ensure that participants knew what they were getting involved in. Full details of the study had to be disclosed in advance before the teachers formally agreed, in writing, to participate. This is known as informed consent, which the British Sociological Research Association (BSRA) describes as being 'necessarily vague' in terms of predetermined rules to follow (2002, p. 29). Such flexibility exists because, for example, there is a clear difference between asking teachers to talk about technologies, and asking someone to disclose their full sexual history. Of course, damage to an individual can occur anywhere upon this spectrum. If I were to go into someone's classroom and give them extremely negative feedback about their teaching, it could have repercussions for their performance, their health, and so on. Even something as simple as me, the manager, pointing out differences in espoused and actual practice could have an impact on a person's confidence or career.

Added to this, there was always the danger of more subtle forms of pressure because of my role as manager, and the false sense of being 'at home' in the workplace. Malone (2003, p. 811) suggests that a 'home' setting can 'camouflage' the issues implicit in such a situation, 'those of institutional power and relationships.' Indeed, she goes so far as to say that 'the most dangerous and difficult place to attempt qualitative research is in a familiar institutional setting, especially when one of the participants is in a position of power over other participants' (ibid). Another area of concern might be using research participants out of 'self interest' (ibid, p. 812), or out of 'self-advancement', as discussed by Mason (1996, p. 29). Additional questions have been raised by Hammersley & Traianou (2012, p.3) regarding how much autonomy and power can be offered to research participants because so many of the final choices and decisions have to be the researcher's. Other concerns relate to issues of data recording, storage, privacy, confidentiality, and anonymity. Hammersley & Traianou (2012, p.5) also suggest that researchers need to look at the bigger picture beyond participants themselves. They point out that 'a study could damage the public reputation of a large organisation, a particular occupation, community group, or national society, and thereby the interests of those involved in it' (ibid).

In this case, two immediate areas of concern arise. The first is the risk that I could manipulate the data for the political purpose of attacking either private or public providers of higher education. The second is the fact that some portrayals of EAP inadvertently create an impression of its teachers being accidental tourists in the world of academia. Such portrayals are dangerous for the long-term future of the subject and for the morale of its more academic practitioners. In both of these potential minefields, the real danger, though, is subjectivity. However, rather than denying its existence, it had to be accepted and addressed through close collaboration with the research participants.

Of course, the biggest issue with this study, from the perspective of outsiders, would be the fact that it took place in an environment where I was a manager – not just that, but a direct manager of several participants. This could be seen to accentuate some of the situations highlighted above, such as gaining consent and adding subtle pressure to the already busy lives of teachers. The act of observing teachers is one where ethical boundaries could become blurred, if it were not clearly stipulated that these were not performance appraisals.

Care then had to be taken in the practice of implementing ethical procedures and also in understanding the nature of insider research. In line with Williams' (1996) emphasis on coming clean in the research story, my initial reason for formulating arguments in favour of insider research was a means of preparation for completion of PhD studies with the dreaded viva. Getting deeper into the literature, I developed a genuine desire to champion this area of research where practitioners have often been shy about trumpeting its benefits for fear of being seen as unscientific. There is much to be gained from conducting what has variously been described in the literature as insider research, inside research, the Insider Doctrine, work-based research, or a further genre of manager-inside research highly pertinent to this study (Coghlan, 2001; Mercer, 2007; Moore, 2007; Coghlan & Brannick, 2009). However, others such as Kerstetter (2012) argue that a great deal of contemporary research actually exists on a spectrum of 'insider, outsider, or somewhere in between' (p. 99). Ultimately, though, to avoid confusion in the narrative, I have opted to use the basic term 'insider research.'

3.2 – Theoretical foundations

The origins of insider research

This study fits Coghlan & Brannick's (2009, p. x) definition of someone doing research in the organisation where they work, at the same time as seeking certification on an academic programme, and thus assuming an 'explicit research role' in addition to a 'normal, functional role.' Taking on this multiplicity of roles, manager, colleague, researcher, and learner too, I would inevitably face challenges along the way. Alongside honesty about my position as manager-researcher, as a means of addressing challenges, Platt (1981) recommends a solid foundation of support from the literature. To begin with, then, it is important to understand the history of insider research.

Such studies, from the outset, present a challenge to traditional notions of scientific research as something conducted by objective outsiders. Simmel (1950, p. 405) portrays the researcher as a stranger who must 'experience and treat even his close relationships as though from a bird's eye view', which is again echoed in such seminal research works as Denzin & Lincoln's (2000). Insider research contends that such outsiders 'will never truly understand a culture or situation if they have not experienced it' (Kerstetter, 2012, p. 100). This is why certain disciplines such as fieldwork-based Anthropology and Sociology have sought out more intimate methods of enquiry in the past half century. Bartunek & Louis (1996) define this as 'going native' in order to understand societies in their natural form. Mercer (2007) illustrates how this epitomises a shift in social anthropology from the study of exotic societies to those closer to home, within researchers' own 'social and cultural backyards.'

This terminology of 'backyard research' has featured in the work of Glesne & Peshkin (1992) and Creswell (2009), who defines it as 'that which involves studying the researcher's own organization or friends or immediate work setting' (p. 177). Again, such features can be mapped to the study herein. Additionally, being an insider can lend itself to a rich and thick description of the context, as is generally required of qualitative research, and thus has been readily adopted by practitioners within this paradigm. Furthermore, insider research supports Vygotskian perspectives regarding cruciality of context and situated cognition. Such forms of research can facilitate deep understanding of development as a process and not just a finished product (Hung & Chen, 2001, p.4). As such, they are congruent to Vygotskian thought where one of the central underpinnings of situated cognition is that it is 'the history of a relationship that causes an outcome' (ibid).

Thus, insider research has not only mapped out its own identity this past half century, but also proven capable of being married to various historical frameworks associated with the qualitative research paradigm. Although it still has critics, its usage has increased substantially in the past couple of decades as evidenced by the amount of studies now conducted in this way, not just in Sociology but in other disciplines such as Education. Mercer (2007) points out that 'the great proliferation of Masters and Doctoral programmes' has partially accounted for this growth (p. 2), but so too has the lack of funding available for teachers conducting 'practitioner research' (ibid).

Definitions and challenges of insider research

Mercer (2007, p. 7) likens the act of 'conducting insider research' to 'wielding a double-edged sword', whilst others have variously described this as 'backyard research' (Glesne & Peshkin, 2002; Malone, 2003; Creswell, 2009), and 'the original sin of ethnographic research' (Moore, 2007, p. 27). This 'forbidden fruit' (Moore, 2007 ibid) involves studying the researcher's own organisation, or friends, or immediate work setting, wherein role conflicts can compromise transparency, disclosure and reportage (Creswell, 2009). Wandering into this forbidden garden could have been further complicated in that I was both manager and researcher, but similar complications could have occurred in the event of being Simmel's (1950) 'stranger'. After all, Mercer (2007, p. 8) narrates the story of Margaret Mead and tales of casual love under the palm trees, where a renowned anthropologist appears to have been misled by her 'native' subjects in a historical representation of their sex lives in the publication *Coming of Age in Samoa* (Mead, 1936).

However, despite this infamous scenario of Margaret Mead's informants 'regaling their inquisitor with counterfeit tales of casual love under the palm trees' (Freeman, 1983, p. 289), the strengths of insider researcher are not simply a reaction to the weaknesses of more detached methods. Mercer (2007, p. 8) points out that the 'potential for distortion' might be even greater in cases of insider research. This could be particularly true in situations where managers want to portray their studies as 'trophies on the mantelpiece' (Breen, 2007) shown off for reasons of self-interest.

Coghlan (2001) suggests that such a dual role, if not handled correctly, could cause conflict and ambiguity. This is then discussed more extensively by Coghlan & Brannick (2009), who outline the different roles that manager-researchers assume, and their potential pitfalls. These include issues of identifying more strongly with the organisation than the research participants or vice versa, and thus losing a sense of subjectivity; making judgements based on tacit rather than explicit knowledge; and being too close to the data in physical and emotional terms (ibid, pp. 61–66.) Mercer (2007, p. 7) echoes this by suggesting that what insider researchers gain in terms of 'their extensive and intimate knowledge of the culture and taken-for granted understandings of the actors' may be lost in terms of 'their myopia and their inability to make the familiar strange' (Hawkins, 1990, p. 417). Similar suggestions are found in earlier literature such as that of Scott (1985, p. 120), who raises the question of how to tell 'where research stops and the rest of life begins', as exemplified in the vignettes of (inter)personal lives.

Furthermore, Hockey (1993, p. 204) maintains that insiders are better able to 'blend into situations, making them less likely to alter the research setting'. Added to this, it is not just teachers who can assume a range of identities. Just as Harry can be teacher, musician, colleague and friend, so too can researchers assume a range of identities on Kerstetter's (2012, p. 99) spectrum of 'insider, outsider, or somewhere in between'. Even Mercer (2007), in comparing insider research to a double-edged sword, admits that 'the insider/outsider dichotomy is actually a continuum with multiple dimensions, and that all researchers constantly move back and forth along a number of axes, depending upon time, location, participants and topic.' Therefore it is possible to be a manager at one point in a relationship, and a doctoral researcher in the workplace at another, because of today's commonplace environment where 'the great majority of students complete (PhD) courses on a part-time basis whilst continuing with their regular jobs, with the result that their own school or college often becomes their research site' (ibid). Ultimately 'there are no overwhelming advantages to being an insider or an outsider' (Hammersley, 1993, p. 219), as what is lost on the swings is made up for on the roundabouts (Merton, 1972, p. 33). There are, of course, practical steps that had to be taken so as to avoid my dual role becoming an Achilles' heel in the research; a source of blood to be drawn on the 'double-edged sword' described by Mercer (2007). Such steps are outlined later in this chapter, but essentially relate to managing a 'pluralism of roles' (ibid, p. 7). Once the parameters of relationships are established and made clear to participants, insider research can facilitate ease of access, 'informed knowledge', 'authenticity', closer relationships, and 'richer data' (Arksey & Knight, 1999, p. 67).

3.3 – Practical considerations

Addressing the issue of insider research

Ways of protecting against the sharp edge of insider research are listed by Coghlan & Brannick (2009). The first of these was to ensure that the study was conducted in the capacity of PhD candidate, with the purpose being professional research rather than disclosure of information to, or about, the organisation. Like a growing number of students in the digital age, my story is one of part-time study whilst continuing with regular employment. This involved travelling along 'a continuum with multiple dimensions' (Mercer, 2007, p. 1) at the same time as developing 'my own interpretation distinct from the orthodoxy of the organization' (Moore, 2007, p. 27). Coghlan & Brannick (2009, p. 68) also point out that doing research as a PhD candidate, if handled effectively, can become a form of 'third-person research' in the organisation, wherein the insider is temporarily playing an outsider's role.

Establishing a clear understanding of my role reduced the tendency to 'dive-bomb' into a purely impressionistic and subjective alternative to 'more arduous' quantitative methods rooted in traditional objectivist epistemologies (Watson-Gegeo, 1988, p. 575). Systematic approaches had to be applied across the entire research process from data generation to analysis, with the 'focus on learning the meaning that the participants hold about the problem or issue, not the meaning found in the research literature or subjective judgements about people and issues' (Creswell, 2009, p. 175). Thus, from the outset, I tried to empower teachers as equal participants in this study.

I began this process of partnership with the design of an information sheet as part of a call for volunteers, sent out to all teachers in an email by a colleague.

Within this, we emphasised 'confidentiality' (Arksey & Knight, 1999, p. 68), alongside the 'pluralism' of my role (Mercer, 2007, p. 7). This issue of 'overlapping personae' (Young, 2005, p. 158) was one stressed repeatedly to those teachers volunteering. For example, at the start of every focus group session, I made clear that '*I am doing this in the capacity of doctoral student in The University of Manchester.*' To have added the phrase '*rather than as your manager*' would have been paradoxical to the concept of assuming another role, and illustrates the crucial nature of language in creating environments that are not at odds with paradigmatic values.

Fostering such an environment was assisted further by the unique nature of the setting, as outlined in the contextualisation chapter. Most research settings have a weight of prior history (Platt, 1981; Edwards, 2002) that, for example, in the EAP context might stretch back over decades. However, because this was a newly formed language centre, we had been working together for less than a year when this study was conceptualised. As such, this reduced the potential for existing beliefs, expectations, presuppositions, and politics to have undue influence. Furthermore, this newness allowed me to portray the research study as a journey of learning and development for each of us. My approach to leadership was characterised by a style of consensus, and emphases on team-building and individual strengths, as with Seed (1958) writing in the context of football management.

Stenhouse (1975, p. 143) further emphasises 'the uniqueness of each classroom setting' as a place of research and also each individual teacher's development as being unique, echoing Burns' (1999, p. 3) reference to the needs of 'these students in this situation and this set of concerns.' Therefore, as a manager, a colleague, a person, and a teacher and researcher, I was interested in the individual stories and needs of those who spend their time in classroom settings. Cultural background played an important role too in that, having worked in former polytechnics, I was more used to flat, democratic structures than hierarchical systems. I would also add that, through being in a position of manager, I was able to influence the organisational culture in a positive way by bringing these values into play, which is another strength of being a manager-researcher (Coghlan & Brannick, 2009, pp. 109–115).

This consensual democratic approach manifested itself in the informal, but organised, atmosphere of the focus group and interview sessions. Similarly, in the observations, I emphasised my roles as doctoral student and teacher developer, distancing these from any appraisal process. This was made easier by the fact that, as a new organisation, the language centre had no official appraisal system in place as yet. As a consequence, all observations were conducted from a developmental stance, using a range of creative, contemporary techniques such as '*catching somebody doing something right*' (Blanchard, 2004). Aside from this, by using the ISTE Classroom Observation Tool (Appendix 2), I was further able to separate work that I had to conduct as a manager from work that I was doing in a research capacity.

When reaching the stage of data analysis, I heeded Cohen et al's (2013, p. 179) call for honesty, depth, and richness of interpretation and reporting, seeking credibility rather than absolute truth (Glaser & Strauss, 1967). Being an insider, I was able to collaborate and corroborate my interpretations with participants, as suggested by Creswell & Miller (2000). One example of this comes from the final stages of analysis where a phrase from Kelly's initial focus group session was echoing and re-echoing in my mind regarding *the bit I really like about teaching.* In order to clarify exactly what she meant by such a loose term as *'bit'*, I asked for a second individual interview, using the actual interview transcript as a source of stimulated recall so she could remember the original context (Calderhead, 1981; Mann, 2005; Borg, 2006).

Talking to Kelly in the light of her recollections, I gained a stronger sense of what she meant by *'the bit'* she really liked about teaching. Essentially, this referred to personal interaction and communication with students in a natural way without the potential barrier of technologies. Having gone through this process of clarification, I was better able to report this from her perspective rather than my own. As such, I was putting into practice not just the strengths of insider research but the underlying values of qualitative research, and a desire to shape the final narrative in the voices of participants. Similar strategies were enacted for all cases, as required, and this collaboration proved invaluable, highlighting the benefits of relationship-based research, which can be more difficult for outsiders. Of course, there was no competition between insider and outsider research. Rather it was a matter of choosing what worked in this context while applying systematic and ethical procedures throughout.

Ensuring consent for the research

Another issue of ethical importance was the previously mentioned matter of gaining informed consent. This was sought at the outset and assurances given regarding anonymity and usage of data. However, it is undeniable that in this digital age the boundaries of identity have shifted, and anonymity seemed not such a major issue for teachers of this generation. Furthermore, talking about technology hardly equates to any deep personal revelation. I would also argue that many EAP teachers aspire to having their voices publicly heard in the broader ELT community's debate about technology, as evidenced by the proliferation of contemporary blogs in this area, and BALEAP's (2008) emphasis on the sharing of ideas.

Therefore, though I opted to offer anonymity as a means of reassurance, this was less of a concern than ensuring that the teachers understood what they were getting into, as advised by the British Social Research Association (2002). Thus I provided full details on the consent forms, and once these were distributed, discussed, and signed, I had established an 'implicit contractual relationship' with participants (Cohen et al, 2013, p. 81). This would serve as a foundation on which subsequent ethical considerations could be structured, but was never intended to be a 'one shot, once and for all affair' (ibid). It was also important that 'no group should be disadvantaged by routinely being excluded from consideration' (BSRA, 2002, p. 14), and so all teachers were invited to participate, which resulted in nine choosing to volunteer. Though participants could have been entering a fog, blind to research discourse (Malone, 2003), I was fortunate that EAP teachers share a professional understanding of it, and a probable 'methodological sophistication' allowing for a 'covenantal' partnership between me, as researcher, and the study's participants (ibid, pp. 805–806). This again helped to address the issue of manager-research, because I was treating the teachers as being equal to me in terms of their background understanding of the subject. Even if my status in the workplace may have been different to theirs, the terrain of this study was one of professional research rather than 'work.'

3.4 – Lessons learned at this stage

On the whole, then, I would argue that, far from being a potential Achilles' heel, my role as manager-researcher has been a strength. Now that I can approach the research context with the benefit of hindsight, through no longer working in the language centre, I am also in a position to see how my role created the potential for this study. This may not have been possible if I had not had the opportunity to manage a programme of teacher development, and conduct research governed by a desire to share the stories of teachers in their own words and actions where possible. In doing this, my research echoes and at the same time differs from other contemporary work, such as that of Douglas Bell (2016) in his study of the positioning and professional identity of EAP practitioners in UK universities. Also carried out within the qualitative paradigm, Bell's research draws on interviews with fifteen internationally recognised EAP scholars, which then give shape to a series of narratives that capture a sense of how the subject or even academic discipline of EAP has developed from the 1960s up until the present day (ibid).

Bell's (2016) research makes a major contribution to EAP in the sense that a series of narratives from some of the most significant theorists in the field has now been preserved for posterity in his thesis, and hopefully future publications. It is invaluable to have a historical record such as that, but in this study the voices that have been captured are closer to the ground and again add to that sense of EAP as a chameleon discipline. This is because our perceptions of EAP seem to be largely shaped by our first-hand experiences of the subject and the socio-political or economic context in which we work. Even in my role as manager within the language centre, I had an element of detachment from the everyday work of teachers in the classroom. This, at times, can create the sort of 'hermetically sealed' environment described by Ding & Bruce (2017, p. 10), where managers are out of touch with the realities of what is happening in everyday classrooms: like the designers of a Music curriculum trying to get the students to understand Mozart when they can't even decipher basic notation. Added to that, another question could be how we reconcile our aspirations to teaching Mozart with situations where the academy itself just wants us to teach students the basics of playing instruments.

Thus, in this situation, by talking directly to ordinary practitioners I could get a better sense of what was happening at the teaching interface despite the possibility of such participants not being able to articulate their experience at the level of theoretical expertise found in studies such as that of Bell (2016). Though there could have been 'minefields' and 'realities' along the way (Malone, 2003, pp. 797–799) as a consequence of being so close to the ground of my own workplace, most of these were addressed by careful planning and consistent application of particular values to the study. At other times, things fell into place naturally – such is the character of real-world research – as in the situation with choosing the cases for final selection. That too, though, was not so much an accident as being in the fortunate position of conducting research in a workplace that I held an intimate knowledge of. By being there as such eventualities took place, I was able to react accordingly.

Similarly, through knowing the teachers, there was less of a danger that they might embellish their stories as in the Margaret Mead (1936) situation. Such an act is difficult when knowing people on a personal level and regarding them as equal partners in the research journey, whether in the context of a vegetarian restaurant, a stage performance, or teaching with technologies in the language classroom. It is in nobody's interest to portray their stories as trophies on the mantelpiece; better to present them as they are, and allow readers to take from this what they choose. However, although the voices of teachers are central to this study, it is an over-simplification to think they speak for themselves alone (Mauthner & Doucet, 2003, p. 418). Therefore, it is important to stress that even though the final narrative has been shaped by giving equality to the voices of teachers, treated ethically and respectfully throughout this research journey, the storyteller's voice is mine, and that too has been aided by what Edwards (2002) deems to be 'deep insider research.' In this study, I have gone as close to the roots of EAP teaching as possible and in doing so have grounded the findings in teachers' everyday practices. Without the benefit of being inside the organisation, it may have been impossible to do that and strip back the various shades and layers of opinion that shape EAP teachers' perspectives on their chameleon subject.

CHAPTER 4

The Drive from Inhibitions to Adoption

4.1 – Contextualisation

Talking about technologies

In the midst of the study, a new colleague arrived in the language centre freshly equipped with a PhD in Education and asked me what exactly I was trying to discover in my research. Was it about technologies, and if so which technologies? Surely, she noted, it would be impossible to keep up to speed with all of the latest developments in a time of such rapid change, as voiced in much of the TPACK literature. The goal, then, in the opening focus group session was not to test teachers' knowledge of technologies, but to get a sense of their perceptions about technology's usage in EAP teaching, and how their past and present experiences had shaped those perceptions.

Thus, the opening question in the first series of focus group sessions required the teachers to discuss prior experience of teacher training and teacher education. Here, I used the term 'training' for pragmatic reasons even if epistemologically I do not agree with the implications of the word. This was influenced by the fact that the term was almost ubiquitous in the language centre in referring to any form of developmental activity. Much of that was to do with the background of the teachers and the habitual usage of such terminology within the English Language Teaching industry. Aside from this, the opening question was not the most critical of the session in terms of the conversations that it was intended to generate. The questions that followed sought to get a deeper understanding of human perspectives on technology, and to get a sense of teachers' expectations about their development.

The second point of discussion began with an outline of the teacher education workshops and the research study as detailed in Figure 4. This then fed into a question about what participants hoped *'to gain from the workshops in the coming months.'* Through personalising the discussion in these early stages,

How to cite this book chapter:
Breen, P. 2018. *Developing Educators for The Digital Age: A Framework for Capturing Knowledge in Action*. Pp. 57–73. London: University of Westminster Press.
DOI: https://doi.org/10.16997/book13.d. License: CC-BY-NC-ND 4.0

it was then possible to further investigate teachers' attitudes to technologies, which was an essential part of mapping their development as educators. The precise question that I asked to gain this information was as follows: '*How do you feel about using technology in general in the EAP classroom?*' This was then followed by a statement that '*this can even be in situations outside the context of our centre at the present time.*' This was the question that created divergence from the loosely pre-planned script, according to the different points made and issues raised by each group. In each session, though, I pointed out that '*it's quite okay to stray off topic.*' For example, with Kelly, Matthew and Patricia, the conversation diverged to a discussion about the potential '*messiness*' of technology, and this eventually led to the whole session tapering out on this issue. However, in another one of the groups, Derek, Emily and James discussed the issue of '*students*' at length; feeding into a final question about '*students' attitudes to the usage of technology.*' Significantly, though, all of them covered the ground that had been intended at the outset, which was to explore teachers' perceptions of technology and get a sense of their expectations about how they might develop over time.

Technology and the human touch

One of the most interesting points to emerge from the first focus group sessions was the manner in which the teachers spoke about technologies, not just from a professional perspective but also a personal one. This is exemplified in the extract below which comes from a discussion that Kelly was having with Matthew and Patricia with regard to their usage of technologies in the EAP classroom. This is also where Kelly talks about that '*bit*' she likes about teaching, and technology sometimes acting as a barrier to that. Here too, she is also touching on a very grounded sense of what EAP and English Language Teaching should be about as she gives us a glimpse into life at the interface of her everyday practice and interaction with students. She is almost making a call for the bright lights and glitz of technologies to be torn away sometimes and the chameleon bared in its truest form.

> '*With the overhead projector and the board and that layout with the tables facing the board, I wonder whether or how we can maintain the interactivity. So for example at the moment we are all sitting together in a circle facing one another and we can see each other and if we don't understand something we can ask each other for clarification. We can say what do you mean and that meaning is kind of negotiated between us but in a classroom if you move all the tables back and you sit in a circle and you don't use that technology you kind of force people to ... erm ... it's personalised and you force people to negotiate the meaning themselves and if they don't understand each other then they have to say what do you mean*

and explain further. (Matthew murmurs yeah.) And that's the bit I really like about teaching, that just doesn't have any computers involved. So I guess that's another thing, just I like to see how to look at computers and see all the exciting things that we can do and not get carried away with it because you know lots of cultural critique is saying that there is so much technology that people don't really interact with each other face to face; it's through Facebook and text messages, and I like to keep the human element in.'

Within the opening focus group sessions, the human element that Kelly spoke of came to be a recurring feature, often voiced through synonyms or similar ideas rather than direct usage of that term itself. According to the participants, technology presented a challenge to some of their traditional ideas about pedagogy, particularly all they had been taught about language teaching. Kelly, Derek, Frank, Matthew and Patricia, in particular, talked about the ways in which technology, rather than fostering interactivity, could create potential barriers between teachers and students. Both Frank and Matthew gave the example of PowerPoint, with the former suggesting that *some teachers will make PowerPoints, throw PowerPoints, do PowerPoints, read from the PowerPoints and students will just sit there, and they're not listening.'*

Matthew went on to describe this as *'a static presentation style'* that most teachers would never use when working with other resources. Labelling this as a *'bear pit'* that teachers are in danger of unconsciously falling into, he elaborated that this transmission style of teaching facilitated by the technology goes against *'everything that you have ever been taught about how people learn, that they have to think for themselves … do guess work … and predict.'* Moving on from this, Harry proposed that such a situation might be okay in what he terms *'subject-specific lectures'* but *'if you're doing anything language related, if you're just going through a whole bunch of slides it's kind of putting a barrier between you and the students. It's kind of about using the technology in a more interactive way and not just because you can.'* Derek, in response to this, echoed Koehler & Mishra's (2009) work[4] on the underlying principles of TPACK when he said that *'it's a case of not just using technology for technology's sake'*. This evoked similar resonance with TPACK philosophy in Emily's subsequent assertion that *'it's about using technology appropriately in such a way that enhances the students' learning.'*

However, there was also a sense that sometimes usage of technology in the language centre was driven by an expectation of usage rather than the foregrounding of student needs. James perceived this to come from a possibly false expectation that *'all students love technology and are au fait with all aspects of technology.'* Kelly, on the other hand, echoed Hamp-Lyons (2011, p. 96) in referring to the all-permeating physical presence of technology, and how she perceived this to be the key driver for its usage. When asked why she chose to use technology, she gave the very simple and obvious response that *'just its being there implies its use.'* Elaborating on this, she remarked that *'obviously there's the electric whiteboard in every classroom.'* Perhaps drawing on her knowledge base in the field of Sociology, she added that *'there's a connection of technology to being professional perhaps so that also implies that it might be expected by the students.'*

In Kelly's case, then, I got a sense that she sometimes felt driven towards usage even though it went against some of her natural feelings and instincts about how people communicate, and what was best for the students. Again, this was a feature of Rosemary's dialogue, where she felt a need to use the technology only at times when it was beneficial to students. This came across most evidently in her assertion that *'sometimes you can focus so much on the technology that you're not actually focusing on the teaching. You're just looking at all the gadgets and the things they can do. You're not focusing on the teaching itself or on the student teacher interaction.'* Rosemary's reference to gadgets had resonance with views expressed by both Emily and Patricia, with the former giving an example of how iPods had been introduced to one context where she worked in the past, and at first had seemed *'a brilliant idea'*, but then turned out *'to be cool for a while, but didn't last long.'* This was because *'after a while the students realised that they weren't really learning, that there was nothing different from a CD.'* This idea of adopting technology purely for short term, populist reasons came across as one of the potential *'bear pits'* spoken of by Matthew. Patricia especially expressed the form of concern voiced by Alvesson & Sandberg (2013, p. 20) when they warn against embracing 'fashions and fads' in society which are a 'hot' topic today, but in danger of going 'cold' tomorrow. Matthew too expressed a worry that *'we've all got used to doing things like PowerPoints and whatever, interactive Starboards and so on, then the next thing comes along and makes us all look like yesterday's news.'* From Patricia's perspective, the biggest problem was the sense of investing wasted time and energy in something that goes out of fashion so quickly. She bemoaned the fact that *'you learn it once and you think you know it. Then the next version comes out and you don't have time to relearn all of the technology every time Microsoft wants to make some more money.'*

Harry, though, unlike most of the others, welcomed the speed of change. He anticipated that this change would probably come even faster with resources such as interactive whiteboards because there is the potential for these tools to achieve much more than their present capabilities. He suggested that in the near future there will be an integration of the existing touch screen whiteboards and the mobile technologies popular with students at this time, where *'everyone's sat there with their iPhones shifting things around'* in a way that is *'a bit more advanced and a bit more user friendly.'* Emily too accepted rapid change as being an inevitability, suggesting that *'I don't think we have a choice on the changes. We just have to keep up with it. And the stronger our foundation in it, the easier it will be for us to adapt.'*

The desire for a foundation in knowledge

Emily's call for a foundation of knowledge added to the chorus of requests for what most teachers still tended to describe as *'training.'* Though terms such as education and development might be preferable, the usage of that word seems calcified in the professional development lexicon of many teachers. The teachers expressed a common set of reasons for seeking the *'training'* that Edge (2003), Diaz-Maggioli (2004) and Mann (2005) all rally against, such as concerns over the speed of technology's advancement; fear of stagnation; confidence-building; and the reinforcement of prior learning. Derek also put forward the suggestion of incorporating a theoretical aspect into this too, so that teachers could learn not just *'how'* to use technologies but also a theoretical rationale as to the *'why'* of their usage. Harry supported this in his reckoning that people should be taught *'not so much about how to use programmes themselves but more about the link between the programme and the classroom … the integration of it rather than how to use it.'*

Though Harry gave the example of *'Second Life'* as a possible resource for learning about integration, the use of interactive whiteboards seemed more relevant to all of the teachers' everyday practice. As Kelly had alluded to, these boards effectively acted as the centre of gravity in every classroom. On the positive side, there was a common recognition of them being easy to navigate at their most basic level and of providing the same affordances as traditional whiteboards, alongside an additional electronic display function. Negatively, such a function could ensnare teachers into the habit of using them as a glorified projector screen. Kelly, for example, echoed an earlier concern of Matthew's when she suggested that *'I guess I'd be worried that I'll just slip into a way where I've just got a million kinds of PowerPoint projections and it might become very static in the classroom.'*

Teachers on the education programme, then, seemed to share a common fear of the technology, at this stage, inhibiting their practice. They were learning about Moodle but this was largely perceived as something that had benefits outside of the classroom – although both Matthew and Harry spoke of integrating the VLE into actual lessons involving the teaching of writing. Because of the physical presence of the interactive whiteboard in every classroom, and the traditional associations of a board as being at the very heart of teaching, going right back to the slate blackboards of the 19th century, these teachers felt ill-equipped without deep knowledge of how to purposefully use the Hitachi Cambridge Starboards. Derek, for instance, gave an example from one of his lessons where *'with how to operate the board, how to push the buttons, the students showed me how to do it.'* Again, another teacher who was not so au fait with technology asked Frank if there were any *'opaque projectors'* because she was unaware that it was possible to scan her slides, and then project these through the Smart Board technology.

This and several other examples supported the need for a workshop in this area, even though teachers had been using these boards every day for months. Without some type of spark or impetus for development, though, there seemed limited possibilities for developing the synergy of pedagogic and technological knowledge that would lead to better usage in the classroom. Providing a trigger for such development (Wilson & Berne, 1999, p. 194) would serve to foster 'a forward-looking, creative, and open-minded seeking of technology use, not for its own sake, but for the sake of advancing student learning and understanding' (Koehler & Mishra, 2009, p. 66). This then set in motion plans for designing a workshop on the interactive whiteboards as laid out in the roadmap of time and activity in Figure 4. That particular focus had been chosen because of the specific technology's role as a central teaching tool within the organisation, and because the earlier needs analysis had shown a demand for knowledge of this. The VLE had already helped foster a sense of communal development in the language centre, and my goal was to somehow replicate that with the IWB in a way that also brought its usage in line with task-based and constructivist views of learning.

4.2 – Theoretical foundations

Integration of interactive whiteboards

There is not a great wealth of information in the literature about interactive whiteboards (IWBs) in the context of higher education, as the bulk of work on them has been done in the primary and secondary school contexts. Branzburg (2008, pp. 1–2) describes such boards as 'being connected to a computer and LCD projector' which can be used for purposes of display, input, annotation, projection, and recording. He goes on to describe Hitachi Starboards, the particular resource supplied by management in this research context. These offer classrooms 'the next generation interactive whiteboard' through multi-touch gestures similar to those of an iPhone (ibid, p. 3). However, he does note that this brand originates in the corporate world, unlike those such as Promethean's Activboard designed 'by teachers for teachers' (ibid, p. 7). Regardless of that, the way he describes the board's affordances suggests that it can already do many of the things that Harry aspired to in his anticipation of *'the next generation of that kind of thing.'*

In the literature that has emerged in the context of higher education, there is a recurring sense that the forms of usage advocated by Branzburg (2008), and Harry in the focus group sessions, are not being realised. Dickenson (2014, p. 14) criticises IWBs as being a 'low-level' form of technology, facilitating integration at an 'adoption' level without 'significantly altering pedagogy (Cuban, 2003)'. This is echoed in the work of Munro (2010), McGrath et al (2011), and Kirk (2012), with the latter writing in an EAP-specific context. The main issue cited by these authors is the lack of innovation, and these boards being used no differently to traditional chalkboards, which have been around since 1801, as pointed out by McGrath et al (2011, p. 7).

However, there is also an underlying sense that IWBs have the potential to reach a level of 'invention' (Cuban, 2003); 'interactive engagement' (Kirk, 2012); and usage from a 'project-based perspective' (Dickenson, 2014), if teachers are provided with the requisite theoretical and practical training (McGrath et al, 2011). Within the literature, positive examples of IWB usage can also be found in various contexts. Slaouti et al (2013) present a vignette of a teacher in the UK Further Education context making a PowerPoint lesson more interactive for students on an IWB, whilst Pim (2013, pp. 22–23) presents an instance of a board being used as a karaoke-type device that allows students to 'digitally visualise rhymes and songs'. The latter example may seem of more relevance to an ELT context, but such facilities could easily be adapted for more academic purposes. There is still a fear, though, as voiced by Emily, of certain technologies being no more than a gimmick that seem hot, or even cool, today and then go out of fashion. For this reason, in the literature, just as in the focus group sessions, the jury seems to be out as to what IWBs really contribute to higher education. One thing that is certain, though, is that they have become established as a centre of gravity amongst the technologies that permeate today's lecture theatres.

Challenges to technology's adoption

Within the preliminary set of focus group discussions, consistent reference was made to inhibitions and concerns regarding technology's usage. This, though, was not an unexpected development because when the voices of teachers are heard in the literature on teaching with technology, there is often an undercurrent of concern. Even passionate advocates of technology such as Punya Mishra and Matthew Koehler, for example, have never portrayed electronic resource as the panacea to every historical challenge in teaching. Teaching existed for a very long time before the arrival of today's high-tech tools, and so too did resources that meet the basic definition of technologies. Mishra & Koehler (2006, p. 1023) point out that these range from 'textbooks to overhead projectors, from typewriters in English Language classrooms to charts of the periodic table on the walls of laboratories.'

Today's technologies, though, are seen to present unnecessarily 'wicked problems' in the classroom (Borko et al, 2009, p. 3). This is evidenced in a study by Velliaris & Willis where one teacher speaks of consciously making a decision to avoid 'technological nightmares' because of technology's failure to act as a 'stand-in for capable instruction' (2014, p. 16). Other teachers in the Velliaris & Willis study (ibid) share the focus group concerns of Matthew and Patricia by talking of the struggle to keep pace with the newest of these technologies.

Adaptation is as much of an issue as integration, and this is accounted for in the literature by an emphasis on the 'protean', 'unstable', and 'opaque' nature of today's Web 2.0 technologies (Koehler & Mishra, 2009, p. 61). Such technologies might include social networking sites and video sharing facilities, as in those listed by Watson (2012) and Motteram (2013).

Other voices reinforce these sentiments from an anti-technology perspective, or out of caution regarding the advantages technology brings to education. Within the 'anti-technology' literature, there is a genuine and often socio-political discontent with what some describe as a 'technocorporate matrix' (Johnson et al, 2008, p. 278) pushing particular forms of technology into the educational milieu. The view that this has proved successful is perhaps backed up by Kelly's focus group reference to a professional expectation of using technology. Such concerns, though, are not new and historical critics are listed alongside the disparaging phrases they have coined by Cummins (2000, p. 537) who outlines how Postman (1992) talks of 'technopoly'; Barlow & Robertson (1994) refer to 'the disinformation superhighway'; and Stoll (1996) speaks of 'silicon snake oil'.

More recent criticisms have come from Neil Selwyn in his 2010 publication *'Schools and Schooling in the Digital Age.'* In writing about teachers' resistance to digital technology use, he states that technologies such as VLEs could be argued (2010, p. 108) 'to depend on the deskilling of teachers and their students, engendering a 'tool' mentality where technology is used to 'yield mechanical tasks and situations of social disconnect' (Monahan, 2005, p. 290).' This echoes Johnson et al (2008), who assert that, despite good intentions, 'the advent of blended learning and e-learning innovations has ostracised, marginalised or ignored those who cannot afford or who are unable to access the latest hardware and software to take advantage of these opportunities' (p. 275). Such an argument goes right back to discussions that came about at the start of the digital age regarding the need for access to match other considerations of teaching with technology. However, this access is not just limited to the provision of computers. Rather, in today's age of heightened internet security, access often involves a struggle to obtain passwords, get through firewalls and so on. This is why many critics are not against technology per se, but rather its surrounding environment.

Even those who combine criticism and commendation where technology is concerned raise issues that resonate with issues raised by the focus groups. They include Zhao et al (2002), who admit to 'the messy process of classroom technology implementation', and Beetham & Sharpe, who see the dangers in an 'often uncritical attitude to internet-based information, and the cut-and-paste mentality of a generation raised on editing tools rather than pen and paper' (2007, p. 5). Similarly, Lea & Jones (2011, p. 377) raise concerns about 'undergraduates being so immersed in web-based technologies in their broader lives that they have difficulties engaging in more conventional study practices such as academic reading and writing essays.' These latter concerns, though, would not emerge from the discussion amongst teachers until a later stage, but they provide a sense of issues lurking in the background with regards to technology's relationship to content knowledge.

Activating and underpinning the existing knowledge base

Though his quote is three decades old, the words of Richard E. Clark regarding the use of media in the classroom remain highly relevant today. In a journal article on 'Reconsidering Research on Learning from Media' (1983), he stated that technologies 'are mere vehicles that deliver instruction but do not influence student achievement any more than the truck that delivers our groceries causes changes in our nutrition.' Though I disagree with the assertion that media can never influence learning, his views on the primacy of pedagogy are not so far removed from the underlying principles of TPACK. His opinions have greater synchronicity with Mishra & Koehler's (2006) position than those of Don Tapscott (1998) and Marc Prensky (2001), who have argued that this new digital age is so radical that the nature of academic study itself is outdated, and thus needs a complete overhaul, involving reconstruction around today's technologies.

Mishra & Koehler (2006) take the position that new media should be seen as a further step in the culture of education and society's use of technology, rather than something wholly radical. This has been expressed by others such as Warschauer (2002), who states that contemporary changes in education are as major as earlier revolutions in language, writing, and print (p. 521). Motteram & Sharma (2009, p. 86) compare the advent of new technologies to past developments such as 'the Socratic method', 'manuscripts in early monastic education', and then books in the wake of Caxton's printing press. Furthermore, and of particular salience to this chapter, McGrath et al (2011, p. 7) nominate the chalkboard as an example of a traditional technology which has evolved since its invention in 1801 into its present interactive, electronic adaptation; 'the form and function' of which are essentially the same as its ancestors'. Similar themes have been explored by Eshet-Alkalai (2004) and Soffer & Eshet-Alkalai (2008), who discuss a pendulum-like historical swing linking the reading of ancient hieroglyphics to today's HTML.

Therefore, a substantial amount of literature supports the notion that the tools of classrooms might be different but the underlying rules are similar. This fits in with Motteram's (2013) argument that education cannot be divorced from the sociocultural context in which it occurs. Thus 'technology's role has been socially shaped within the field of language teaching, and language teaching has changed profoundly too' (ibid, p. 184). In order for teachers to develop their technological knowledge, they need to draw on traditional understandings of how to manage and adapt to change. They need to take mental charge of technologies, bringing these tools into their 'cognitive space' (Mann, 2005,

p. 108), and allow their pedagogic strategies to become the classroom's centre of gravity rather than any individual resource, whether Moodle or an IWB. In order to do this, Warschauer (1998) suggests having personal philosophies of teaching, whilst Mann (2005) states that a crucial first step is the establishment of foundations for individual development.

Experienced teachers, though, are not working from a base of freshly dug trenches in an unfamiliar site. The architectural structure of pedagogic and content knowledge is already in place, and therefore what is needed is a procedure known in the construction industry as 'underpinning'. Essentially, this involves a process of adding new material such as concrete to the existing infrastructure of a building so that it can maintain its stability in a new set of circumstances. This new set of circumstances might come about in the aftermath of an earth tremor, for example, or in anticipation of one. Technology for some teachers, such as those in the Velliaris & Willis study (2014), might appear to be a never-ending source of such tremors. However, the way for them to guard against this is to draw on their existing knowledge base of teaching, as referred to by Shulman (1986), and Koehler & Mishra (2009).

Even though teachers might be confronted with the tremor of a new resource, such as an IWB, for example, they should not feel like novices in its presence. Rather they should relate the use of this tool to what they already know about 'the processes and practices or methods of learning and teaching' (Koehler & Mishra, 2009, p. 63). By doing this they are taking charge of the resource and controlling the trigger of their own development. Such development, according to the Vygotskian perspective of Manning & Payne (1993, p. 62), comes about as a result of synergy between past knowledge and new experience. That belief, then, in knowledge as a spiral, shaped the workshop on whiteboards which, as stressed before, had not been so universally welcomed as Moodle even though several teachers identified this as a 'training' need.

4.3 – Practical considerations

Demystifying interactive whiteboards

The *Merriam Webster Dictionary* (2016) informs us that the transitive verb 'demystify' originates in the very modern times of 1963, and provides the definition 'to make (something) clear and easy to understand: to explain (something) so that it no longer confuses or mystifies someone' (30-11-2016). Interestingly, the example sentence that it provides relates to the demystifying of computers, and in the Oxford English Dictionary too, they use the example of '*this book attempts to demystify technology*' (accessed 30 November 2016). The term has also featured in a 2003 article by Mark Warschauer on '*Demystifying the Digital Divide*' and in the EAP literature from Hyland & Hamp-Lyons (2002). As such, it seemed an appropriate title for the second in the series of teacher education workshops, with this one happening as part of what the organisation had labelled as a Staff Development Day, in the middle of the academic term.

I approached this workshop differently to those focusing on the Moodle Virtual Learning Environment. Firstly, I realised that the use of a whiteboard, compared to a VLE, goes right to the core of a teacher's identity, and has particular symbolism for English Language practitioners of a generation schooled in the teaching paradigm of presentation, production and practice (PPP). Admitting an inability to use this resource fully might cause awkwardness in a room full of colleagues, as suggested by Patricia in the opening focus group session. There she told the other participants that *'nobody wants to walk in front of their co-workers and say I don't know how to do this or I'm particularly bad at that.'* Kelly agreed with this in adding *'Yes, it's quite scary to admit that you don't know something about an aspect.'*

From a TPACK perspective this is also interesting because at this stage Kelly's focus seems to be on 'aspects' of individual technologies rather than on more holistic ways of using them in the classroom. This might be why, as mentioned earlier in this chapter, she had also spoken of creating an environment, possibly within her own comfort zone, where there is no technology involved, and she can fall back on communicative approaches, and a knowledge base that has probably served her well in the past. However, what seemed certain at this stage was the demand for increased technological knowledge on the part of teachers. This knowledge, though, featured more of a process of underpinning than laying new foundations because teachers had been working with these boards for quite some time. In order to consolidate existing knowledge and simultaneously facilitate new knowledge, I decided firstly to take a flipped-classroom approach to this workshop. The flipped classroom is one where students do core work in advance of classes rather than during classes (Tucker, 2012), and is a concept that has its roots in the work of Alison King (1993) and Eric Mazur (1997), though neither of these authors used the term directly in their writings. For the purposes of the workshop, the flipped materials came in the form of an eight-page booklet that I designed for sending out to teachers in advance of the workshop. The opening section of this booklet can be seen in Figure 5 – referring to the website geographypages.com – with a sub-heading shaped by issues that had arisen in the earlier needs analysis. This was a question about whether these boards were a case of 'smoke and mirrors, or a means of enlightenment for the students'.

Essentially, this booklet steered teachers through basic usage of the IWB, right up to utilisation of its more complex functions. The former included basic recording and storage facilities whilst the latter featured the design of lessons combining the IWB's capabilities with other technological resources, such as the integration of PowerPoint, or video and audio. The purpose of this was to provide a learning platform for those who were only using the board as a glorified projector screen whilst at the same time not patronising or wasting the time of those more fluent in usage. As with the Moodle workshop, the objective

---

Interactive Whiteboard Training

Smoke and mirrors or a means of enlightenment for the students?
Session conducted by Paul Breen.

According to www.geographypages.com "the main features of an IWB are the interactions between resources such as CD-ROMs, website pages, Word documents and PowerPoint slides and the pupils / teachers. Tools such as highlighters and coloured pens will also be available. Images can be called up quickly, and demonstrations can be made of tools such as rulers and protractors. Students can come up and 'draw what they mean' on the board."

But how does this relate to the teaching of academic English and what can we do with them to enhance the student experience? This workshop will examine some basic ways of using interactive whiteboards, mainly taking examples from English Language Teaching as the means through which we will explore the pedagogic rather than technical benefits of interactive whiteboards.

To do so, you must firstly consider the ways in which you (1) use the interactive whiteboards in your classroom and (2) want to use these in the future. Now, make a list of these and consider whether each action or planned future action is shaped by (a) pedagogy (b) technology or (c) a combination of both.

Figure 5: Opening section of the IWB 'training' document.

was not just to provide technical information. There had to be discussion about the pedagogic rationale for using interactive whiteboards, and the challenges they presented in the classroom, as raised in the initial focus group sessions. A recurring example of that came in the way that teachers voiced concern about them being a barrier to interaction, and encouraging a regression to delivering rather than activating learning.

Intramuscular approach to development

Staff development days are sometimes characterised by 'top-down' training and the prevalence of style over substance that contributes little to teachers' real and busy lives (Diaz-Maggioli, 2004). Partly this is because such training sessions occur as part of an 'episodic, fragmented approach' (Darling-Hammond & Richardson, 2009, p.3). Workshops delivered in this manner tend to be governed by a 'drive-by' or 'one-shot' approach. Sykes (1996, p. 1) writes that 'the phrase "one-shot workshop" entered educational parlance as shorthand for superficial, faddish inservice education that supports a mini-industry of consultants without having much effect on what goes on in schools and class-rooms.' Admittedly, this type of session does have a role to play in other areas of education, such as library inductions or basic admin training for both teachers and students. However, the contribution that these episodic sessions can make to long-term development seems minimal.

Thus, it was important for me to establish a linkage between the session on IWB usage, and the broader teacher development programme. That was done in the first instance by adopting the 'flipped classroom' approach, which supported a view of development as a 'sustained, coherent, and intense activity' (Darling-Hammond & Richardson, 2009, p. 3). It was made explicit to teachers that the workshop served as the mid-point in a broader developmental process, rather than the start of something that would last little more than an hour and fade into memory during the next coffee break; another recurring image of 'training days' according to Diaz-Maggioli (2004).

The expression that I have deployed for such a process of sustained and intense learning over a period of time is 'an intramuscular approach to teacher development' (Breen, 2013). This comes from medical terminology, where we find two common forms of injection, subcutaneous and intramuscular, with the latter being 'a technique used to deliver a medication deep into the muscles' so as to facilitate long-term storage and gradual release into the bloodstream (Cafasso, 2015). Common examples of this form of medication include hormone treatments and the flu vaccine (ibid). Though such injections may indeed involve a single shot from a syringe, the impact is long-lasting. This fits in with Richards & Farrell's (2005, p. 23) description of workshops as 'an intensive, short-term learning activity that is designed to provide an opportunity to acquire specific knowledge and skills.' Thus, that was the value set I brought to the table in preparation for the delivery of the workshop. In order to ensure that the learning was not forgotten very quickly, it was essential to provide context-specific ideas that could be put into practice. If this was not just to be a one-shot exercise, there had to be some form of learning that would lead to developments in actual classroom teaching.

Actual delivery of the IWB workshop

Teaching, educational development, and research rarely run as smoothly as we anticipate, and it emerged in the run-up to the Staff Development Day that I could not manage at a macro level, and organise the workshop at the same time. Therefore, a colleague named John volunteered to run the session for me, provided I gave him all the materials and guidance beforehand. This colleague was not participating in the research programme as such because he was a teacher of Mathematics and Science, rather than EAP. Additionally, he claimed no expertise in the use of interactive whiteboards, which seemed to go against the Richards & Farrell (2005, p. 23) suggestion that workshops should normally be conducted by someone who is recognised as an expert in the particular subject being shared or delivered. However, we came up with a strategy of using this lack of expertise to our advantage in the workshop.

This teacher of Science and Maths agreed to run the workshop as an interactive seminar-type session where he was a partner in the learning process with the other teachers in the room rather than as an expert imparting knowledge. This turned out to be very interesting because we had effectively a full house of participants: over twenty teachers, not just of English for Academic Purposes, but other subjects too. John took centre stage in the crowded classroom, with the IWB switched on behind him, and set the context for his audience. He had taken over the running of the workshop because of my time constraints, but felt that he needed to admit his own lack of knowledge in the subject, and a need for communal assistance.

The way that he delivered this message was both welcoming and humorous, breaking the ice in a session that could well have fallen into the bear pit of being mechanical and 'technocentric' (Papert, 1987). The audience warmed to John as he invited them to participate and to come up to the board itself at regular intervals to demonstrate a particular technique or activity that they had used in their lessons and wished to share. Because John, the person leading the session, had no inhibitions, this mood spread throughout the room, and effectively neutralised such fears as those voiced by Patricia and Kelly in the focus groups. John's actions and activities fed into a sense of it not being necessary to understand every aspect of the board in order to produce activities that were beneficial to students. He was also indirectly giving credence to Derek's technique of putting the teacher in the position of learner, and getting the students to help out at certain moments. The mood in the room was one of relaxation and humour, perhaps more typical of the inevitable social gathering in a pub at the day's end than the soulless atmosphere of 'training' days described by Diaz-Maggioli (2004).

The aftermath of the IWB workshop

Leaving the scene of John's workshop, teachers' voices buzzed with a sense of anticipation and activation of new ideas. Heading for refreshments, ideas developed collectively would remain warm long after the coffee and the croissants had gone cold. The boards might no longer seem such a cold presence at the heart of classrooms. Rather, they might become a warm dough with which teachers could mould and shape their own ideas. Going against the view that such sessions should always be conducted by experts, giving John the leadership role had served to 'activate' teacher learning in the manner espoused by Wilson & Berne (1999, p. 194). The trigger for such learning (ibid) had come about by getting teachers to see that it doesn't have to be scary to admit lack of knowledge about an aspect of technology, and even those who are not experts in terms of a technological resource can draw upon their existing knowledge base to make it a part of their practice. Teaching, rather than tools, thus remains the classroom's centre of gravity.

Of course, it was important not to base perceptions of the workshop being a success purely on conjecture or first impressions. From the outset of the research study, the goal had been one of giving teachers the right to speak for and about their own profession, so as to provide representation of a 'plurality of interests, voices, and perspectives' (Greene & Caracelli, 1997, p.14). Thus, it was crucial to explore how the dough of interest had built up over time when the day's coffee and croissants had gone cold. To do that, I arranged another series of focus group sessions that did not explicitly ask about the workshop or the use of interactive whiteboards. Rather, I allowed the conversation to flow naturally and focus on the teachers' own ideas about the developments that had occurred in their practice following the first two workshops.

Thus, I started with the question of *what has been happening in the weeks since the two workshops, particularly as regards Moodle?'* The reason for emphasising Moodle here is that this was the tool that teachers had had longer to work with, since focusing on its usage in a workshop. Gradually, that fed into a question of *'following on from this, how have the workshops affected your attitudes to using technology in the EAP classroom?'* By asking such a question, I could establish linkage to the attitudes outlined in the initial focus group session and get a clearer sense of whether or not there had been any developments in thought and practice. After this, the discussion was allowed to flow freely until it reached a point of talking about whether there were *'any other comments you would like to make on the workshop or the ways in which your perceptions or ideas have changed since?'* Here, teachers were not being led towards any particular answers or constrained by a rigid format, but at the same time being guided towards a relevant thread of discussion.

Kelly, in the first focus group session, had expressed an interest in how technology *'can really be interactive and communicative.'* Others voiced the same desire in different words but in that first session, when the interactive whiteboards got mentioned, it tended to involve references to technical aspects, as in Derek and Harry discussing problems in writing upon them. The focus of such conversation changed slightly in the second set of discussions, with Harry providing one such example of a change in practice that seemed more pedagogic than technological, or perhaps an intersection of both. In conversation with Patricia, he made the following statement as regards a change that had occurred in his practice between focus group sessions. Though one teacher cannot be taken to represent the whole group, there are elements within this that resonated with the broader group experience.

'What I've tried to do is stop using the whiteboard, and to use the interactive whiteboard instead. I've been sort of using Word as an ongoing notepad basically which has been really quite good because it's left me with

> *loads of notes at the end of class that I can then sort of erm recycle and reuse. And I was using; James showed me a programme which allows you to take notes and put them into a flow, like mind maps and things so I've sort of used those to bring notes together and conduct reviews with that and that's been, that's been quite helpful actually and especially cos another thing again with the same programme is just using words if you've got a big computer and being able to demonstrate to students how to write is a lot easier if you're able to type it up and show how to put quotes and show how to redraft. So basically I've been doing fancy moving stuff around interactive whiteboards.'*

There are a couple of significant factors as regards Harry's statement. Firstly, he does not say that the workshops have activated these developments, which supports the view that development is indeed intramuscular. The workshops as entities on their own have not necessarily been drivers for development, but have served as more of a trigger for subsequent learning, often taking place through collaboration with other colleagues. This supports elements of the Communities of Practice literature, but at the same time shows a need for formal cultivation of knowledge in the first instance. In this extract, we see how Harry interacted with James and through that interaction managed to realise the aspirations he had spoken of at an earlier stage, to have the IWB reflect the affordances of mobile technologies in the classroom.

These developments were not limited to Harry's work alone, and obviously James's too, if he had been helping to foster such developments. Patricia also spoke of how she *'did end up using the whiteboard more confidently since time moved on after the sessions on that stuff.'* This actually happened at a point where she and Harry were discussing techniques they had picked up in the workshops and were using in the classroom, albeit to different levels at this stage. This was because Patricia, in conversation with Kelly, felt that she had fallen *'out of the habit'* of using some of the ideas. She did, though, give examples of her usage of the annotation function on the whiteboards where teachers can *'put something into Word and pull it up as a file on the interactive whiteboard and then you can underline things and write in answers for gap fills and matching and all that stuff.'*

This is significant because that was something explored during the course of John's workshop, and also because the close analysis of text is a key feature of EAP teaching as highlighted in much of the literature in the field, and also in BALEAP's (2008) Core Competencies for teachers. What this seemed to suggest was that once teachers address some of their inhibitions as regards the usage of technology, they begin to explore and develop other areas of the knowledge base for teaching. Interestingly, Kelly also talked about how she would use the IWB for its core purpose of *'interactive things'* and as a reference point but then *'move to the other boards as well'*.

This suggested a greater synergy between her new technological knowledge and her existing knowledge base that had previously seemed to contradict each other, especially in terms of maintaining the communicative aspect of language teaching. Rosemary too described how, in relation to the IWB, *'I use that on a regular basis with students, so for example I've brought up a document or PowerPoint. You can bring it up, you can annotate it and save it.'* Interestingly, Matthew did not make so much reference to the boards even though in the opening focus group sessions he had talked a lot about the potential *'bear pits'* of reliance on technology and regression to transmission-style teaching. Possibly this was because a lot of his discussion in the second focus group session related to Moodle and using that for interactivity. The IWB didn't seem to have captured teachers' imaginations in the same way.

4.4 – Lessons learned at this stage

In this chapter, the teachers' voices have come more to the fore, and hopefully through those voices there is a sense of knowledge building through a combination of shared practice and different forms of activation. Going back to earlier architectural images, that knowledge does appear to have been building very slowly, much like the Olympic Stadium in the distance. However, as we approached the halfway stage of the six planned workshops, I was getting a sense of the infrastructure being in place to facilitate further developments, especially in establishing the synergy required to create instances of TPACK. Of course, such synergy remained more of an aspiration than a reality at this point because radical transformation was never going to occur overnight, and there is no magic formula for making this happen. The process takes time, and also requires an element of self-direction on the part of teachers, as suggested in the literature by those such as Mann (2005).

Focus group sessions showed that the participants themselves were growing in confidence when talking about technology, less inhibited about not understanding every aspect of the resources at their disposal. Through the discussions in the focus groups too, such as when Harry casually talked about James showing him how to use the whiteboards, there was a sense of informal learning occurring in the workplace outside of the more formal context of the workshops. This has real echoes of Wenger's conceptualisation of Communities of Practice, especially in teachers' own development becoming 'their enterprise' (1998, p. 79). However, it also appeared that such development needed some form of trigger or activation to take shape in the first place. This was what the workshops had provided at the start, though there seemed a growing sense of teacher learning taking on a life of its own.

CHAPTER 5

The Shift to a More Individual Focus

5.1 – Contextualisation

New directions for individual teachers

Over time, teachers in the language centre began to exhibit characteristics of autonomy and a sense of greater control over their own learning, building on the knowledge from the first couple of workshops by developing and sharing ideas together on a more informal basis. This was apparent not just in staff room interactions or through online collaboration, but also in the decisions teachers were making with regards to the new knowledge gained in the later workshops. They were also making their own choices about how to react to this new knowledge. There was great interest, for example, in learning about *Advanced Usage of Moodle*, but there was not the same passion for learning about technologies being used for purposes of feedback and lecture capture. What seemed to be happening was that teachers developed a preference for a particular resource that worked well in their classroom and then stuck with this. In doing so, they showed an appreciation for the values of TPACK, and also a changing perspective on what they deemed to be expected of themselves in terms of technological knowledge. It was as if they had accepted that depth is the force that matters in terms of knowledge and not width, as in Patrick Kavanagh's (1967) assertion about poetic experience. The teachers now appeared to realise that they didn't need to know the full A to Z of technologies available to EAP practitioners, such as those listed in Watson (2012). In coming to such acceptances, they were becoming better equipped to deal with the nimbus of technological change forever looming on the horizon.

As manager and researcher, I could see this happening through my everyday experience and informal discussions, but empirical observation alone could not provide sufficient evidence for claims of development in knowledge and action. It was also not enough for me to simply use the voices and perspectives

How to cite this book chapter:
Breen, P. 2018. *Developing Educators for The Digital Age: A Framework for Capturing Knowledge in Action*. Pp. 75–88. London: University of Westminster Press.
DOI: https://doi.org/10.16997/book13.e. License: CC-BY-NC-ND 4.0

of teachers in group discussion as a single barometer, regardless of how much data this produced. Even at the focus group stage I had to begin making plans for reducing the number of voices I could study in detail, and then choosing a set of cases for deeper analysis. Though it may have been interesting to investigate the perspectives of all nine participants on a more longitudinal basis, that could have sacrificed quality for quantity.

Thus, as I began moving towards the final focus group session, I had started to formulate plans for shifting from nine to four teachers to also attain Kavanagh's 'depth' and 'not width' (1967). By this stage, further workshops had taken place, which had dealt with a range of subjects. The first of these concerned *Adapting traditional approaches to feedback in the Digital Age*, and involved bringing a guest speaker from outside to run a session in the language centre. That worked well for some, but for others it involved reference to too many technologies, and had the impact of causing a return to such inhibitions as those voiced at the outset of the focus group sessions and this research study. The next workshop was on *Use of Blogs and Wikis in the classroom*, before a further session on *Advanced Usage of Moodle*, which Emily played the major part in helping out with. Then the final workshop provided as part of the teacher education series looked at *Use of technologies as a means of capturing lectures and recording feedback*. Interestingly, aside from the session on Moodle, these workshops did not appear to spark a communal interest in the same manner as the earlier ones, which continued to get a mention in the focus group sessions. However, the session on lecture capture did spark an interest on the part of some individuals.

In the third and final set of focus group discussions, I asked teachers '*if there have been any changes or developments in how you are using technology following the recent workshops, the staff development day, and any other training you have had recently.*' That then fed into a more open discussion where questions were now even less rigid and pre-structured than in previous sessions. This was to allow a more natural discussion to take place, determined by teachers' own voices rather than prompts from me as researcher. Emergent details included the information that some of the teachers had begun to use particular tools on an individual basis in their own classrooms. This was discussed most vigorously in one session that included James, Kelly, and Matthew. Here, the discussion centred upon both possible and actual usage of tools for providing feedback, such as those detailed in the session on *Use of technologies as a means of capturing lectures and recording feedback*. Very quickly, it emerged that each teacher was now acting more individually, making strategic decisions based on the practical needs of their own students, as advocated not just in the EAP literature, especially BALEAP (2008), but also that of TPACK. Kelly, for example, had started to talk of experimenting with Camtasia whilst Matthew continued to pursue greater knowledge of Moodle, adapting this in such a way that it could be used for the purpose of giving feedback. By doing so he was reconfiguring tools for a 'customized pedagogic purpose' in the manner advocated by Koehler & Mishra (2009, p. 66).

Throughout the programme, teachers had worked closely together on tools and ideas from the workshops, with usage of Moodle exemplifying this. Then, the workshops had been based upon the staple tools of the language centre's classrooms: interactive whiteboards and the Virtual Learning Environment. In contrast, the latter sessions had taken more of a cafeteria approach. For example, in the session on *Adapting traditional approaches to feedback in the Digital Age*, the speaker presented ideas on a set of tools ranging from Turnitin software to a screencasting programme named Jing, which has audio and video facilities. Exposed to a greater range of tools, teachers could now pick and choose the resources they wanted to explore. Alternatively, they could choose to ignore these and concentrate on the staple technologies.

This also meant that rather than everybody being engaged on a common enterprise, smaller communities of practice began to emerge. James, for example, had been exploring a resource named Teacher's Pet alongside another colleague. This set of tools, originally designed for use in primary and secondary schools, provided the ability to transform content into worksheets, crosswords, flashcards, and word search exercises. Even though he was only using this resource with one other teacher, James spoke of it being *'a collective work in progress.'* Kelly and Matthew's work evidenced the same spirit, with their efforts involving different resources and partners. Kelly had been busy exploring Camtasia, while Matthew continued with Moodle.

Beforehand, in terms of work, exploration, and discussion, there had been clear links between everyone's work but now practices had started to diverge. This meant that the nature of discussion was less consistent, with each group, and to some extent each individual, concentrating on different issues. Rosemary, for example, spoke of looking at things like Camtasia and Prezi, which she said *'looked amazing and great but we don't have the time at the minute and you need that time, initially you need that time to sit down and look at it, and work it out.'* Continuing this theme, she added that *'because we don't have the time whilst we may be interested in it it's very difficult to then make it part of your working day.'* Rosemary, in saying this, had touched upon another important issue regarding the context of the study at this stage.

Teachers' busy classroom lives

Rosemary had touched upon an issue of critical importance, echoing Anne Burns' (1999, p. 14) assertion that teachers lead 'busy classroom lives', which creates difficulties in allowing time for research. In this context, though, it was not just time for research that was lacking, but time for exploration. Rosemary knew of interesting tools being available; *'some great stuff out there, but we need some initial time to explore what the possibilities are.'* Others voiced the same concerns about time and heavy workloads, particularly in Rosemary's session alongside Frank and Derek. Once the discussion veered towards the issue of time, it stayed there for several minutes, twined into a discussion on uptake of resources. Frank spoke of exploring Camtasia as a feedback tool and finding out that it required *about thirty minutes per essay*, which was *quite a lot of time to spend, with the workload.* Derek went further than this in his criticism of workload, stating that *the system here militates against getting that kind of time.*

Despite such concerns, a search for solutions characterised the final set of focus group discussions. In most cases, when teachers identified a problem or obstacle, they subsequently looked for ways to address this. For example, Frank raised the issue of people no longer even having time for *training* as the academic year reached its busiest period. This was not specifically related to the teacher education programme but to other areas such as understanding a new student attendance system named ISAMS. Frank suggested that *if someone doesn't have time to do the personal training, they could watch the video like a YouTube instructional video.* Derek and Rosemary pointed out possible drawbacks of this, particularly *if you have questions that the video doesn't answer* (Derek). Despite this, there appeared to be a desire on the part of teachers in all focus group sessions to use technology not just as a solution for teaching but for addressing everyday challenges too. Kelly, for example, discussed how she had used Camtasia as a means of making up for teaching time that was lost as a consequence of Bank Holidays.

It was clear, though, that time was an issue, and that the focus group sessions had started to outlive their original purpose. As teachers started to diverge in their usage of technologies, there was less common ground for discussion and this inevitably meant that factors such as time and workload became more of an issue. Though interesting in terms of contextual knowledge and valuable in light of sociocultural understanding, this risked digression from the main focus, which was concerned with transitions in knowledge and practice as a consequence of the teacher education programme. Thus, after several hours of group conversation, it was time to narrow the funnel and hone in on specific areas of individual teachers' knowledge and practice. For that to happen, there had to be longer, more personalised interviews with a smaller group of teachers who would then serve as cases for further exploration.

Natural selection in choice of participants for interview

At the outset, around twenty teachers participated in the teacher education programme organised as a series of workshops regarding the integration of learning technologies with traditional approaches to teaching. Because the programme was voluntary, the number of participants was not set in stone, although nine members of this group opted to take part in the focus groups. Over time, as the research journey took shape, this group became smaller and four cases (*Harry, Kelly, Matthew and Rosemary*) were eventually selected in a multi-case study approach, allowing analysis to occur across and within cases

(Baxter & Jack, 2008, p. 550). The final choice of cases resulted from a combination of personal suitability and wider circumstances.

This study had taken place over the course of an academic year and a period of eleven months had passed between its original needs analysis and the wrapping up of focus group sessions. Normally, in the life of an organisation, a year is not such a long time. However, as outlined in Chapter 1, this was a brand new venture. Much like the Queen Elizabeth Olympic Park taking shape down the road in Stratford, the language centre was starting to grow at an astonishing rate. At its opening, student numbers totalled less than one hundred, but within eighteen months this had risen to over one thousand. Consequently, the centre required a greater number of teachers and an associated increase in people to fill management positions. Generally, such positions came to be filled by internal candidates because of their contextual knowledge and the fact of many being highly qualified to begin with. Emily and Frank featured amongst such candidates, rising up very quickly from teaching roles to positions of management. These new positions entailed a greater amount of administrative work and simultaneous reduction in teaching hours. Thus, even though Emily continued to be a leading player in the development of Moodle, for example, there appeared to be a natural and logical need to reduce the participation of managers in the research.

This was not to say that Emily and Frank would not have made excellent candidates at the interview stage but the focus of this study is on teachers, and teaching was no longer the essence of their practice. Patricia too had assumed management responsibilities, but then had to withdraw from the workplace for personal reasons towards the end of the academic year. Around the same time, Derek and James also left the language centre for differing professional reasons. Derek, having explored the domain of EAP, opted for a move back into ESOL teaching in a Further Education context. Similarly, James was offered a lecturing position in one of the University of London's prestigious constituent colleges, and decided to accept the role because such opportunities are rare in the world of EAP.

As a consequence of these withdrawals and changes in circumstances, the four remaining teachers were offered the chance to participate in semi-structured interviews over the next three months. Significantly, some of the earlier contributions from Harry, Kelly, Matthew, and Rosemary had been the most clearly mapped out in terms of developments in knowledge and practice. This meant that even though there was a significant element of natural selection in the final choice of candidates for interview, these four teachers served as excellent cases for the final analysis. Even without the various background circumstances, they may well have formed the chosen cases if different criteria had been applied to the selection process. Further to this, they serve as fine examples of the diversity found in the lives of EAP teachers, and particularly those who are newer to the profession. Again, choosing such candidates is what separates this study from other important monographs and work in this field, such as that of Bell (2016).

The reality of natural selection being a deciding factor does not make the study any less systematic than it ought to be. Rather, it falls in line with the values of the research paradigm that I had chosen to follow. Since qualitative research designs are constantly 'evolving' (Robson, 2002, p. 166) and 'emergent' (Creswell, 2009, p. 175), researchers have long been expected to commence with a wide field of focus to capture the dynamics of unfolding situations (Nisbet & Watt, 1984, p. 78). Through following this approach, the focus is narrowed, clarified, and delimited on its gradual passage towards the data analysis stage; a process which has been likened to a 'funnel' by Bogdan & Biklen (1982, p. 55) and Hammersley & Atkinson (1983, p, 175). This narrowing of the funnel, though, should not mean loss of depth or decrease in trustworthiness in the reporting of the research. Hence it was crucial to structure and report accurately on the next stage of the process.

5.2 – Theoretical foundations

Getting to the heart of individual practices

Three decades ago, Lee Shulman suggested that teacher education programmes needed to employ a growing and diverse body of case literature, across contexts so as to 'provide teachers with a rich body of prototypes, precedents, and parables from which to reason' (1986, p. 14). Mishra & Koehler (2006, p. 1018) suggest that such studies can serve as 'the first step towards the development of unified theoretical and conceptual frameworks' to act as examples of best practice, which they perceive to be sorely lacking. Chapelle (2010, p. 60) further proposes that cases rooted in actual practice could serve as 'exemplars' that better inform the broader field of ELT than larger scale quantitative summaries that can sometimes lack 'the detail needed to use research results to improve instruction.' One obvious and seminal example of such a study in the context of EAP is again that of Bell (2016) in his efforts to harmonise the voices of leading experts in the field to develop unified conceptual frameworks around notions of practitioner identity.

Those discussions, though, were quite different, and did not necessitate a forum for shared development at the outset, which the focus groups provided in this study. In Bell's (2016) evaluation of practitioner experiences, the participants held a wealth of knowledge and experience in the field of EAP. Back at the start of our teacher education workshops, many of the participants were new to the context of higher education, access to learning technologies, and even the subject to some extent. They needed to work together and the focus groups facilitated a form of 'intersubjective depth' (Miller & Glassner, 1997, p. 106) by placing an emphasis on participants' stories being shared. This meant that in practical terms Kelly, at the outset, might have felt quite reluctant to admit in an interview situation that she had inhibitions about using technologies, and even viewed them as a barrier to interaction. However, once she heard others in the various focus group sessions voicing similar concerns, she grew in the confidence necessary to express her views. As others did the same, this allowed for the emergence of a narrated reality of context-rich, and 'locally produced accounts' as with Silverman (2005, p. 154).

On the whole, then, the focus group sessions were used as 'material for thought, reflection, and further investigation' (Arksey & Knight, 1999, p. 77). This further investigation featured the use of interviews, observations, and analysis of learning materials accessed with the full permission of teachers, particularly those placed on Moodle. Aside from prolonging engagement, in the study, and providing material to facilitate thick descriptions of the setting, this incorporation and analysis of additional sources served as 'triangulation techniques' to ensure trustworthiness (Lincoln & Guba, 1985, pp. 359–360). Though some characteristics of these multiple methods overlapped in terms of their positioning in the overall timeframe of the study, interviews served as a natural progression from the focus groups. This meant that interviews had to be organised in a manner which was just as systematic, and informed by principles that would bring the data collection activities into line with Mertler's (2008, p. 68) funnel so as to 'constrict' the emphasis towards 'very precise characteristics' of each case within the study.

Rationale for conducting semi-structured interviews

Drawing upon an analogy first made by Wiseman and Aron (1972), Cohen (1976) compares interviewing to fishing in that both activities require 'careful preparation, much patience, and considerable practice if the eventual reward is to be a worthwhile catch' (p. 82). Drawing on the same metaphor, the best catches are often facilitated in a lone situation as exemplified in Ernest Hemingway's opening line from *The Old Man and the Sea* where we find the protagonist working alone in a skiff in the Gulf Stream (1952). Furthermore, towards the end of the focus group sessions, teachers had begun to express their views far more freely than at the outset. Indeed, at several points it was frustrating that the possibility of further discussion on an issue raised by a particular individual was sometimes reined in by the needs of the group as a whole. Examples of that came at times when a participant would mention a resource that nobody else had heard of or used, and then the conversation regressed from discussion to something more basic and descriptive.

For that reason, I felt that I needed one-to-one interviews in order to progress the study further, and to get to the heart of the developments that I was trying to trace. In the literature, Arksey & Knight (1999, p. 89) point out that there are three major interview formats 'differentiated in terms of degree of structure or formality; structured, semi-structured, and unstructured.' In the context of this research, after careful consideration, I opted for a semi-structured approach defined by Borg (2006, p. 190) as being flexible on account of being 'directed by a set of general themes, rather than specific questions.' This was because that approach mirrored techniques I had used in the last of the focus group sessions, where I basically entered the forum for discussion with only one pre-selected question. This worked well, but at the same time it did so because I was in the presence of three other people. The individual interviews would be held one-to-one in a situation that in some ways felt as natural as going for a coffee in the language centre café, but at the same time had to entail some degree of formality. The challenge, then, was to make the exchange seem conversational, as discussed by Kvale (1996) and Borg (2006), at the same time as being professional and serious.

To strike such a balance, I recognised the need to engage in a process of ensuring shared meaning-making (Ellis & Berger, 2003) at the same time as being able to prompt and probe in order to allow people to talk about their own experience in their own terms (Arksey & Knight, 1999, pp. 99–100). I tried to achieve this by having a prepared script at the outset of each interview from which I could digress or re-order questions where necessary (Lam, 2000). The aim was to 'generate plausible accounts' rather than attempting to unearth 'pictures of reality' (Silverman, 2005, p. 154) or to squeeze the discussion into a focus determined by me rather than the teachers.

Using stimulated recall to strengthen semi-structured interviews

One of the issues or features of any longitudinal study based on the perspectives of its participants is that people forget things with the passage of time, especially in light of busy personal and professional lives. In order to counteract this, I used a technique which Calderhead (1981, p. 122) defines as 'stimulated recall', whereby a variety of devices are used to 'aid a participant's recall of his thought processes at the time of that behaviour.' When employed correctly by researchers, this stimulates a form of structured reflection thought to be more accurate than memory alone. For example, during an interview, Harry might not immediately recall his reference to *the next generation* of technologies, but would do so when prompted. If this is eliciting Harry's experience and not mine as researcher, then this is not 'contaminating' the data with subjectivity (Reason and Rowan, 1981).

This approach to prompting discussion is not without its critics, though. Borg (2006) highlights the main criticisms as being 'the adequacy with which teachers can accurately report information (e.g. thought processes) that is no longer in their short term memory' and 'the extent to which the prompts used to assist teachers' recall may influence the way in which they report their thinking' (p. 211). Yinger (1986) also voices concerns about the accuracy of information gained through stimulated recall interviews but asserts that they remain the 'primary source of data for interactive thought' (p. 267). After all, 'teachers cannot teach and talk about their thoughts at the same time (i.e. concurrent verbalization is not possible) and thus retrospective verbal accounts are required to examine interactive thinking' (Borg, 2006, p. 210).

However, the strongest defence of stimulated recall as a means of generating discussion is that despite being a technique first introduced decades ago, it fits in very well with the expectations and demands of the digital age. With the advent of social media, streaming media, and the increasing digitisation of society, we are now effectively living in an environment of almost endless simulation and stimulation of our memories. It is increasingly difficult, for example, to erase our digital footprint from the world wide web. Thus, in this present age of technology and a particular study of teachers using technologies, there is sound justification for incorporating techniques of stimulated recall such as those employed in the introductions to interviews.

5.3 – Practical considerations

The early stages of data analysis

Coffey & Atkinson (1996, pp. 10–11) define analysis as being a 'pervasive activity' throughout the life of a research project. This means that analysis does not begin when data is collected, but is part of advance planning and then continues during the process. Creswell (2009, p. 184) similarly describes data analysis as 'an ongoing process involving continual reflection about the data, whilst Leedy & Ormrod (2005, p. 133) talk about digging deep to reach 'a complete understanding' of the phenomenon under investigation. Furthermore, the analysis and exploration of existing data allows researchers 'to make decisions about the future direction' so as to create scope for a 'narrowing of the funnel' and to decide upon the 'true focus' (Mertler, 2006, p. 8).

Therefore, in advance of semi-structured interviews, I conducted a first cycle of data analysis, drawing on the research literature for guidance. Being a pervasive activity, this analysis started at the time of conducting the focus group sessions – recorded and then transcribed into text units stored as computer files. Building upon this, the next stage involved the construction of a theoretical prism through which to interpret data, so as to identify recurring themes, patterns, and categories for establishment of coherent linkage. As such, I created a framework of codes based upon the TPACK literature. Having established this framework as a basis for moving forward, the next step was to choose a systematic and replicable technique for compressing the volume of original data, so as to explore underlying concepts.

A process of 'thematic analysis' provided a means of unearthing these concepts (Braun & Clarke, 2006, p. 8), and lent itself to the flexibility required of qualitative research through not being 'wed to any pre-existing theoretical framework' (ibid). Coupling ideological freedom with such systematic processes of evaluation, thematic analysis has the potential to unwrap the richness of 'messages contained in talk data' (Joffe & Yardley, 2003, p. 56). Furthermore, this allowed me to divide the data corpus into two sections, allowing for deep-focused analysis of the four main cases, at the same time as incorporating background cases and thus providing an accurate portrayal of the whole data set (Braun & Clarke, 2006, p. 11).

Thematic analysis must be as systematic as any other form of Content Analysis, and thus Braun & Clarke (2006) delineate the process into six clear stages. The first of these is 'familiarising yourself with the data' which involves a constant moving back and forward between the entire saturated data set, coded extracts of data, and the production of analysed data for 'repeated patterns of meaning' (2006, p. 15). They deem this to be a process of 'immersion' characterised by an *'active'* reading of the data, repeated until a 'bedrock' for subsequent analysis has been established (ibid, pp. 16–17). Creswell (2009, p. 183) further likens this process of deeper understanding of the data to 'peeling back the layers of an onion.'

Following this advice, I read the transcripts repeatedly, supported by notes and memos, and repeatedly listened to the recordings as well, asking such questions as *'How did X say that?'* or *'When Y and Z's speech overlapped, who was it that actually spoke first?'* This, of course, was slow and painstaking at times, cutting across data sources, but was invaluable in capturing a sense of the whole dataset. The fact that it had been digitally recorded as well meant that storage and retrieval was made easier, and that I could cut back and forwards across sessions to cross-reference, compare, interpret, and re-interpret particular instances of dialogue.

This deep reading fed into the second stage of Braun & Clarke's (2006, p. 17) framework, which is labelled as 'generating initial codes' and involves a systematic process, yet again, of breaking down chunks of text into the format of a single word or phrase that can be more readily understood. This was done by following Creswell's recommendation of using some combination of predetermined and emerging' codes' (2009, p. 187). Although case study data analysis is most commonly associated with data-driven approaches (Stake, 1995), the choice of TPACK and its associated sociocultural variables as the conceptual framework necessitated a theory-driven (deductive) element as well. Added to this, I followed Creswell's suggestion of using 'in vivo' coding, where appropriate, based on the actual language of the participants (2009, p. 186).

In practice, this was achieved by going back and forwards through the text, reading and re-reading, assigning and reassigning, placing and replacing labels to the point of refinement. Through this process, I reached a better understanding of key themes and issues emerging from the focus groups, and was able to formulate a structure for the interviews, combining a set of generic and individually tailored questions. Simultaneously, I could move on with the next two steps in Braun & Clarke's (2006) framework for thematic analysis. These were labelled as 'searching for themes' (ibid, p. 19), and 'reviewing themes' (p. 20).

The results of this would act as a foundation for the fifth stage of 'defining and naming themes' (p. 22), so as to feed into the final stage of 'producing the report' (p. 23). That, of course, would not come until much later, but in light of Coffey & Atkinson's (1996) statement about analysis being a pervasive activity throughout the life of a research project, even at this stage it was important to have some sense of how the whole tapestry might connect.

Homogeneity of the four chosen cases

Section 5.1 provided a rudimentary outline of choices made regarding selection of candidates for individual interviews. Though there was an element of natural selection in the first instance, deeper analysis of the focus group data provided further 'methodological justification' for choosing cases, as advocated by Seawright & Gerring (2008, pp. 295–296). This also helps to capture the 'exclusive distinctiveness' of the chosen group (Cohen et al, 2013, p. 161). Homogeneity existed in the first instance for everyone in the focus groups because of context, practice and characteristics unique to English teaching professionals. However, the four chosen cases *(Harry, Kelly, Matthew and Rosemary)* had an additional range of characteristics more commonly found in what Patton (1990) describes as a 'purposeful sample.'

Firstly, they remained active in the EAP classroom in this specific context, unlike those who had left or progressed into management roles. Further homogenisation came about through similar instances of interest, experience, concerns, and ambitions expressed within the focus group sessions. For example, Matthew and Harry shared an espoused interest in the affordance of new, more integrated technologies, and a frustration with some of the potential *'bear pits'* of existing tools. Some of these concerns echoed Kelly's inhibitions regarding the use of technology as a facilitator for communication, and Rosemary's concerns about lack of time inhibiting her experimentation. Although each of the teachers had concerns regarding usage of technologies for the betterment of students, one of the strongest homogenising factors was the emphasis that they placed on finding solutions to problems. That came across in Rosemary's struggle to make time for extra learning, and Harry's efforts to introduce and integrate the use of tablets in teaching. Kelly's work with Camtasia added further evidence of this, as did Harry's aspiration to blur the boundaries between educational and social media resources.

Further to this, each of the teachers appeared to be taking more of a cafeteria-style approach to their choice of technologies. Indeed, an amusing, though suitable image at this stage might be that of how superheroes from different TV shows often have a choice of weapon that characterises them. Just as we have come to associate the crossbow or the lightsaber with certain fictional characters, various technologies were becoming synonymous with particular teachers – Harry's iPads, Kelly's lecture capture software, Rosemary's Moodle, and Matthew's exploration of various tools to help cross that elusive bridge between the classroom and the outside world.

These and other examples will be discussed more deeply in later chapters, but the aim here is to give a sense of how the early analysis managed to 'illuminate' certain issues at the heart of the research (Yin, 2009, p. 26). It also reinforced the study's theoretical direction because it was becoming possible to identify and trace elements of TPACK in the four teachers' espoused practices. Although this was not yet fully formed in terms of Mishra & Koehler's (2006) framework, the seeds had been planted, and possibly 'cultivated' (Wenger & Snyder, 2000) by the teacher education programme. However, it was up to the teachers, rather than me, to make that judgement.

Setting up the actual interviews

Since the teachers appeared to have elements of a TPACK knowledge base already in place, this allowed me to shape the interviews around questions that would probe the extent of this. At the same time, I wanted to find out about other developments in their practice, and their thoughts on what might have activated any such changes in their knowledge or actions. Although these interviews took place when the teacher education programme had ended, the teachers' work and usage of technology was continuing, as before. The first stage of data analysis had allowed me to create a tailored set of questions to go along with those that were more generic, and given me the requisite information to use authentic forms of stimulated recall. Prior to the interviews, I spoke to the teachers and said that I was analysing the data. This allowed me, in the first instance, to ask for any clarification where needed. Secondly, this attention to detail created a positive impression and illustrated my dedication to producing an accurate synthesis of developments over time. The fact of studying the transcript in such immersive detail also helped to foster a sense of value in each contribution and every single word.

On a practical level, it was also easier to set up interviews than focus groups in terms of space, timing, generating discussion, and recording dialogue. We had the interviews in tinted glass booths used for one-to-one tutorials with students, and these created a professional, but comfortable, atmosphere. I allowed teachers to choose their own times for interview, and made sure that they were still happy to participate in the research project. Once these foundations had been established, the first set of interviews took place; the results of which are discussed in subsequent chapters.

Questions followed a similar pattern, with some adaptations for each teacher. For example, all of the teachers were asked *'what approaches have worked best for you in the EAP classroom?'* and *'how much of the initial workshop participation has influenced your present approach to teaching and lesson design?'* Alongside this, I asked everyone when they used technology in their lessons and then why they chose to use technology in their lessons. However, some questions had to be phrased slightly differently for each person. Such a situation arose with references back to the focus group discussions, where I drew upon a light form of stimulated recall in making the earlier transcripts available to the teachers so that they could see what they had said.

Using this stimulated recall, I prompted slightly different discussions with Rosemary and Matthew, for instance. With Rosemary, I raised the following points for discussion – *'At the time of the focus group sessions you were talking a lot about experimentation and also about time constraints and so on. Has this experimentation or time issue changed or developed in any way?'* During Matthew's discussion, on the other hand, I adapted the phrasing slightly – *'So at the time of the focus group sessions you were talking a lot about your usage of things like Moodle, PowerPoint and other technologies. Has this continued or developed in any way?'* These sample excerpts also highlight the conversational manner in which I conducted the interviews and tried to create a sense of a linkage between the different stages of the research journey. The fact of being able to refer back to what was said in the focus group sessions also engendered a sense of honesty and transparency in the interview process. For example, I was always open to showing teachers the written form of their focus group dialogue if they requested that.

5.4 – Lessons learned at this stage

Though this chapter has concentrated on the shift from focus groups to individual interviews, there is still a clear linkage to the journey as a whole. That story will be told in further detail in the chapters that follow but for now, it has been important to show the why and how of spoken data collection. This data allowed me to get a stronger sense of theoretical direction, particularly in terms of TPACK, and teachers' placement on such a knowledge spectrum. At the same time, I remained aware of limitations in any study based on the voices of participants alone, and the differences in 'espoused theory' versus 'theory in action' as introduced by Argyris & Schön (1974).

Therefore, because of the qualitative emphasis on reconciling data from different sources (Chapelle, 2010), I was aware of the need to access further data that could provide information on theory in action. There were two ways of doing this, with the first being to analyse teachers' usage of particular technologies through materials produced for classroom or self-access usage. That, of course, would be easier in the case of a resource such as Moodle than for iPads. Thus, something more than analysis of materials would be required in order to gain a stronger understanding of theory in action.

Observation of lessons would become the means by which this was achieved, and that is discussed in Chapter 6. Such observations had already been carried out at earlier stages of the programme and these are discussed too. This chapter, then, has served as a useful foundation for evaluating the focus group data and using that to shape the interview questions, at the same time as strengthening belief in the authenticity of their discussions. The desire to provide vignettes of practice in the classroom was not triggered by doubt in the teachers' claims, but by a strengthened belief in the importance of them. As a consequence of this importance, not just for the local context but the broader domain of teaching and TPACK, it was essential to consolidate a sense of trustworthiness in the overall research story.

CHAPTER 6

Observations in the Thick of Practice

6.1 – Contextualisation

Teachers' thoughts on observations

Teacher observations have been a regular feature of the English Language Teaching profession for decades. Indeed, one of the strengths of the DELTA is that teachers must be observed as part of their formal certification. In my research paper on the professional development of two DELTA trainees at the outset of their career (Breen, 2013), one of the teachers (*Caroline*) spoke about the benefits of being observed. She spoke of how useful this was in terms of learning, and being exposed to new techniques, interactions and approaches. Specifically, she stated that *'it helps you realise things you weren't aware of in your own teaching'* and went on to highlight the benefits of *'someone else coming in the classroom'* to *'suggest techniques that you've never tried, but could actually work quite well.'* Indeed, she cited observations as one of the main strengths of the DELTA compared to other courses such as the CELTA, because of the extent to which it combines a range of different types of observations, over a period of time, including those of peers and even mentors. On the whole, the DELTA had made Caroline *'a lot more aware of how I need to continually learn and how learning how to teach is not just something you kind of do once and then can do for the rest of your life.'* This is a view that is echoed throughout much of the teacher education literature from Wallace (1991) onwards, particularly in the sense that 'training or education is something that can be presented or managed by others; whereas development is something that can be done only by and for oneself' (p. 3).

Caroline's experience on the DELTA offers strong support for the view that observations can be developmental if organised in the right atmosphere. Logically, then, they could bring benefits to a programme of teacher education and teacher development. However, a great deal would hinge upon the creation

How to cite this book chapter:
Breen, P. 2018. *Developing Educators for The Digital Age: A Framework for Capturing Knowledge in Action*. Pp. 89–100. London: University of Westminster Press.
DOI: https://doi.org/10.16997/book13.f. License: CC-BY-NC-ND 4.0

of an appropriate atmosphere. Patricia captured a sense of this in one of the early focus group sessions when she had a brief discussion on *'peer observations'* with Kelly. She stated that *'I have seen them go beautifully and learned lots of things from them and everybody was really excited but it does require a level of trust.'* Matthew voiced similar thoughts on a slightly more expansive level in one of his individual interviews where he talked about how it was important *'to create that atmosphere where people feel free to share ideas.'* He went on to make a call for *'collective interaction'* in suggesting that *'there should be much more of people pooling resources and pooling ideas and observing each other and that kind of thing.'*

Here, he seems to be making quite an interesting demand in that he is not separating out observations from other aspects of *'collective interaction.'* All too often, teacher observations are conducted in a way that has semblance with Diaz-Maggioli's (2004) description of training days. These are the sorts of events and observations conducted in an environment that bears no resemblance to the world of everyday practice. Borg (1998, p. 278) stipulates that observational data should 'portray what teachers do in ELT classrooms, as well as how they talk about the rationale for their work.' Elsewhere, he argues that events and activities observed in classrooms can serve as a better method of data collection than teachers' retrospective accounts (Borg, 2003, p. 34). Thus, in conducting observations, I hoped to be able to get more of an insight into what was happening in the teachers' classrooms than simply their own verbal account of events, as offered in the focus group sessions.

Setting up observations and recording data

During one of her individual interviews, Kelly described an *'experiential'* teaching situation where *'the students were doing presentations in groups and the teacher's role was basically to sit to one side … as a kind of silent observer.'* Though in this case she, as teacher, could *'step in if there was some help necessary'*, she explained that *'the students were basically left to do the presentations and run the groups by themselves.'* She went on to say that this worked well *'because they were empowered and I think that's probably a key idea is that empowerment.'* Ultimately, students *'were in control of their own learning'* and the teacher was *'mainly a silent observer.'* Kelly's usage of the word *'empowerment'* encapsulated a sense of the atmosphere I wanted to create as a visitor to the teachers' classrooms.

Although I accepted that observation would 'change the nature of the class, perhaps in some negative ways' (Malone, 2003, p. 798), it was important for me to minimise the sense of intrusion. I needed to be a silent observer at the back of the room, positioned there for research, not appraisal, purposes. Yet, inevitably, there was a need also to incorporate some elements of the standard appraisal process since Goodwyn (1997, pp. 108–110) points out that, historically, teacher observations have been shaped by the 'industrial model' which is designed to create a 'two-way' process of evaluation. This means that objectives for the observation will also be negotiated in advance, and feedback offered when the session has concluded. As with workshops, observations should not take place by means of a 'one-shot' (Meltzer, 2010) or 'drive-by' formula (Darling-Hammond & Richardson, 2009). They have to be contextualised, offering something practical in the longer term, and the benefit of these observations was the unique form of feedback at the end.

Teachers were basically presented with access to vignettes of their practice, shaped by notes on their lessons recorded through the adapted ISTE Classroom Observation Tool, shown as Appendix 2. Here, the term vignette is used in the sense of providing a brief sketch of practice that serves as a portrait of their broader lives and activities. The use of such vignettes to capture a sense of people's everyday practice can be found in Wenger's (1998) depictions of the lives of claims processors, and Motteram & Sharma's (2009) study into using blended learning as a teaching methodology. In a further study of three teachers working at the interface of technology and language learning, Slaouti, Onat-Stelma & Motteram (2013, p. 69) define vignettes as offering 'a mind's eye picture of a specific instance' of practice.

Using the ISTE Classroom Observation Tool, I agreed with the teachers that I could take notes throughout my time in their classrooms. This was discussed as part of a meeting held before the observation, as suggested by Goodwyn (1997, p. 109). The purpose of this meeting was to establish a suitable time for going into the classroom, and to explain what would happen during the observation, which would last up to one hour, with me sitting at the back of the classroom taking notes. After the observation, I would type up my notes and have a second meeting to discuss what I had written. By doing so, I was creating a 'two-way' process (ibid), and giving teachers a say in the interpretation of what I had witnessed or recorded. As a result of the feedback from observations, teachers would get a chance to reflect upon their practice, and take mental charge of their own development (Mann, 2005). With each source of data collection, from focus groups to observations, I wanted to stay true to the underlying values of the study and ensure that it was being shaped by teachers' perspectives (Greene & Caracelli, 1997, p.14). In the case of the vignettes, it was no longer just their words that shaped the reporting of the data but also their actions in the classroom and interaction with students.

6.2 – Theoretical foundations

Challenges posed by teachers' espoused and actual practices

Much of the literature on teacher observation talks about the benefit that it brings in terms of validating spoken claims (Marx et al, 1998; Borg, 2003; Borg,

2006; Pierson & Borthwick, 2010). Indeed, throughout the history of qualitative research, participant observation has been the backbone of social enquiry (Atkinson & Hammersley, 1994, p. 249), going back to its origins in field work by anthropologists and sociologists (Silverman, 2005, p. 111). Teachers too have spoken of its benefits, as reported in this study through the voices of Matthew, Patricia and then Caroline from my 2013 'DELTA' article. However, it is still important to note that what people say they do in practice, and what they actually do, may be quite different (Freeman, 2002; Donaghue, 2003; Silverman, 2005). Donaghue (2003, p. 345), writing in the specific context of ELT, discusses the notion of 'espoused theory' versus 'theory in action', first introduced in the work of Argyris & Schön (1974), and also examined in Judson's (2006) study of connections between the way that teachers integrate technology, and core beliefs about teaching and learning. In this pertinent study, the author discovered that teachers' actual practice with technologies betrayed epistemologies they proclaimed adherence to (ibid, p. 581), when observed through a model known as FIT-COM (*Focus on Integrated Technology: Classroom Observation Measurement*).

Donaghue (2003, p. 345) further states that espoused theory, in the context of teacher education, involves the actions people claim to engage in, whilst theory in action is what a participant really does in the classroom. Her study is of particular importance to this research context because she is interested in how developments occur in the aftermath of prior learning. Thus, she provides the example of sessions at an IATEFL Conference which might be interesting for participants but do not result in any changes to practice. She suggests that there is often considerable difference between intake (what comes from the instructor), uptake (elements which the trainees find interesting) and output (what they actually use in their classroom practice). She then gives reasons for this as being 'context difference'; lack of understanding about the theory behind the practice and the techniques; or lack of time, creativity, and adaptability to transfer this new knowledge into classroom practice (ibid).

Challenges posed by the chameleon nature of EAP

One further complication in terms of using observations as a tool for evaluating the development of knowledge and action is that the very nature of EAP's knowledge base remains contentious, as outlined in previous chapters. There is no single agreed understanding of what EAP is as a discipline, as outlined in work such as Bell (2016), though on the other hand there are as many perspectives on what Economics, for example, should be as a discipline. However, what seems to be universally agreed is that the context in which teachers are working largely determines perspectives on the subject. Teachers on an intensive and generic summer pre-sessional course are therefore going to have a very different perspective to those working on in-sessional courses within specific academic departments. In the case of this study, teachers worked across programmes which were foundational for pre-degree students, at actual degree level for Business Diploma students on the course that Harry taught, and then graduate level for pre-Masters students.

Naturally, these courses and the students taking them coloured each teacher's perspective on what EAP as a subject was supposed to be or do. Hence, once again, the comparison to a chameleon discipline springs to mind, as argued in Chapter 1. During the focus group sessions and individual interviews, I asked teachers for their thoughts on what should happen in an EAP classroom and EAP teaching situations. Generally, the responses supported the argument of perspectives being shaped by practical experience, particularly the immediate demands of the teaching situation. However, as the discussions grew more theoretical towards the end of the focus group sessions, the teachers demonstrated awareness of different perspectives on how EAP should be taught. Harry, for example, became more focused on discipline-specific work. Matthew prioritised language and preparation for the real-life and future study contexts in which that was used. Such an approach, though, is very different from many contemporary theories of how EAP should be taught. The danger, then, is of teachers acting out scenarios that are not typical of their everyday practice, and of playing to the expectations of the observer, as regards what EAP is supposed to be.

Role of TPACK in the teacher observations

Another potential pitfall for both teachers and me, as observer, was in trying to force the presence of TPACK into teaching situations. This means that teachers might try too hard to integrate technology because that is what they believed to be expected of them, or I might be tempted to portray certain actions as instances of TPACK so as to fast-track evidence of development. However, the way to avoid this was to solidly establish the fact that the goal of the observations and the study as a whole was not to find or measure instances of TPACK but to triangulate or support claims coming out of the teachers' spoken data. Indeed, the framework itself was intended only as a theoretical prism through which developments could be understood, and was used only to serve this function during the course of the observations. Ultimately, the most important reason for carrying out observations was to provide an accurate glimpse of what was happening in teachers' classrooms. Those observations have been shaped into the following vignettes of practice.

6.3 – Instances of teachers' everyday EAP practice

Vignette from Harry's classroom

In the opening months of the teacher education programme, Harry taught a group of eighteen Foundation students the English for Academic Purposes component of a Business & Humanities course. Those students were of mixed language ability, gender, and nationalities, including Arab, Chinese, and Russian. The lessons took place on a weekly basis in a classroom equipped with the language centre's standard trappings of technology –computer, projector, and interactive whiteboard. However, there was limited space for movement, as the room was too small for eighteen students. That, alongside differences in language levels, posed challenges for Harry.

This particular lesson involved 'Teaching differences in facts & opinions' through material adapted from Oshima & Hogue's writing textbook (2007). I began the observation ten minutes after the lesson had started. By this point, students had started reading a text and analysing information so as to find answers to exercises in the textbook, concerned with finding supporting evidence in paragraphs. At this stage the technology in use, recorded through the ISTE Classroom Observation Tool, was a straightforward combination of desktop computer and interactive whiteboard, with these being used for the purposes of presentation. Interestingly, PowerPoint's potential *'barrier'* (Focus Group 1; hereafter, FG1) was the main vehicle of demonstrating information. However, rather than simply lecturing students and *going through a whole bunch of slides'* (ibid), he engaged in conversational information exchange with the class, through eliciting examples of facts and opinions at whole-group level.

This had the feel of a 'chalk-and-talk presentation' style of writing on a board whilst delivering a standard textbook lesson (Mayer, 2005, p. 2). There was none of the innovation that he had aspired to in getting students shifting things around interactively, in partnership with the teacher, as advocated in FG1. Even though there was fifteen minutes' worth of engagement and negotiation of meaning with the students in the post-reading task, echoing focus group examples of working on students' writing processes, his emphasis seemed to be on 'comprehension' rather than 'output' (Mayer, 2005, p. 476). The primary instrument of teaching was Oshima & Hogue's textbook, to whose exercises the students returned post-discussion.

Again, once this new set of exercises was completed, answers were elicited at whole-group level, and the process of exercise followed by answers, and back to exercises continued. Thus, on this day, in this particular instance, there was not so much usage of technology, or indeed 'the methods, practices and techniques of communicative language teaching' related to the tasks of an academic context (BALEAP, 2008, p. 8). However, in a post-lesson discussion, Harry pointed out that the purpose of the tasks and exercises was to stimulate knowledge of using supporting evidence in academic essays. As such, he felt that he had introduced the students to this concept, and was *getting what I wanted done with the lesson done.'* He also stressed problems caused by the physical layout of the classroom.

Therefore, even though on first impressions, it might seem that Harry was not drawing on a base of TPK or TCK, in this vignette it could be argued that he was showing knowledge of pedagogy applicable to teaching specific content

(Koehler & Mishra, 2009, p. 64). This echoes Shulman's original PCK conceptualisation with its emphasis on providing the 'most useful forms of representation' of particular ideas, and 'formulating' the subject to 'make it comprehensible to others' (1986, p. 9). With these particular students, in this particular classroom situation, Harry had actually opted not to use the technology *just because you can*' (FG1). Rather, he taught the students what they needed to learn, with the resources at his disposal, and the main resource in this particular lesson happened to be a standard textbook.

Vignette from Kelly's classroom

During the first focus group session, Kelly seemed most comfortable talking about communicative aspects of teaching, rather than the academic context. Although she was teaching two classes at this time, and I observed both, it seemed particularly important to get a sense of how she translated her communicative strategies into the academic context of a postgraduate pathway course. This was a Graduate Diploma course, which is essentially EAP for students hoping to progress onto Masters degree programmes, mainly in disciplines such as Humanities and Law. Although Kelly was new to EAP, a Programme Manager had asked her to teach on this course as a consequence of holding a Masters degree specifically related to the Social Sciences. I also felt that with this background knowledge and disciplinary experience, she might feel more comfortable and natural in being observed, having earlier spoken about the 'scary' aspect of the public view (FG1).

In this observation, Kelly's class took place in a standard language centre classroom equipped with computer, projector, and IWB. The focus was on complex noun phrases and looking at texts to see the role that these play in the construction of paragraphs and in aiding the cohesion/flow of paragraphs. Further emphasis was placed on the function of language and the way in which noun phrases can be used to deepen the information within a paragraph and its component parts; namely sentences. The texts used for this exercise came from other subjects taken by students on the programme, and as such had a discipline-specific focus. The content thus had notable differences from her past experiences of teaching General English.

The session started off with a 'word cloud' displayed through a PowerPoint slide on the IWB. The purpose of this was to introduce students to the vocabulary they would encounter when reading texts at a later stage of the lesson, and appeared to engage them from the outset. The group as a whole seemed focused on the task and the vocabulary, in a classroom atmosphere that was positive and conducive to learning. After the word cloud activity had finished, the next stage of the lesson was a combination of a split dictation and chopped up sentences in which one student had to dictate whilst the others constructed paragraphs out of the sentences. Kelly took particular care in setting up dictation and matching activities. She checked comprehension of instructions and monitored progress, using strategies that combined traditional ELT approaches with those of a more academic context.

Having completed the split dictation and paragraph construction, students then moved on to searching the paragraphs for examples of noun phrases. This was done in pairs, before answers were checked at a whole-class level, and brought up on the IWB system's visualiser. Noticeably, there was very good rapport with the students. Kelly tried to practice what she preached by incorporating *a human element* (FG1) through focusing on student needs, monitoring the class constantly, and grading her language appropriately. I also noted a smooth transition between activities, and a gradual movement from guided input to more autonomous, task-based work.

During the course of the lesson, Kelly assumed various roles: facilitator, presenter, helper, guide, provider of resources, and source of knowledge. There was an effective combination of activities through the use of a word cloud activity, a split dictation, chopped up sentences, eliciting, modelling of language, highlighting of target language, guided reading activities, and the use of reflective questions. Students were engaged in a number of learning activities, and were shown the function of a form of language they had come across in their academic texts, before being given a sense of how this could be used. Technology played an important role in the teaching and learning activities, particularly as a presentation device, conducting a warmer activity, and in modelling answers to the tasks that students completed.

On the whole, then, Kelly demonstrated far more technological knowledge, operating in synergy with pedagogic strategies, than she had given insight into during the first focus group session. She seemed far more comfortable in using technological resources than her early dialogue suggested. There was none of the *static* teaching that she feared (FG1), and when she used technology, she incorporated communicative teaching strategies as a means of keeping the students engaged. In a matter of weeks, she appeared to have found new ways of interacting. Perhaps she was starting to find a place for *the human element* (ibid) in the activity system of her classroom, and getting a better sense of her own place in an EAP activity system.

Vignette from Matthew's classroom

Having completed the first focus group session, Matthew's dialogue suggested a desire for innovation that was sometimes frustrated or inhibited by a lack of technological knowledge. It was interesting, then, to see him for the first time in an EAP teaching situation, having previously observed him in the General English classroom. There are two additional points of note regarding the class content. To begin with, the course that he was teaching on this day was known as English for University Study (EUS). This was a pre-foundation course for students with low IELTS entry scores, designed as a bridge into more demanding academic pathway programmes: effectively a cross-breed of General English and English for General Academic Purposes. Secondly, at this stage of development, Matthew was fond of bringing his interests into the classroom, through activities related to theatre and music; echoing Thornbury's (2000) focus on bringing the self into the classroom.

The class was composed of mixed nationality students with an IELTS range of 4.5 to 5.0. The lesson, which was taking place in a standard classroom equipped with computer, projector, and interactive whiteboard, began with feedback on homework. Students had been required to find a newspaper article 'of reasonable complexity' (Matthew's words) and upload this onto Moodle, which was an instance of 'putting stuff online' as advocated in FG1. However, not all students had managed to upload their work. As a consequence of this, Matthew then had to think on his feet, as also referred to in FG1, by appearing to draw on what Shulman (1986, p. 12) defines as 'strategic pedagogical knowledge', which is 'brought into play as the teacher confronts particular situations or problems' (p. 13).

He did this by fitting the task to the situation at hand, arranging students into groups, where they verbally summarised the homework as he monitored progress. When this was complete, fifteen minutes into the lesson, students presented two items of vocabulary from their article, giving the word, meaning, and part of speech. Matthew pointed out that the purpose was to build and demonstrate knowledge of vocabulary across a range of topics. Ten minutes later, when this was done, he moved onto another vocabulary exercise, facilitated by PowerPoint. In teams, students had to guess the endings of words related to relationships (e.g. beaut________ – noun, beaut________ – adjective). This exercise was time-bound, and completed quickly, before Matthew explained the importance of predicting the form of missing words in a gap-fill activity (e.g. tasks common in language proficiency exams).

Once the various tasks of contextualisation and reinforcement had been completed, the emphasis shifted to a reading task in the textbook on the theme of relationships between people. When that ended, students had to look at a piece of writing related to creating their own characters and situations, such as a conversation between Macbeth and the witches from Shakespeare's famous tragedy (1606). Generally, this could be difficult to set up in an EAP classroom with students of such a low IELTS level. However, in FG1 Matthew had spoken of 'fun' in the classroom, and this was what he tried to create; bringing something of 'the outside world' into class, and facilitating the 'interactivity' he had spoken of in the same focus group session.

Although the class worked in terms of interactivity, and students seemed to enjoy the concept of role-playing, this was probably not the best example of Matthew's attempts to integrate technology, pedagogy, and content. Just as in his FG1 dialogue, there was a sense of drawing on an ELT knowledge base, particularly in the area of Communicative Language Teaching (CLT), rather than showing awareness of the key differences between the content and processes required for teaching and learning in an EAP class compared with a general ELT class (BALEAP, 2008, p. 8). The lesson as a whole created a sense of Matthew being at a 'mid-way point' of transition in terms of moving gradually from General English to the teaching of EAP, as described by Martin (2014, p. 18), but doing so out of choice rather than from lack of knowledge about disciplinary expectations. In discussions afterwards, he agreed with this analysis but also explained that he had chosen this creative approach to teaching the lesson because of student levels and earlier disengagement. Therefore, like Harry, he appeared to be prioritising student needs when it came to decisions regarding pedagogy, content, and technology.

Vignette from Rosemary's classroom

Rosemary, in the early focus group sessions, had suggested that there was 'a time and a place' for technology (FG1). It would be interesting, then, to see the role played by technology in this observation of a Foundation EAP lesson for a group of primarily Chinese students with basic entry IELTS scores of 4.5. The session took place in a standard language centre classroom equipped with computer, projector, and IWB, in addition to a portable whiteboard.

Prior to the session, Rosemary explained that her objective was to get students working on analysing articles from their personal reading diaries, and preparing to give a presentation on this. The *'main idea'* was to promote understanding of the task by getting students to generate their own ideas so as to create a sense of direction in their forthcoming presentations. As such, Rosemary had suggested that the use of technology would be limited. However, this fell in line with her focus group sessions where she had emphasised the importance of sometimes *'focusing on the teaching'* and *'student-teacher interaction'* rather than *'looking at all the gadgets and the things they can do'* (FG1).

Rosemary opened her lesson with an introduction to the objectives, and checked who had done their homework: preparing topics for presentations. She then assigned students to groups, and asked them to discuss those topics. Before the discussion, Rosemary instructed the students to *'use pen and paper to jot down ideas about what is wanted or expected from presentations'*, reinforced by her illustration of the task on the whiteboard. Because of language levels in this class, she then reinforced her instructions by eliciting responses from students about what needed to be done.

However, several students had not brought in copies of their articles despite having been told to do so, and then had to work from memory. Interestingly, once the group work began, one student asked if he could take out his laptop to access the articles. Rosemary agreed to this so long as he interacted with the others, which triggered two more students taking out their computers. Though this could have created a sense of division within the groups, Rosemary managed the dynamics well; supporting principles within the TPACK literature of adapting tools around the task, rather than vice versa.

Once the students had discussed their reading tasks for around twenty minutes, Rosemary then elicited answers and wrote these on the mobile whiteboard, asking additional questions where necessary. After completion of whole-class feedback, students again returned to group work, focusing this time on planning their actual presentations rather than understanding the content of texts in their reading diaries. This time, though, Rosemary did not monitor the discussions. Instead she sat at the top end of the classroom, and conducted one-to-one tutorials with students about their presentations. By then, there was much less to see and I concluded the observation.

On the whole, despite limited use of technology, observing this lesson proved beneficial because it served as an instance of prioritising content over technologies. In this instance of practice, Rosemary preferred traditional methods of teaching to using newer technologies but was able to adapt her plans to incorporate students' personal computers when required. Perhaps she could have used technology in the delivery of this lesson, but it may not have added anything to the pre-determined emphasis on content. Such an emphasis on content lies at the heart of Shulman's (1986) original PCK framework, from which TPACK subsequently evolved. Within Koehler & Mishra's (2009, p. 66) definition they speak of 'a forward-looking, creative, and open-minded seeking of technology use, not for its own sake, but for the sake of advancing student learning and understanding.'

In this observation, Rosemary emphasised comprehension of the presentation task, which was largely based around understanding texts at this stage. That understanding, as she suggested in post-observation discussions, might have been further aided by use of Moodle outside of class. However, in the context of this lesson, she did not feel that there was any substantial way in which her objectives could have been better realised with usage of technologies. Perhaps one area of improvement was that if all students had been asked to bring in personal computers, it might have guaranteed them access to the texts around which they were basing their presentations.

6.4 – Lessons learned at this stage

Observations proved a useful mechanism for matching espoused and actual practices, but this was not a spying mission into teachers' classrooms. Instead this quartet of vignettes served four key purposes. Firstly, they provided foundations for reporting an instance of practice in the work of each teacher. Secondly, in the majority of cases, they provided support for values and ideas expressed during the focus group sessions. Following on from this, they unearthed new areas for exploration through individual interviews or analysis of teaching materials. Finally, these observations allowed me to establish links not just to the teacher education or cognition literature, but also to TPACK and the underlying PCK framework from which this has evolved.

Out of these four central purposes, the provision of a vignette for each person is perhaps the most important in terms of reporting the overall story. This is because a key aim of this study is to share its story through the voices and experience of participants where possible. Reflecting back on the opening chapter's discussion about identity formation, these vignettes of practice have offered a portrait of the teachers on both a personal and professional level. Furthermore, through arranging meetings with the teachers after the observations, I was able to get a sense of their perspective on the lesson and a rationale for why they had chosen particular approaches or adapted original plans. This was highly valuable, especially in Harry's case where he was able to explain why this particular lesson was far from an ideal snapshot of his practice, even though it met the needs of 'these students in this situation and this set of concerns' (Burns, 1999, p. 3). Indeed, all four teachers enacted these values in their practice and I was able to understand that there was a clear rationale for their choices because of the two-way process of negotiation before and after the observations, as recommended by Goodwyn (1997, pp. 108–110). This also supported the benefits of being on site as an 'insider researcher' as discussed in greater detail in Chapter 3.

CHAPTER 7

Resources and Technology Use

7.1 – Contextualisation

Overview of post workshop developments

Over the course of the teacher education programme, individuals developed
an interest in a diverse range of technologies. Some of these had been the focus
of workshops, such as those on Moodle, developed over time in a community
of practice. Others had been adopted as a result of individual interests
and explorations. Earlier, I compared this to superheroes and their weapons
of choice – Harry's iPads and Kelly's lecture capture software, for example.
However, unlike comic book characters, teachers' work is rarely reduced to use
of a single resource. Furthermore, in the classroom, resources are used more as
vehicles than weapons, echoing Richard Clark's (1983) comparison of media
to 'the truck that delivers our groceries' but does not necessarily change eating
habits. Perhaps then it is more pertinent to speak of the Batmobile and TARDIS,
than a crossbow or lightsabre, when drawing comparisons to preferred choice
of technologies. Regardless of individual choices, though, the focus was still on
teaching. The main goal of the workplace was not to showcase technologies, but
to provide a foundation of language and skills for students' progression to university. Therefore, student needs shaped a great deal of the teachers' practice,
as evidenced in observations and interviews. Other factors also influenced the
uptake of technology, as will be highlighted throughout this chapter.

Some factors had been in existence from the outset of the workshops, and
others acquired in the course of teachers' learning journeys, but amidst developments, one feature stood out most strongly. This was a gradual shift towards
self-directed development, in which these teachers took charge not just of their
own learning, but also of shaping other developments within the language centre. As such, they became 'brokers' of new activity, as discussed in the work of
Wenger (1998) and Kimble et al (2010). The latter describe this as a process

---

How to cite this book chapter:
Breen, P. 2018. *Developing Educators for The Digital Age: A Framework for Capturing
Knowledge in Action*. Pp. 101–114. London: University of Westminster Press.
DOI: https://doi.org/10.16997/book13.g. License: CC-BY-NC-ND 4.0

of becoming 'interlocutors' in the transfer of knowledge from one context to another (ibid, p. 439) so that in its most transformative enactment, there is a collective adaptation of practice (Engeström, 2001, p. 137).

In some ways, this increased self-direction and brokering of activity had been happening from the outset, but it intensified towards the end of workshops, and then became most noticeable in occurrences over the course of the subsequent academic term. By now, these four teachers who form the cases in this study had completed a range of workshops and even additional developmental sessions, sometimes organised by themselves for colleagues. Here again, this suggested a changing role for these teachers within the workplace community of practice, becoming leaders, offering assistance to less experienced or confident members of the group. Again, this has echoes of Wenger's (1998) study, and the earlier work of Lave and Wenger (1991). Further to this, but again connected to Communities of Practice theory, in subsequent interviews, it became apparent that the four teachers were becoming better able to articulate their personal philosophies of teaching.

Articulation of personal philosophies

The notion of personal philosophy informing teaching practice recurs throughout the literature, and in its most basic sense refers to a synergy between teachers' professional knowledge and their interconnected 'universe of prior activities, tools, values, and norms of practice' (Schlager & Fusco, 2003, p. 209). Matthew, for example, has an avocation for drama and theatre, shaped by past experience on both personal and professional levels. This appears to underpin a personal philosophy of creativity in the classroom, evidenced by incorporation of story-telling, image, and dramatic techniques. That may partially explain why, in the opening focus group sessions, he highlighted one of technology's *'bear pits'* as being lack of interactivity, and he feared regression to a bygone style of teaching where PowerPoint just becomes a more high-tech version of the traditional chalkboard. Later on, in discussion with Kelly and Patricia, he felt bound to the use of technology, even in circumstances where it went against his natural instincts. Yet, by the end of the workshops, he appeared to have a greater handle on use of technology, and less fear, or even professional guilt, about shaping usage of resources around his natural instincts rather than vice versa. This suggested growing confidence not just in practice, but in teaching philosophy too.

Growth in confidence also characterised the work of the other teachers, with greater openness in both adoption and resistance to particular technologies. The introductory focus group sessions had featured a lot of discussion on the drawbacks of technology. This included a sense of resources inhibiting teaching, particularly from a communicative perspective. Kelly, for instance, had concerns about how her teaching might become *'static'* if she relied too heavily on the affordances of the interactive whiteboards. Even the physical context or layout of the classrooms had an inhibiting effect on her work – *'with the overhead projector and the board and that layout with the tables facing the board, I wonder whether or how we can maintain the interactivity.'* Because of the high-tech classroom, she felt unable to adjust the room to her own needs, and this curtailed what she described as *'the bit I really like about teaching'*, which was *'the human element'* of interaction with and between students.

Reshaping of personal and shared practices

By the end of the workshops, participants had grown in confidence as regards doing their own thing outside of formal teacher education sessions. Again, Kelly provides an excellent example of this. By the time the workshops had formally ended, she appeared to have gained considerable confidence in adapting the use of technology to meet her own needs, as evidenced by observations and focus group data. This adaptation included greater confidence in managing the physical space of the classroom and her interaction with the students. Despite technology's ubiquitous presence, Kelly now had the confidence to see her teaching as the EAP classroom's centre of gravity. This not only suggests a shift in philosophy, but also perceptions of context. Previously, the presence of technology had weighed heavily upon teachers' sense of what practices they were supposed to enact in the classroom. Now they integrated technologies with the focus of their teaching rather than vice versa. One instance of this, again from Kelly's teaching, came in changing approaches to lesson design. In the early focus group sessions, Kelly and others spoke of challenges in working with PowerPoint as if this resource served as the modelling tool around which lessons were moulded, but in later stages of development, PowerPoint had become more of a vehicle for content.

Harry too had grown in confidence, becoming a broker of new activity in his introduction of iPads into teaching within the language centre. Rosemary, of course, at an earlier stage had also assumed this role with the creation of revision quizzes on the Moodle VLE. Though she first designed these for use with her own students, she later introduced the idea and means of doing this to other teachers, not just of EAP, but a range of subjects including Mathematics where there was a significant uptake of quizzes. Rosemary thus brokered new activity not just within her immediate community of practice, but in relations 'with other tangential and overlapping communities of practice' as in Lave and Wenger's original definition (1991, p. 98). There was a growing sense, then, in general, of teachers taking greater charge of their own learning, and of doing this outside of any formal 'training' context. Though this ties in to some extent with the Communities of Practice literature, there also appeared to be a Vygotskian element to the manner of development.

7.2 – Theoretical foundations

Self-directed professional development

Literature on self-directed development goes back several decades, to form an important part of the 'detailed topography of the development landscape' (Mann, 2005, p. 104). Mann (ibid) further adds that a crucial first step is for the individual to establish foundations for their own development, which in this instance happened through the process outlined in Chapter 1. Teachers first recognised a need for some form of education in the use of technologies, and then attended the series of workshops at the heart of this study. Subsequently, through a combination of learning from these sessions and a range of other sociocultural influences, including the workplace community, the participants began a journey towards more self-directed practices.

The importance of such self-direction is highlighted in work that stretches back as far as Gibbons & Norman's (1987, p. 110) use of the term 'self-directed professional development.' Others have referred to this in similar terms across a range of disciplines and professional contexts, including Manning & Payne (1993), Bailey, Curtis, & Nunan (2001), Crookes & Chandler (2001), and Diaz-Maggioli (2004). Significantly for this study, Mishra & Koehler (2006) also make reference to the importance of teachers taking charge of their own mental development as a means of facilitating the synergy of TPACK. Manning & Payne's (1993) Vygotskian-based study of teacher cognition provides a further framework for helping teaching professionals become more 'proactive' (p. 362), and self-regulated (p. 369). They attribute the origins of self-directed professional development to Vygotsky's work on thought and language, and recommend that in order for development to occur, teachers need some form of prompting to move from within their 'zone of proximal development' (1993, p. 361).

This prompting or scaffolding generally takes place through a combination of support from more experienced practitioners in the first instance and then socially-shaped interactions with others. Kimble et al (2010, p. 437) see innovation as stemming from 'collaboration and knowledge sharing across professional or organizational boundaries.' Vygotsky (1978, p. 56) suggests that development is not circular but proceeds 'in a spiral, passing through the same point at each new revolution while advancing to a higher level.' This means that development comes about through an interaction of past knowledge and new experience (Manning & Payne, 1993, p. 362). Similarly, Mann (2005, p. 108) talks about the creation of 'a cognitive space' where teachers take mental charge of their own development.

This sense of new learning occurring at a juncture with existing knowledge interlinks the teacher education and teacher cognition literature. Mann's (2005) reference to teachers taking mental charge of their own development echoes work that stretches from Calderhead (1990) to Freeman (2002), and then Borg's (2006) seminal synthesis of teacher cognition literature. This also connects to the aforementioned belief that 'teacher learning ought not to be bound and *delivered* but rather *activated*' and that this activation is triggered only when teachers come to an understanding of their own knowledge (Wilson & Berne, 1999, p.194). Warschauer (1996), citing Garret (1991), also refers to how computers can serve as a medium through which teachers enact their 'pedagogical philosophies' with the learning activities they create.

Emphasis on personal philosophies of teaching

Every teacher has a personal philosophy of practice, even if this can be difficult to measure, and not easy to articulate. Added to this, it is difficult to evaluate the relationship of 'thought-to-practice' (Roehler et al, 1988, p. 164) and even to argue that teachers have time to consciously and consistently act out their philosophies in the heat of classroom interaction (Pajares, 1992). Therefore, when used here, the concern is not with micro-aspects of teaching. Instead, the definition prioritises a focus on broader epistemological positions, echoing John Dewey's emphasis upon an overarching 'pedagogic creed', as described in his seminal 'declaration concerning education' (1897, pp. 77–80).

The 'creed' in this context is particularly focused upon the intersection of pedagogy, technology, and content, in line with the TPACK framework, and significantly pedagogical philosophy features heavily in early CALL literature. Warschauer (2000, p. 42), writing about uptake of technology in a study conducted in Hawaii, nominates teachers' main influences as being 'the general institutional context and the particular beliefs of each individual.' This connects to earlier references to 'pedagogical philosophies' where it is not 'the what' that matters, whether tools or content, but rather 'how' these are put into practice (Warschauer, 1996, p. 6). Technology thus serves as an advanced medium through which 'a variety of methods, approaches, and pedagogical philosophies may be implemented' (Garrett, 1991, p. 75). However, use of technology is not a philosophy in itself. On the contrary, it is the teacher's 'underlying pedagogical philosophy' that shapes the way in which they use computers in their classroom (Becker, 2000, p. 11). Such a stance resonates strongly with the underlying philosophy of TPACK, as defined by Mishra & Koehler (2006), and Koehler & Mishra (2009).

The adoption of personal philosophies, though, should not be taken as 'context-neutral' or as 'generic solutions to the problem of teaching' (Mishra & Koehler, 2006, p. 1032). This is because of 'the situated nature of learning' (ibid), as also frequently referred to in the work of Lave and Wenger (1991). Mishra & Koehler further stress that 'technology use in the classroom is context bound' and 'generic solutions do not value the individual teacher' (2006, p. 1032). Perhaps that is especially true of the heavily situated context of English Language classrooms, and particularly when working within the chameleon discipline of English for Academic Purposes.

The importance of teaching philosophies in an EAP context is stressed by Kirk (2012), who contends that 'a leap into TEAP' requires consolidation of both philosophy and practice. This echoes some of the earliest EAP literature, including Pennycook (1997), who suggests that teaching should be guided by a broader philosophy than simply 'the local and the everyday defining what we do' (p. 255). That should not be taken as a challenge to situated learning, but as a call for awareness of 'language as social practice' which 'cannot be isolated from its social, cultural, and ideological contexts' (ibid, pp. 257–258). Pennycook thus advocates a philosophy that takes into account the broader ecological systems of education and society. Rather than divorcing the EAP classroom from what happens in the wider world outside, it has to be part of a broader 'ecosystem' (Fenwick & Edwards, 2010, p. 9) that, in today's digital age, has to incorporate technologies, and the outside world's 'mesh of connections' such as the domain of social media (Kear, 2011, p. 38).

Influence of institutional philosophy upon practice

Borg (2006, p. 275) highlights the fact that contextual factors such as availability of resources and institutional policy impact on what happens in classrooms. This ties in with Warschauer's aforementioned writings on how the institutional context influences uptake of technology (2000, p. 42), echoed by other expert voices in this area such as Chapelle (2000). Diaz-Maggioli (2004) has also argued that 'school culture' and 'school climate' are key contextual factors in teachers' professional development, as indeed does Hadley (2014) in the slightly different context of outlining how neoliberal values are shaping work practices in today's universities. Further to this, Mariam Attia (2011) talks about the role of 'institutional philosophy', which is an area that hitherto had not been covered in such great depth within literature specifically relating to the uptake of ICT in educational contexts.

Attia's use of the term 'institutional philosophy' arose from her PhD study that explored 'the role of teachers' early learning experiences in shaping their pedagogical beliefs and practice specifically in relation to technology use' (2014, p. 1). Interestingly, that PhD study took place in 'a private institution of higher education in Cairo, Egypt' (ibid), making it comparable to the language centre herein. There, teachers worked in an 'environment of ubiquitous computing and networking' not always matched by institutional systems that helped make the most out of technology's affordances (Attia, 2011, pp. 196–197). Obstacles to adoption of resources included time, technical support, and lack of learning opportunities (pp. 198–201). However, the study's participants also believed that 'teachers play a significant, active role in their own development' (ibid, p. 198), which is boosted by 'peer collaboration' (p. 201). That combination of factors thus means that Attia's works (2011; 2014) can provide valuable theoretical guidelines for studies of teacher development, particularly when there is a focus on practitioners' uptake of technology.

7.3 – Practical considerations

Sociocultural environment and collaboration

By the end of the workshops and the advent of a second academic year, a great deal had changed in the language centre. Much had changed in London too, as time raced towards the completion of the Queen Elizabeth Olympic Park, a couple of miles down the road, as a javelin flies, in the regenerated Stratford region. Hackney Marshes had been cleared, and foundations laid for a shiny new stadium of layers connected together in the style of muscles in a human body. Across the way, another structure rose magnificent and mysterious against London's spring-blue skies. Towering close to 400 feet, this spectacle of modern art spiralled between clouds and the last of autumn's golden leaves. Officially named the *ArcelorMittal Orbit*, London's people and papers had shortened it to a single word. The Orbit, waiting patiently, watched over the last stages of construction on the Olympic site below. Fittingly too, from a distance, observed through a train window on the way to work, it could have passed for an incarnation of Vygotsky's developmental spiral (1978, p. 76).

Down the train tracks, beyond the glass mountain of Liverpool Street station, developments gathered pace in the language centre too. The storms described in Bruce Tuckman's (1965) team development model had long since passed, as the workplace matured and established its boundaries. Hundreds of new students arrived from various corners of the world, creating a simultaneous demand for more teaching staff. This time around, upon arrival, new teachers found a thriving community and benefitted greatly from unofficial, informal apprenticeships offered by those already in the workplace. Alongside these 'newbies' and the more established staff members, Harry, Kelly, Matthew, and Rosemary carried on with everyday affairs of teaching, and movement along the continuum of development (Richards, 1998).

From the outset of the teacher education workshops, collaboration with colleagues had been at the heart of this development. That continued, as time passed, and gave birth to new levels of innovation. Harry's work with iPads served as a continuing example of this. Back in the focus group sessions, he had aspired to using '*the next generation*' of resources, and had actively pursued that interest by encouraging the language centre to make mobile technologies an established part of its activity. To do this, he fought for the right to purchase a set of iPads for students, for specific use on an International Diploma course. Then, aside from introducing and integrating these new tools into the language centre's activity system, he also advocated adoption of a newer version of

Moodle, which would function better alongside mobile technologies. As such, he was not just developing on a personal or professional level but also continuing to act as a broker of activity within the broader workplace, as suggested by Wenger (1998), and Kimble et al (2010).

In instigating this programme, Harry had to collaborate with a range of colleagues and also senior managers in the workplace. As such, he had to change and even challenge existing institutional policy and philosophy. This firstly involved championing the benefits of iPads, gaining the required funds to invest in these technologies, and then affirming their place in the language centre's activity system, by proving their benefits for students. In doing this, he also shared best practices with colleagues, particularly Matthew, who grew more interested in the use of iPads as the academic year progressed. Matthew's interest concerned ways in which these resources might be used specifically for the teaching of language on the English for University Studies course, as described in his earlier vignette of practice. Harry's interest, on the other hand, largely featured ways in which 'content' and language could be taught together. As such, this involved liaison with colleagues across a range of disciplines because the International Diploma course primarily featured such subjects as Business, Economics, and Organisational Behaviour.

Harry was not the only person to instigate changes in activity. Across programmes, a culture of innovation had developed. This was not just carried out on the part of those teachers chosen as cases. Others made equally significant contributions, including those who had participated in various workshops and focus groups. Emily, for example, embarked on exemplary practices in the use of Moodle both as a resource for teachers and as a means of self-access for students. However, for the purposes of this study, it is important to primarily report the practices of the chosen cases who each contributed to the language centre's broader environment in their own ways. Kelly tried to introduce Camtasia as a means of providing feedback to students but felt that her efforts were not supported by the institution to the same extent as the iPad programme. Therefore, over time, her focus shifted away from technologies and towards content to a greater extent, particularly in the Graduate Diploma English course that she was still teaching on. The same happened to some extent with Rosemary, who spoke of facing time constraints on the very demanding Foundation English programme, when asked about continuing use of technologies, during individual interviews.

Matthew, in teaching on the EUS course, had taken a different stance as regards the ways that he wanted to use technology in the classroom, as summed up in his first individual interview. There, he asserted that *unless the classroom is a bubble which doesn't really reflect life then you should be using social networking within the classroom.* As such, he was trying to enact a different form of collaboration by interacting with a wider sociocultural domain in *the real world outside of the classroom.* This, though, was not only facilitated by social media but also through *new and authentic* tools such as podcasts, accessed online or created by the students themselves. One particular set of podcasts that he used as an exemplar and also encouraged students to access and use was *The Guardian* podcast series, which had been in existence since 2004, and could be accessed through the newspaper site, and also on iTunes, Soundcloud, Audioboom, and Mixcloud.

Student influence on teacher choices

Matthew's instigation of podcast recordings exemplified efforts to shift learning beyond traditional classroom boundaries, and get students working on authentic activities outside of class. Sometimes he enacted this by instructing his group in a particular language point, and then sending them out to use that language in a real-life interview situation, which was recorded on their mobile phones and uploaded onto the Virtual Learning Environment. Similarly, Harry used real-life situations to stimulate autonomy, language, and understanding of subject matter in the International Business Diploma course. Drawing upon the language centre's surrounding area, he developed lessons and assessments around the affordances of Old Spitalfields' Market, with its hundreds of stalls offering everything from antiques to modern fashions. Armed with iPads, Harry's students firstly interviewed market traders about their particular business. Then, working in groups, they formulated plans for developing or consolidating that specific business. When finished, they shared their ideas with the rest of the class in a formal group presentation.

By developing lessons such as these, Harry and Matthew enacted instances of important theory in their teaching practice. Firstly, from a pedagogic perspective, they showed understanding of the BALEAP (2008) framework in fostering a strong sense of 'personal learning, development and autonomy' (p. 5) on the part of students. This could only be achieved by concise instructions from the teacher at the outset of the session. Such lessons also serve as instances of Vygotskian thought in practice because of the need for activation of student learning with higher level input at the outset. Furthermore, technology appeared to have become a natural and normalised part of Harry and Matthew's everyday practice (Bax, 2003). Their work with iPads and podcasts could be related to the TPACK framework through their reconfiguration of resources for 'customized pedagogic purposes' (Mishra & Koehler, 2009, p. 66). Further to this, the nature of their lessons demonstrated 'an open-minded seeking of technology use, not for its own sake, but for the sake of advancing student learning and understanding' (ibid), as had been similarly voiced in the focus group sessions by Derek and Emily.

Drawing upon those earlier sentiments of Derek and Emily, it would be wrong to suggest that an increased emphasis on student interaction had stemmed from the teacher education workshops. This had been evident from the outset in everyone's dialogue, including Kelly, and Rosemary who expressed a view that *'sometimes you can focus so much on the technology that you're not actually focusing on the teaching.'* She went on to say that *'you're just looking at all the gadgets and the things they can do. You're not focusing on the teaching itself or on the student teacher interaction.'* This gives a sense of technology being an obtrusive presence in Rosemary's classroom, just as Kelly had depicted technology as inhibiting communication at the outset.

Later in the study, Rosemary retained her focus on students but now came across as having greater control of *'gadgets.'* During individual interviews, she outlined some of her favoured technologies as being Smartboards, Moodle, PowerPoint, quizzes for self-study, and music as a *'stimulus'* for motivation. Regarding changes in usage throughout the study, she felt that *'we're definitely moving in the right direction … we've been using more* (technology)'. Interestingly, in light of her roots, her character, and her early work as an instigator and broker of Moodle, unlike any of the other cases, Rosemary analysed usage of technology through a group prism, rather than individual.

This again cropped up when talking about her own reasons for choosing to use technology in the classroom. Eventually, though, the focus shifted back towards the students as she stated that *'I don't see the point in just using technology for the teacher'*, and then introduced a recurring sentiment on the issue of self-access. Echoing views shared with the other teachers, she remarked that the VLE *'can benefit students outside of the classroom … you've got the wikis, you've got the quizzes that you can set up, the forums where students can interact, and rather than just the lesson ending you can continue on with students. So yes, Moodle is beneficial.'* Though depicting a different concept of life beyond the classroom walls, Rosemary's closing words echo some of Harry and Matthew's practices. Of course, each of the teachers used the VLE for self-access purposes, even though they did so to a different extent, in association with a combination of other resources.

Personal philosophies and self-direction

Though the workplace environment evolved over time, becoming busier and less personalised as the language centre grew, teachers adapted well and even shaped sociocultural change. In doing so, they demonstrated a greater sense of self-direction, not just in terms of their own learning, but in taking charge of the context in which they were teaching. Examples of this, already listed, include Harry sending his students out to Spitalfields with iPads, and Matthew's efforts to replicate *Guardian* podcasts, or create some afresh. Kelly and Rosemary's sense of self-direction also increased, particularly in shaping the direction of the courses they were teaching on, to a greater extent. In some instances, they also shaped institutional policy and philosophy. Rosemary, for example, became a leading advocate of teachers using Moodle in a consistent and meaningful manner on the Foundation programme.

Of course, just like instances of TPACK, examples of self-direction and demonstration of personal philosophies are difficult to 'tease out' in practice (Mishra & Koehler, 2009, p. 66). This is because self-direction and personal philosophies effectively belong to the field of autonomy, which is a difficult area to define, let alone quantify. Therefore, in order to get some basic understanding of the teachers' underlying philosophies, I shaped an individual interview question around the *favoured practice* referred to in Simon Borg's seminal text on teacher cognition (2006, p. 94). The purpose of this was not just to understand practice and philosophy in the closing stages of the research study, but to track its evolution through earlier dialogue in the focus group sessions, as in the particular instance detailed below.

During his final interview, Harry stated that *'you can't just experiment with technology'* because *'you need to have the way of teaching to go with it'*, echoing Steve Kirk's (2012) assertion that 'practitioners first need to turn technology into *techknowlogy*, before it can be *enrolled* into pedagogical practices.' In Harry's case, technology – much like music – had been a lifelong passion. When I then asked if his practice had changed, he insisted that it had *'remained reasonably consistent'* whilst stressing that *'the resources I've been able to use to implement that approach have been better.'* However, his perspective on subject matter appeared to have changed because at the outset he talked about EAP as *'all about writing essays.'* Yet, by the time of the final interview, he appeared to have altered his understanding of EAP to incorporate a stronger element of discipline-specific work. This was evidenced in his statement of creating situations where *'the students are being exposed to real language, the kind of language that they need to understand'*, and *'making the most of student knowledge and emergent language, the language teaching, integration of content and language.'*

One such instance of Harry's work with emergent language and discipline-specific texts arose in *'pronunciation classes with very small groups of Chinese students.'* Here, he was involved in *'recording very short pieces of text, like very short introductions and focusing in on the pronunciation areas within there.'* In doing this, he was using the technology and the pedagogy to teach content, which was language-related, but pedagogy remained central to his actions, and this had been a consistent feature of his sense of practice throughout the study. On the whole, then, Harry's philosophy appeared to strongly resonate with Koehler & Mishra's depiction of Technological Pedagogical Knowledge (2009, pp. 65–66), with some characteristics of Technological Pedagogical Content Knowledge (pp. 66–67) in there too. However, language as content, as later discussed, remains problematic.

Although Harry's case has been studied in the greatest detail here, each of the teachers spoke of favoured practice in their own unique manner. Rosemary, for example, moved the emphasis away from technology to more traditional expectations within English Language teaching. She stated that *'favoured practice with regards to EAP is motivation.'* Thus, she prioritised issues such as *'setting up a positive classroom atmosphere'* and *'creating dynamics in the classroom'*, as well as making *'sure that students understand'*, and creating *'student centred, student focused lessons.'* Here, there is less emphasis on fostering autonomy or creating awareness of disciplinary difference, and hence less of an association with those aspects of BALEAP's (2008) principles for competency. However, since Rosemary's practice appears to have been shaped by the nature of her classes and learners within them, she also exhibits a sense of addressing needs of 'these students in this situation' (Burns, 1999, p. 3); which falls in line with BALEAP's (2008) recurring emphasis on 'student needs' (pp. 3, 6, 7, 8 & 10).

Likewise, Matthew drew heavily upon his ELT background in espousing particular practices he valued in the EAP classroom. Echoing Rosemary, he attached great importance to the teacher's position as facilitator, through *'appealing to different learning styles'* and *'working towards collaborative learning'* so as to give students a sense of the university environment. Again, this shares common ground with the BALEAP (2008) competencies, particularly those relating to 'student critical thinking' and student 'autonomy in academic contexts' (p. 3). Technology, particularly use of visual images, also featured heavily in depictions of his favoured practice. From the outset of this study, he had advocated integration of real world language into the EAP classroom, though voiced concerns over lack of technological knowledge.

By building up the required technological knowledge, Matthew then felt better equipped to realise his aspirations for wedding the classroom *'bubble'* to more *'authentic'* contexts. Increased technological knowledge, alongside his existing ELT pedagogical knowledge base, strengthened his overall TPK, and allowed him to realise his aspirations in actual practice. One instance of this came about in his changing use of audio. At the outset, he conducted listening sessions exclusively within the classroom. Then he moved to a point of uploading these onto the Virtual Learning Environment and having students listen to them in their own time. Gradually, this evolved into students having to go out and find or create their listening resources, such as podcast recordings, to share in the classroom. That brings his work in sync with BALEAP's (2008, p. 10) demand for student autonomy, which they define as 'both independence and interdependence (Little, 1991; 1994 cited in Blin, 2004).' Echoing basic elements of Bhatia's (2004) work, they further suggest that there should also be 'development of a social, and even political autonomy through which a group of learners will collectively take responsibility for and control their learning' (BALEAP, 2008, p. 10). In scaffolding students towards such definitions of autonomy within his classes, Matthew was enacting a core belief that EAP classes should prepare students for the real-life contexts in which they will interact and study, as stated in his individual interviews. Technology, at this stage, thus appeared to have become less of a bear-pit in his work, and more of a vehicle for the teaching values he wanted to enact.

Kelly, who features heavily in the next chapter, also showed signs of her philosophy shifting slightly according to the evolution of her knowledge base, but at the same time staying true to long-held underlying principles. Indeed, by the latter stages of the study, she had moved full-circle, through exploration with different technologies, back to a point where she was arguing for renewed emphasis on more natural approaches to teaching and learning. Conversely, by building up a stronger sense of TPACK's components, she then had the confidence to re-examine earlier attitudes towards technology, and argue in support of those from a more informed position. Instances of this included her perspectives on the teaching of reading and writing where she lamented the sometimes *'superficial and shallow'* manner in which today's students approached researching and planning their academic essays.

She then used the washing machine as a simile for technologies in education. Though more convenient and labour-saving in some aspects, she argued, machines in themselves do not bring about revolutionary change. She posited that *'with any form of technology or development people like to believe this is going to make everything a lot easier'* and that feminists *'touted the invention of the washing machine'* as one that was *'brilliant'* because *'women are going to be doing less housework.'* Yet *'women do exactly the same amount of housework now as they did with the kind of pre-industrialised thing.'* Thus, she appears to believe new technologies are not a 'panacea' (Warschauer & Meskill, 2000, p. 315) for age-old problems, whether that relates to the burden of housework expected of women, or traditional challenges that students face in writing essays. This interpretation is further supported by her dismissal of *'the myth'* that even if *'it may be quicker'*, the actual content is improved just because *'you've an iPad or a computer, or quick access to an electronic journal.'* The challenges, she contended, do not disappear as a consequence of *'having an app or an iPhone or an iPod, or an electronic whiteboard.'* Continuing this theme, she expressed the view that real change comes from within, and not from technologies, which will always be the case in language teaching *'until you can get a syringe and you can literally inject people with the language and the theory.'* Ultimately, then, as seen in her closing quote about language injections, Kelly is a case in proof that developing a greater sense of TPACK does not equate to becoming a 'technology junkie', which of course was never its creators' intention.

7.4 – Lessons learned at this stage

This chapter has tried to show how the four teachers developed over time, after the teacher education workshops and towards the end of the timeframe for the original study. Through their practice and some of their words, it was evident that they were becoming more self-directed as well as developing philosophies of teaching in line with the TPACK framework. That self-direction was linked in the first instance to the development of technological knowledge, but a range of other variables impacted on the acquisition of new learning, beyond the context of the formal workshops. Teachers were indeed 'taking responsibility for personal learning endeavours' (Brockett & Hiemstra, 1991, p. 29) and this was happening not just because of who they were as professionals, but also the personal characteristics they possessed.

These four teachers were not just bringing about change in their own practice, but also changes to the local environment in which they worked, as in Rosemary's efforts with Moodle. Since any research journey must have further resonance than that of its immediate surroundings, developments within the language centre can provide significant lessons for teacher educators not just here, but in the broader EAP and higher educational domains. This again is particularly important in a qualitative study, where like the poet Patrick Kavanagh's quote at the start of this book, in the slightly different context of literary writing, 'it is depth that counts, not width' (1967).

However, for the study to be of broader interest beyond the immediate context, it was essential to understand to what extent such transitions in knowledge had been embedded for the longer term. In order to address that, the chapter that follows is going to focus largely on Kelly's practice and dialogue so as to understand how such a process of embedding might occur. By doing so, the aim is to consolidate the lessons learned in this chapter as regards the ways in which elements of TPACK are enacted in practice, and how such enactments are not dependent upon instances of using technology. This further strengthens the central argument of this work, which is that even within this theoretical framework for teaching with technology, pedagogy remains central to everything, and the teacher continues to be the chess piece around which the class is built (Stevick, 1996, p. 180).

CHAPTER 8

The Embedding of Development

8.1 – Contextualisation

Conceptualising the spiral of knowledge

Set against the Olympic Stadium, Anish Kapoor's *ArcelorMittal Orbit* reached its full height of 376 feet in November 2011, twice the reach of Nelson's famous column in Trafalgar Square. This monument shaped from twisted steel stood as the receptacle of differing symbols merged into one form, given life over the course of several years, in a time of great change. Described by *The Independent* newspaper as 'a continuously looping lattice' (2010), it would offer a legacy to London beyond the coming victories of such athletes as Jessica Ennis, Mo Farah, and Greg Rutherford upon the track and field in their own specific disciplines, whether the long jump or the 5,000 metres. But watching it rise into the clouds from a distance, taking on almost mythical proportions, to paraphrase Boris Johnson, then the city's Lord Mayor, onlookers could not help but wonder what it actually represented. London 2012 Chairman Sebastian Coe declared it 'an indelible memory, a declaration of legacy, and a definable landmark' for Londoners and other visitors from around the world. Its creators, though, portrayed it as more of a developmental symbol; a sign of the physical and psychological journey that athletes have to undertake in their continuous quest for improvement. Through this theme of continuous development, the sculpture can serve as an inspiration for the story of how teachers develop in their practice over time. This is because the original objective of the tower's designers was to create something vague or mystical that could indeed be all things to all men. Women too, for as the design panel themselves pointed out, the body shape beneath the hard steel exterior is unmistakably feminine (ArcelorMittal, 2010).

Thus, for some, this mysterious scarlet tower is a flamenco dancer bowing to the crowd, and for others a helter skelter connecting uncluttered concrete skies to the city's high-rise landscape of shards and gherkins. But for an EAP

How to cite this book chapter:
Breen, P. 2018. *Developing Educators for The Digital Age: A Framework for Capturing Knowledge in Action*. Pp. 115–125. London: University of Westminster Press.
DOI: https://doi.org/10.16997/book13.h. License: CC-BY-NC-ND 4.0

manager looking out of a train window every groundhog day on the way to Liverpool Street, this tower becomes the incarnation of a language teacher's developmental continuum. This is because each time it rises in a knotted loop, simultaneously it appears to fall back on itself in the manner of a spiral. Though locked together by eight winding strands, strange tunnels, and rings scattered off the Olympic flag, it always seems loose enough to breathe, tumbling back to earth; grounded in the soil and the environment that it has sprung from, but at the same time reaching out not just to the broader city of London but the whole sporting world. In that image too of being grounded in its own specific context and at the same time reaching beyond that, there is a further sense of how this chameleon sculpture evokes various layers of imagery in the mind of an EAP practitioner. Perhaps too, it is an appropriate image through which to introduce a chapter that has Kelly as its main subject. This is because sport plays such a definitive part in her personal life. Significantly too, as a marathon runner, she is engaging in a historical sporting activity which owes its present-day incarnation and very existence to the Olympic games, as a consequence of having been reconfigured for the Athens competition of 1896.

Kelly and differing strands of development

Chapter 3 provided personal vignettes from the life of each teacher, and Kelly's case featured a story of running in Brighton's annual marathon. This, though, was not something that happened out of the blue. Just like those Olympic athletes already mentioned, this involved months of preparation for Kelly, as she built up gradually towards being capable of running the 26.2 miles in a marathon. At the same time, and in a similar way, she was developing as a teacher through her work in the language centre. Sometimes she taught in the specific discipline of International Relations on the Foundation programme, and other times EAP on the Graduate Diploma. Then she later took on an additional role as one of the language centre's Plagiarism Officers, and her efforts came to be characterised by staying late in the workplace, before heading off for a run in the evenings.

None of these differing parts of her life could be divorced from the others because they each contributed to her development as a person. In teaching, the boundaries of the personal and the professional are so blurred that they weave together as one. Though certain disciplines may be suited to creating distance between personal and professional selves, the English Language classroom is generally not a place for masking or shielding self-identity. This is because the core principles of English Language teaching emphasise a need for interactivity, personalisation, and communication in every lesson. Perhaps this was why, at the outset of the focus groups, Kelly's greatest concern appeared to be the need to *'maintain the interactivity'* and to negotiate meaning with students, rather than dictate.

Of course, it is important to remember that at the start of her journey in the language centre, Kelly had come from what was primarily a General English teaching background, in terms of her classroom teaching experience. Through that, she had acquired a particular experience of 'training' which was quite different to an EAP or higher educational context. When asked about her views on teacher education at the start, she suggested that *without training you do get out of the habit and then six months have passed and you haven't really looked at another book.* Added to this, in these early stages, Kelly expressed a strong sense of the institution being responsible for instigating and generating interest in training, particularly *'managers.'* Although she had completed a Masters degree in Sociology and had a strong sense of autonomy in her personal and intellectual life, her professional background had been characterised by lack of power in the workplace. Generally, private language schools offer a career cul-de-sac with few perks or opportunities for teachers. This is evidenced by their habit of using zero-hour contracts long before such a term entered the political parlance of our times.

Though not entirely a 'novice teacher' (Alexander, 2010, p. 4), Kelly had come to the language centre at a point in her developmental continuum where she needed some spark to ignite unrealised pedagogic potential. Like the others in this study, and many teaching professionals at the start of their careers, she was too talented for the private language school cul-de-sac. Thus, embarking upon her new position and the associated workshops, Kelly faced a challenge akin to preparing for a long distance run, albeit one that was lifelong rather than building up to a single marathon. In doing so, she would make a slow transition from ELT to EAP practitioner, but this did not mean abandoning everything in her existing ELT knowledge base.

8.2 – Theoretical foundations

The five tenets of teacher development in Vygotskian theory

The process of development is personal to each teaching professional and not simply a product of 'quantitative increments, but qualitative shifts as the unique past experiences and previous knowledge of individuals interact with the present learning event' (Manning & Payne, 1993, p. 362). Added to this, 'the life history' of new teachers contributes greatly to interpretation of what is provided in 'teacher education programs' (ibid). However, consistency comes in the fact that there are five established tenets of development within a Vygotskian perspective (ibid, pp. 362–366). As with the interlocking links of the *ArcelorMittal* sculpture, these tenets wind through one another in the form of a spiral towards what we might consider a high point, rather than end point. That high point is essentially the development of upper-level knowledge, which is then mediated and given expression through practice. In the case of this study, upper-level knowledge could be evaluated in terms of its being mediated through practical enactments of TPACK's core components.

Manning & Payne's (1993, p. 362) framework for relating Vygotskian theory to teacher education lists 'self regulation' as a first essential tenet of development. This involves teachers taking greater charge of autonomously orchestrating their classroom environments and utilising 'higher mental processes', which should include both cognitive and affective aspects (ibid). Practically speaking, this provides a challenge to any mechanistic sense of the classroom environment dictating teachers' practices. Of course, as seen in this study, in the first vignette of Harry's practice and Kelly's early focus group discussions, it can be a challenge to transcend the environment. Though theorists such as Thornbury (2000) may see any such attempt as absurd, the great strength of Manning & Payne's call for self-regulation is that it raises teaching above an endless cycle of 'putting out fires' (1993, p. 363).

Having developed self-regulation, teachers then need to build on their sense of 'metacognition' as a second tenet of development (1993, p. 363). Such metacognition refers to an understanding of one's own thought processes, and connects closely to the notion of being a reflective practitioner. This means not just being able to control the classroom or take charge of it, but to understand mistakes in strategies, for example, and then to correct these. Often such awareness comes about through social interactions, which gives shape to the third tenet of this Vygotskian perspective, which emphasises the role of 'Vygotsky's concept of the zone of proximal development' (ZPD). That can be defined as 'the distance between what one can accomplish independently as compared to what one can accomplish when aided' (ibid). As such, the concept of a ZPD is connected to the idea of 'scaffolding' as a form of development (Bruner, 1985), which is also referred to in the BALEAP Competency framework (2008, p. 8), and therefore highly commensurate with the EAP context at the heart of this study.

The fourth tenet of Manning & Payne's Vygotskian framework is the 'internalization of knowledge', which involves passing through a series of psychological planes shaped by dialogue. Ultimately, the end of this passage through different points of interaction leads to greater self-direction, which is on a slightly higher psychological plane than self-regulation. However, when self-direction is achieved, the teacher functions more independently, and has the ability to instigate verbal mediation with the self (1993, p. 365), which is the last of the five tenets in this teacher education framework. This, though, can be difficult to understand and even harder to evaluate because it involves 'talking to oneself in relevant ways when confronted with something to be learned, a problem to be solved, or a concept to be attained' (ibid). In other words, the high point of development from a Vygotskian perspective comes when teachers have confidence in their own mental voice, rather than reliance upon external factors to shape their decision making. The challenge, of course, is to know when that mental voice has matured, and also accept that finding such a voice should never be seen as the end point of development.

The spiralling nature of a teacher's developmental continuum

Teaching is best viewed as 'a continuous process of becoming' and one which 'can never be finished' (Mann, 2005, p. 105), since it is part of a journey along a continuum that should be both 'professional' (Goodwyn, 1997, p. 115), and 'developmental' (Richards, 1998, p. 48). This echoes the more historical work of Vygotsky (1978, p. 56) who suggests that development is not circular but proceeds 'in a spiral, passing through the same point at each new revolution while advancing to a higher level.' As such, the highest levels of development come about through heightened awareness of the interaction between past knowledge and new experience (Manning & Payne, 1993, p. 362), as outlined in the previous section.

Thus, in Kelly's case, development should theoretically occur at the point where she was able to synergise her existing ELT knowledge base with new understandings of EAP, pedagogy, and technology gained through the teacher education workshops. Alexander et al (2008) discuss this in *EAP Essentials*, one of the seminal texts in the practice and principles of teaching English for Academic Purposes. They suggest that 'the process of adjustment from general English to EAP teaching can involve some major shifts in approach' but that this should 'not mean abandoning good teaching practice' (p. 5). Even though 'EAP and other kinds of English teaching share an underlying core of methodology' in key areas of language learning and classroom management, teachers from an ELT background 'sometimes begin to feel insecure and leave their most valuable skills at the EAP classroom door' (ibid). That could be seen in elements of Kelly's early dialogue where she felt that the expectations of the EAP higher educational context involved a need to utilise technology in all circumstances, even though at times this seemed to inhibit natural communication with the students. Thus, she seemed torn between what she knew best, up to that point in the ELT classroom, and these new, daunting expectations of the more academic context. The fact that Matthew, coming from a similar background, voiced the same challenges suggests that Alexander at al's (2008, p. 5) dilemma is faced by many 'new recruits to the tribe' of EAP's academic discourse community (p. 6).

This emphasis on joining a community, wherein new members are aided by more experienced practitioners, has elements of both Wenger's (1998) theories regarding apprenticeships, and Vygotskian perspectives. In the Communities of Practice literature, though, there is not the same emphasis on eventual progression towards self-direction. For me, Wenger's primary focus is on a sharing of voices rather than a shift towards being able to internalise those voices, and use them to shape our own mental voice. TPACK, though, does emphasise the role of reflection and self-direction because it makes a demand of teachers to 'ask questions of their pedagogy' (Mishra & Koehler, 2006, p. 103). Furthermore, like Manning & Payne's Vygotskian model, TPACK's is constructed of interlocking but inseparable tenets which should culminate in acquisition of mental reflection and self-regulation, when 'a dynamic equilibrium' has been established amongst all of the framework's constituent parts (Koehler & Mishra, 2009, p. 67). However, the literature affirms that this cannot be achieved overnight, with Alexander et al (2008) suggesting 'a considerable time lag before principles … begin to inform practice'; perhaps making it more of a marathon than a sprint.

8.3 – Practical considerations

Developments in Kelly's professional practice

At the outset of the teacher education programme, Kelly had expressed discomfort with technology, struggling to juxtapose human elements of teaching with the ubiquitous hardware of the language centre's classrooms. Gradually, though, as her technological knowledge increased, she used her existing ELT knowledge base and beliefs in what teaching is supposed to be, to adapt the hardware to meet the particular needs of students. Subsequently, she changed the focus of activity to extend beyond the classroom through greater use of Moodle at first. In doing so, she seemed to have repositioned herself as a teacher, not just physically but philosophically, in how she managed communication with and between those students.

By the time of the third focus group session, Kelly described further changes in her practice, and actions shaped by new knowledge of, and access to, technologies. She talked about having contended with an unusual set of Bank Holidays created by the particular circumstances of the time period, where the Royal Wedding of Prince William and Catherine Middleton coincided with the end of an Easter week that was already late in the calendar year. This caused a situation that was not deliberately planned but ended up with workers having the unusual scenario of three short weeks in a row, beginning on Good Friday and ending with the May Bank Holiday. Six months prior to this, in an article in *The Daily Telegraph*, Wallop (2010) predicted that this would 'create a nightmare for many employers.' As in many other professions at the time, teachers on intensive foundational courses that were scheduled to a very strict time-frame related to university progression could not just 'down tools for weeks at a time' (ibid), particularly in situations such as that of Kelly, where some of her classes happened to fall on Mondays and Fridays.

In order to meet this challenge of what she called these '*accidental Bank Holidays*', she drew on the support of the language centre's IT department to introduce and use Camtasia Studio as a self-accessible resource for students. This is a software suite used for creating video tutorials. These are recorded by means of screencast or video screen capture, usually alongside audio recordings, and are generally used in a teaching context for either the presentation of information or the provision of feedback to students. Having been introduced to the theory behind this resource in the last of the workshops on *Use of technologies as a means of capturing lectures and recording feedback*, Kelly then sought practical help from someone she describes as '*the Head of IT.*' In doing all of this, she professed that '*I think that accident of the Bank Holidays kind of sparked usage of technology.*' Following on from this initial spark of activity, brokered through the IT department, Kelly then expanded on an existing base of PK and PCK to shape her learning materials and subject matter around the affordances of Camtasia Studio. Although the Head of IT said that she could '*record lectures*', she '*didn't want to do the video.*' Instead she '*used the PowerPoint slides*' in a '*programme where you can record them.*'

As before with Moodle, she was making pedagogical choices, drawing on elements of PCK and TPK. This time, though, because she was also using the technology to shape the content in particular ways, it could be argued that she was starting to find that synergy between technology and content, which facilitates TCK. At the very least, she was aware of the need to work on ways of reshaping content and technology to fit the needs of learners. She manifested this awareness in her analysis of the technology's effectiveness, in that '*it was quite successful in the way that some of the students went and watched it and listened to it*', but others had difficulty accessing it because of formatting and downloading. Despite the challenges, she hoped to '*use it a bit more maybe*', and went on to explain that she had started '*playing around with it in the staffroom*', alongside a more experienced colleague named Kenneth who hailed from a teacher education background.

What was interesting in Kelly's case was the way in which she adopted different tools for her own purposes, and changed her teaching and learning activities through doing so, first with Moodle, and then Camtasia. She used Moodle to reshape communication with students, and the balance of activity, and had discovered how Camtasia could reshape both provision of lectures and feedback to students. Just a relatively short time before, she had come across as being inhibited by the presence of technology, and the fear of having '*to admit that you don't know something about an aspect*', as stated in the opening focus group session. Yet, by the end of the teacher education programme, she was contentedly using one '*aspect*' of a tool such as Camtasia, whilst not being fluent in other aspects of its usage, and, rather than being inhibited, showing excitement at possibilities of further discovery.

The snowballing of knowledge

Although Kelly suggested that the most immediate spark for change in her practice came about '*because of the Bank Holidays*', she also discussed other significant influences. The first of these related to issues of exploration and collaboration, as examined in the previous chapter. Regarding such collaboration, in the third focus group session, she concurred with James and Matthew on the benefits of working with someone who is *'more of an expert.'* James exemplified this in his assertion that he sometimes consulted Emily about things he was having difficulty with, because he happened to sit across from her in the staff room, and preferred this direct approach to *'faffing and fooling around if I'm not getting anywhere.'*

Kelly told James *'I am the same really'*, and that when a need occurs, she will *'go and ask someone what to do about it, and see if anyone has any ideas.'* Similarly, she found assistance *'just from overhearing other people, and talking about things usually.'* She then added that overhearing people sparked a sense of *'getting a bit curious'* about the subject matter, *'and asking them what's happening, getting pulled into conversations, and seeing the demonstrations.'* This created a scenario of *'them showing you something'* and *'then it snowballing from there.'* This combination of professional eavesdropping and taking directions from more expert users again seemed to reside at an intersection of Vygotskian and Communities of Practice theory.

Kelly's specific reference to *'snowballing'* is particularly useful for evaluating developments that occurred in terms of actions and knowledge, during and after the teacher education programme. Firstly, there appeared to be an increased presence of community, collegiality, and collaboration in the staff room. This then translated itself into an exploration of resources, and a sharing of knowledge and opportunities. Through this sharing of ideas, Kelly's understanding of technologies 'snowballed', which suggests rapid growth from something starting out quite small. This context of ideas being shared, and bigger developments growing from small seeds strongly echoed Wenger & Snyder's (2000) work on how communities of practice can sometimes form through an initial cultivation. In this case, there was no deliberate cultivation of community, but the workshops appeared to have sparked forms of collaboration, not just for those who took part in them, but for others in the broader activity of the language centre. Thus, the snowballing that Kelly spoke of happened not just on an individual but also a group level.

Embedding and resurfacing of knowledge

Although Kelly had been proactive with Moodle and Camtasia, alongside the exploration of other resources such as Teacher's Pet, by the time of the individual interviews, her usage of these tools appeared to have dipped. During her first interview, she admitted that with some technologies her interest had continued, but with others it had waned over time. For example, she pointed out that *'it has reached a bit of a dead end with Camtasia'*, but *'not because of anything to do with the software itself'*, or that she was *'suddenly reticent about using it.'* Instead, *'the best way to put it is that things got in the way'*, which caused her to become *'distracted'* and then to *'not push for that enough'* in terms of getting support for the resource from *'different managers or the people who hold the purse strings basically.'* That echoes Engeström's (1999, p. 19) reference to the impact of socioeconomic factors on an individual's actions. Kelly appeared to have reached a point where her usage of varying technologies was going to 'snowball' but then was not given further impetus for this, and so she went back to reliance on the instruments most readily available to her. This was a combination of IWB, Word, Moodle, and the Graduate Diploma's core *Oxford English for Academic Purposes Upper-Intermediate* textbook, written by Edward de Chazal et al (2012).

However, this should not be taken as a regression back to reliance on the tools of the past. Rather, it shows an effective integration of TPACK's various categories and the ability to use resources where appropriate, as provided, or as readily accessible. Furthermore, the knowledge she had gained of other instruments had not gone away, as feared in the very first focus group session where she spoke of getting *'out of the habit'* and forgetting about *'training'*. Now, in referring to Camtasia, she expressed a view that *'I suppose what's interesting is that as we're coming to the end of term now it's resurfacing, the idea of using it again is resurfacing.'* This reference to *'resurfacing'* of usage and knowledge implies that there had been developments in terms of both actions and knowledge in Kelly's practice. She appeared to have embedded TPK in such a way that it was no longer dependent on recent education, or usage of a particular instrument. Rather, that usage was now shaped to a greater extent by the particular needs of students. She had found a way of using and integrating technology into her practice 'not for its own sake, but for the sake of advancing student learning' (Koehler & Mishra, 2009, p. 66).

Summary of developments in Kelly's practice

Overall, Kelly's journey featured fast development at the outset in getting to grips with technology, and then consolidation as she sought to develop her practice in line with contemporary ideas of what should happen in the EAP classroom (BALEAP, 2008; de Chazal et al, 2012). To some extent, as her technological knowledge developed, she placed it to one side and concentrated more on the content aspect of teaching. As later seen in her second vignette of practice, she moved towards *'more of an idea of what English for Academic Purposes is and the different kind of skills that students need.'* In this case, she concentrated a great deal of her efforts on usage of text processing and text production, as in BALEAP (2008, p. 8).

This is evidenced in her second vignette of practice, as later described, which involved looking at the function of language in a text, as a strategy for students' production of written output. Through doing so, she demonstrated understanding of both substantive and syntactic structures (Shulman, 1986, p. 9) within EAP preparation for postgraduate studies. She talked about getting students *'to notice the particular structures in their context and then to analyse it and to let students apply that by themselves'* whilst also having a focus on *'what's on the syllabus.'* The latter statement strongly echoes BALEAP's emphasis on syllabus development (2008, p. 7). Thus, Kelly, over the course of the programme, had moved from an early prioritisation of communication and interaction, towards understanding how to locate 'the methods, practices, and techniques of communicative language teaching' within specific academic contexts (ibid, p. 8). This in turn required a particular set of tasks and processes in order to make the subject matter comprehensible to students (Shulman, 1986, p. 8). As a consequence, content rather than technologies became the focus of work with her Graduate Diploma students preparing for entry to postgraduate courses. The focus shifted to breaking down and reassembling academic texts to develop academic literacy, rather than communicative language teaching. However, some base principles of English Language teaching remained, particularly in motivating students and facilitating discussion. This, like technology, became something that she could choose to dip in and out of, though.

Ultimately, this meant that Kelly's practice shifted towards a broader sense of 'overall educational purposes, values, and aims' (Koehler & Mishra, 2009, p. 63), rather than 'short term learning for learning's sake' (ibid), as is sometimes a feature of General English teaching. By making this shift towards a more academic context, she achieved greater synergy with the BALEAP Competency Framework which situates technology as something in the background that needs to be understood and integrated into delivery so as to 'reflect academic practices' (2008, p. 8). Having acquired a better synergy of TK with other elements of knowledge, Kelly seemed better equipped to then make strategic choices about when to use particular technologies, based around an emphasis on the subject matter, as suggested by Shulman (1986, p. 9). She had now progressed on her developmental continuum to the point of having a better understanding of what an EAP teacher should be able to do, particularly in terms of integrating elements of textual analysis into her work.

8.4 – Lessons learned at this stage

Through choosing Kelly as a focus for analysis, this chapter has provided an instance of 'knowledge growth in teaching' (Shulman, 1986). It has shown how knowledge is developed over time, and part of that development entails elements of Manning & Payne's (1993, p. 362) framework of relating Vygotskian theory to teacher education. Over time, as Kelly developed, she became more self-regulated, building on her metacognitive capacities in line with the spark provided by workshops, and collegial collaboration. This allowed her to enter into a dialogue with the self to a much greater extent, as evidenced through her ability to make autonomous choices about what technologies to use in the classroom, and then what to prioritise in class.

As such, by the end of the teacher education programme, Kelly had become self-directed to a greater extent. Additionally, she had developed an advanced perspective on the role of content, and moved beyond any simple desire to progress on a linear continuum of technological knowledge alone. Rather, her actions and dialogue towards the end of the programme strongly supported the notion of moving back and forth upon a developmental spiral. Like viewing the loops of the *ArcelorMittal Orbit,* or running the laps of a marathon route, this involved 'passing through the same point at each new revolution while advancing to a higher level' (Vygotsky, 1978, p. 56). The points that she passed through in her journey could be seen as a combination of TPACK categories, and the existing knowledge base of English Language teaching, providing a platform for her development as an EAP practitioner.

Simultaneous to her development as an EAP teacher, she developed a more comprehensive understanding of how to use and how to choose technology in her lessons, again going back to what she knew best when appropriate. Starting out, she had voiced concerns about the dominance of hardware over humanware, as spoken of in Warschauer & Meskill (2000, p. 315). However, by the end of the programme, she had turned that relationship upside down, as if now viewing technology as being no more than a vehicle 'to help reshape both the content and processes of language education' (ibid). Relating this to Manning & Payne's (1993) framework, something had happened to spark a more significant change in Kelly's practice than simply making choices as regards one resource over another. She was now asking significant questions of her own pedagogy and her subject, as in higher-level elements of the TPACK framework (Mishra & Koehler, 2006, p. 103). By doing so, she had internalised knowledge and was better able to instigate verbal mediation through her own mental voice (Manning & Payne, 1993, p. 365).

Ultimately, though, Kelly became a better EAP teacher because inhibitions about technology were no longer obstructing the delivery of content. She had learned how to embed new knowledge in a place where it could resurface when needed. Though there may seem nothing revolutionary in this, a great many teachers, across disciplines, struggle to find such self-direction. There is therefore much to be learned from a case such as Kelly's in terms of her progress and the consolidation of this into her everyday practice. Of course, as with all teacher development, it is important to stress again that teaching is best viewed as 'a continuous process of becoming' and one which 'can never be finished' (Mann, 2005, p. 105). There is always something more to learn, and each new learning experience involves fresh movement back through the developmental spiral towards the juncture where past knowledge and new experience intersects to form new knowledge (Vygotsky, 1978; Manning & Payne, 1993). Thankfully for Kelly and all those in the teaching profession, the journey of development is more of a marathon than a sprint, albeit with a few precocious bursts of speed along the way.

CHAPTER 9

Blended Learning's Consistent Presence

9.1 – Contextualisation

Evolution of blended learning practices in the language centre

One of the chief examples of technology becoming an indivisible part of the higher education landscape is in the usage of blended learning through Virtual Learning Environments (VLEs). Garrison (1988) defines such learning as a 'balanced approach between teacher-centered relationships found in face to face education' and 'the tendency to stress learner centered relationships in the emerging electronic environment.' Further to this, blended learning encourages an emphasis on self-access for students, which has been an important focus in the work of BALEAP (2008), and ELT in general, for over two decades (White, 2003). Significantly, in its solitary direct reference to technology, BALEAP's Competency Framework advocates 'the use of new technologies to support autonomous learning' (2008, p. 7).

The 'marriage of new technologies to old teaching' (Ham, 2010) had been embraced with passion by the teachers in this study. Thankfully too, from a teacher educator's perspective, this had come about as more of 'a love match' than a 'shotgun wedding' (ibid). Many of the teachers' actions in the EAP classroom, right from the start of the teacher education programme through to the finish, again supported Warschauer & Meskill's (2000, p. 315) argument that while 'computer technology is not a panacea for language teaching', it can provide ways of helping to 'reshape both the content and processes of language education' (ibid). Harry's integration of iPads into the International Diploma programme served as one example of this, whilst Rosemary's development of interactive quizzes proved to be an instance of change not just in EAP but across a broader range of subjects.

Such developments within the language centre reflected changes in the world outside, as advocated by Matthew from the outset of focus group sessions.

How to cite this book chapter:
Breen, P. 2018. *Developing Educators for The Digital Age: A Framework for Capturing Knowledge in Action.* Pp. 127–142. London: University of Westminster Press. DOI: https://doi.org/10.16997/book13.i. License: CC-BY-NC-ND 4.0

Cultural momentum, particularly in the evolution of social media, has added to the drive towards using technology in education (Maddux & Johnson, 2011, p. 2). As Matthew said of *Guardian* podcasts, '*it's just been made, it's incredibly new and authentic; why on earth would I not source that online, why would I not use that technology in the classroom?*' Through such a statement, Matthew envisioned a sense of blended learning that reflected the philosophy which seemed to gradually emerge from within the language centre.

Although, in the beginning, the blend had essentially involved a twinning of Moodle and classroom teaching, by the later stages of the study, a whole new series of combinations entered the fray. Though Moodle remained a staple part of the language centre's technological resource, a new generation of tools added diversity to the enactment of blended learning approaches. As the centre grew, a new generation of teachers arrived too. Significantly, though, a sense of continuation characterised the Community of Practice that had grown up around the use of Moodle in the centre's formative days, largely driven by the brokering efforts of Rosemary and Emily. In many cases, new teachers would arrive in the centre, be shown the ropes of the Virtual Learning Environment in a formal capacity, and then be left alone to explore, experiment, collaborate, and shape their own stake in the technological landscape, as the 'first generation' of teachers had also done. In some cases, they then took charge of reshaping the blend or content of their courses, effectively stamping their own character and philosophy upon the VLE. Or, more accurately, the VLE became a vehicle for enacting their philosophies.

Thus, the language centre had matured considerably in the later stages of the study, which was probably as much to do with collaboration as with the original series of teacher workshops that had simply served as a 'trigger' (Wilson & Berne, 1999, p. 194). Rosemary supported this view from the mid-point of the study with a statement that '*I've noticed as well how the subject teachers and the English teachers are looking at each other's Moodle pages and trying to sort of work together, which works a lot better; everyone looking at each other's.*' Through this simple collaboration, Moodle gradually evolved into more than a simple repository, and began to take on the characteristics of Robin Mason's (1998) trajectory of development in usage of Virtual Learning Environments. Since it is important to understand the ideology of Mason's (1998) framework, unlike in previous chapters, the contextualisation has been shortened here to put increased emphasis on theory and practice.

9.2 – Theoretical foundations

From evolution to revolution

Mason (1998) suggests that for teachers to make full use of a Virtual Learning Environment when designing online courses, they need to go beyond the notion of it as a mere repository for content, and undergo a 'pedagogical revolution' (p. 3). Such a revolution comes about in a three-stage process of development, beginning with a 'content + support model' which 'supports the notion of relatively unchanging content materials' (ibid, p.6). This is the most basic of the three stages, where the VLE is essentially used as a means of storage for course materials; a de facto dumping ground for a collection of PowerPoint slides and worksheets. Within such usage, there is little effort made by teachers 'to infuse technology into the learning experiences of their students' (McGrath et al, 2011, p.2). In effect, it becomes a manifestation of using technology 'for its own sake' rather than for 'advancing student learning and understanding' (Koehler & Mishra, 2009, p. 66). Yet there can be little dispute that contemporary higher education is weighed down by a great virtual heap of Microsoft Word documents and lecture slides left to decompose, out of date, on VLEs that are not being used to their full potential.

This is why Mason (1998, p.6) advocates a shift away from 'predetermined content', and a reliance upon 'relatively unchanging content materials which can be tutored by other teachers', or accessed by students who have not attended particular lecture sessions. Though beneficial in its own way, when the blend of content and support is utilised properly, this system only lends itself to 'rudimentary amounts of collaborative activity'. As such, he goes on to argue that there is a greater need for a 'wrap around model' as a second stage of development in a pedagogic revolution. He describes this second stage as defining 'those courses which consist of tailor made materials (study guide, activities and discussion) wrapped around existing materials (textbooks, CD-ROM resources or tutorials.)' Such a model 'tends to favour a resource-based approach to learning, giving more freedom and responsibility to the students to interpret the course for themselves' whilst also making the teacher's role 'more extensive' since 'less of the course is predetermined' (ibid). Instead, much of the activity on the VLE is socially constructed through real-life discussions, engagement with students and a mix of various 'event-based activities' (Valiathan, 2002, p. 1).

Following on from the 'content + support model' and the 'wrap around model', the third and final stage of pedagogical evolution comes in the form of an 'integrated model' (Mason, 1998). This is defined as being 'at the opposite end of the spectrum from the first' because it 'consists of collaborative activities, learning resources and joint assignments' so that the distinction between content and support is dissolved, 'and is dependent on the creation of a learning community' (p. 6). Thus, online learning becomes established as 'the heart of the course', and effectively 'dissolves the distinction between content and support' (ibid). In practical terms, this means that teachers are using 'new technologies to support autonomous learning', as advocated by BALEAP (2008, p. 7). Mason (1998, p. 10) suggests that the scaffolding of such autonomy entails a shift away from teacher control of the classroom environment, towards developing a 'carefully constructed online environment to create a self-sustaining learning community.'

The creation of such a community falls in line with the underlying values of this study, in emphasising the importance of collaboration serving as a scaffold for self-direction. Finally, although Mason's (1998) framework deals with usage of Virtual Learning Environments, its underlying principles can be moulded around the usage of other technologies too. For example, Harry's iPad project bore the hallmarks of the 'integrated model' (ibid, p. 6), as did some of the features found at higher levels of the English for University Study course which Emily managed, and Matthew worked upon.

Blended learning as a spark for growth

Blended learning, as a methodology, provides an effective 'starting point for getting teachers to work with technology in their practice' (Motteram, 2013, p. 7). Educating teachers in the first instance can pave the way to ongoing competency, defined by BALEAP (2008, p. 2) as 'the technical skills and professional capabilities that a teacher needs to bring to a position in order to fulfil its functions completely (Aitken, 1998).' Historically, though, it has been a challenge to situate or balance the role of technology within teacher preparation (Papert, 1987; McCormick & Scrimshaw, 2001; Harris, 2008; Harris, Mishra & Koehler, 2009.) Warschauer & Meskill (2000, p. 315) conclude that 'the key to successful use of technology in language teaching lies not in the hardware or software, but in 'humanware'; our human capacity as teachers to plan, design, and implement effective educational activity.'

Wenger (1998) also emphasises the need for personalisation and an interactional dimension to learning in the workplace. Technology needs to become a natural, normalised part of teachers' busy lives. Due to its modular structure, Moodle, in particular, can become a teacher's personal enterprise, beyond the remit of 'institutionalized processes' (Wenger, ibid, p. 10). The fact of it being a shared enterprise also helps address challenges endemic to the EAP context. These include lack of formal training (Hamp-Lyons, 2011), and 'the intensive nature of EAP courses', which creates difficulty for teachers in finding time 'to judiciously investigate and integrate technology in their teaching' (Gilbert, 2013, p. 140). Though not a panacea for such problems as time, training, and the 'lone ranger' nature of teaching (Samaras & Gismondi, 1998, p. 716), blended learning approaches can minimise the dangers of 'being focused on the enabling of technology at the expense of its impact on human endeavour' (Romeo & Russell, 2010, p. 54).

Just as in other professions, 'mutual engagement, shared repertoire, and joint enterprise' (Wenger, 1998) can spark the 'knowledge growth in teaching' advocated by Shulman (1986). Such knowledge and expertise are deepened by 'interacting on an ongoing basis' (Wenger et al, 2002, p. 4). Thus, even though the 'hardware' serves as the vehicle for interaction, it is through social interaction, exploration, and collaboration that development takes place. The VLE too can serve as a fixed point in Manning & Payne's (1993) Vygotskian spiral of teacher growth, serving as a locus for 'the interaction of new knowledge and past experience' (p. 362). The process of growth can also be tracked because the VLE provides a natural receptacle for 'a body of common knowledge, practices and approaches' that contributes to understanding the history of organisations (Wenger, 2000, p. 5). Thus, through looking at work on a VLE, it should be possible to see how teachers develop not just as individuals, but as part of a group. Such analysis might also offer insight into different perspectives on the 'blend' at the heart of this methodology.

Variants in the notion of a blend

Although the term 'blended learning' is now taken as synonymous with integration of classroom instruction and web-based technologies, there are other blends at play in the everyday practice of teachers. Educators have been using technologies for decades; resources that range from 'textbooks to overhead projectors, from typewriters in English Language classrooms to charts of the periodic table on the walls of laboratories' (Mishra & Koehler, 2006, p. 1023). Further to this, Motteram (2013, pp. 5–8) illustrates how the range of learning technologies available in the 21st century has proliferated, and 'become central to language practice' (p. 5). Several instances of new technologies blended into traditional ELT/EAP teaching approaches have been described in Gilbert (2013), including the example of an EGAP (English for General Academic Purposes) group project conducted by Jarvis (2009). Here, groups had to undertake web-based research on chosen topics of interest, write draft reports, consider feedback from classmates and instructors by sharing and collaborating on drafts posted on the course website, and then deliver a presentation based on the final paper. Such a project has particular relevance here because of its resonance with Harry's usage of iPads, especially in his Spitalfields' project.

Thus, the 'blend' is not simply limited to usage of VLEs or other electronic tools but can be found in any combination of resources. However, it has to be remembered that 'the selection of computer-assisted language learning can entail considerable change in the culture of the classroom ... unlike the selection of course books' (Chapelle, 2010, p. 57). Despite this, there has been a tendency in the ELT literature to downplay the importance of content, as with Freeman (2002, p. 6) describing the integration of subject-matter into language teaching as 'messy and possibly unworkable.' This appears to present a challenge to the viewpoint that EAP requires subject-specificity to survive within the current university system (Alexander, Sloan, & Porter, 2011; Macallister & Kirk, 2013). If a synergy between content and language is seen as messy, then that could have implications for the provision of EAP within contemporary higher education, and particularly in the UK.

However, others in the literature have conceptualised a blend that does work and marries together the elements Freeman (2002) sees as disparate. This is the combination of subject matter *(content)* and the traditional primacy of language within the pedagogic creed of ELT. Various labels have been attached to this combination of language and subject matter, including CLIL *(Content and Language Integrated Learning)*. Though this name originates from around the time of Marsh (1994), the actual usage of this theoretical and pedagogic approach has featured for decades in second language instruction in the work of Krashen (1981 & 1982), and Hutchinson & Waters (1987). Brinton, Snow, & Wesche (1989) talk of a similar construct known as Content-Based Second Language Instruction (CBI), which seems to more closely resemble hallmarks of ESP, and EAP in its modern discipline-specific incarnation. Çelik & Simpson (2013) have also tried to situate the content aspect of TPACK within ELT by arguing that 'language lies somewhere mainly between content and pedagogy, and that 'language is the context' (p. 8). On the whole, then, there are very different approaches and interpretations of how to blend content into language teaching contexts.

The role of students in shaping a blend

McGrath et al (2011, p. 2) talk about the need for teachers to 'infuse technology into the learning experiences of their students.' This emphasis upon students is one that recurs throughout the literature, mirroring many of the discussions that took place in the focus group sessions for this study. However, just as with teachers, the emphasis must be firmly placed upon 'humanware' rather than 'hardware' (Warschauer & Meskill, 2000, p. 315). Again echoing Koehler & Mishra's (2009, p. 66) reference to an 'open-minded seeking of technology use', Borko et al (2009, p. 5) emphasise the need for research 'to illuminate technology's impact' on teacher and student learning because 'education can ill afford glitzy technology for the sake of glitz'.

Thus, there has to be a clear purpose and pedagogic rationale to using technology for the benefit of students, as seen in those examples offered by Jarvis (2009) and Gilbert (2013). Others, such as Oliver & Trigwell (2005, p.17), have argued that the entire notion of 'blended learning' should be 'radically reconceived' to incorporate greater account of learners' needs. Beetham & Sharpe (2007, p. 1) suggest that those needs should include transformative aspects which feed into the broader ambitions of post-compulsory education. This could include preparation for 21st century work and citizenship (Trilling & Fadel, 2009; Spires et al, 2012). However, others have argued that technologies in themselves are not transformative, echoing the PCK literature by emphasising the role of content-based learning (Harris, Mishra & Koehler, 2009, pp. 393–395). Even in this age of using such high-tech vehicles as a means of instruction, the essence of content is driven by teachers who remain the primary drivers of what happens in the classroom, and ultimately the main 'chess piece' (Stevick, 1996, p. 180) around which learning manoeuvres are shaped, albeit in a more 'blended' context.

9.3 – Practical considerations

Moodle as a measure of development

Throughout much of the literature on TPACK, CALL, and blended learning, there is a sense that for technology to find an effective synergy with pedagogy, it has to become a normal part of everyday practice (Warschauer, 1996; Bax, 2003; Mishra & Koehler, 2006; McGrath et al, 2011; Motteram, 2013). In this study, the embedding of technology has reshaped the practice of all four teachers being evaluated, not just in the classroom, but in their work with students outside of class as well. Moodle serves as the best example of this, and was becoming embedded in practice from as early as the second focus group session. This, of course, happened to a different extent for each teacher. Rosemary, for example, concentrated most of her efforts on an in-depth understanding of Moodle, whilst Harry pushed the VLE to one side, at first, whilst exploring the usage of more mobile technologies. Kelly and Matthew, on the other hand, dipped in and out of using other resources but kept Moodle as a staple around which other activities could be built.

i. Kelly's usage of Moodle and a broader blend

In the first focus group session, Kelly made very little reference to use of Moodle, despite having gone through an introductory session in its usage. By the time of the second focus group, she had been involved in more workshops and a greater amount of collaboration with other teachers in the workplace. This appeared to have given rise to recent developments in her actions and knowledge, which then reshaped her professional practice in terms of how she was using this particular resource in her teaching. In that second session, she stated that she was using Moodle more '*with regards to structuring and organisation*' and getting students more involved. Here, rather than being a barrier to communication, as in the first focus group session, the technology helped facilitate interaction, and this had come about through new technological knowledge of the resource, and pedagogical awareness of how to teach with it. In the first session, she had talked about the potential for an interactive element, and getting students to contribute and publish things online. However, she was not translating that into practice, even though she could see that it was a possible strategy in terms of addressing the tension brought about by technology's physical barrier to communication.

Gradually, though, as the study gathered pace, Kelly moved on from the straightforward usage of Moodle as a communication device, towards more advanced usage that suggested shifting perspectives on the objectives of EAP teaching. This included a greater drive towards fostering autonomy on the part of students, as described in BALEAP (2008, p. 5). Now, Kelly began to test possibilities of integrating audio into the VLE, and to focus on *'writing skills'* by guiding students towards *'entering into debate on their own.'* In the third focus group session she echoed some of Matthew's assertions with the statement that *'they're using it (Moodle) for their homework and they're communicating on it, which they would be doing anyway on Facebook or wherever.'* Here, once again, new knowledge was having an impact on activity. In trying to make Moodle more communicative, she was trying to alter the activity of students outside of class, and attempting to translate practices of social media into a more academic context. She was also getting to grips with blended learning as a methodology, and enacting this in her practice.

Those new strategies to develop students' *'writing skills'*, and to *'debate online'*, not only showed an increased synergy of technological and pedagogical knowledge to form TPK, but also illustrated how such knowledge feeds into teaching competency, as defined by BALEAP's framework (2008). There appeared to have been a change in her focus on writing skills, alongside her sequencing of teaching and learning activities (2008, p. 8). Added to this, she expressed increased awareness of skills needed in academic contexts, for both teachers and students, as she talked about how *'they can check when their assignments are'*, which is *'obviously a good kind of management tool or planning tool for the teacher and for them as well.'*

Significantly, her actions were not just in sync with BALEAP's core competencies, but also meeting key managerial and curricular aspects of Koehler & Mishra's (2009, p. 63) definition of the elements of pedagogical knowledge. She was now using Moodle as a course management tool on two separate levels. She, as teacher, controlled one level, where she used the VLE as a means of helping students plan for presentations and assignments. At a second level, she facilitated debates and discussions linked in to the content being studied in their specific subjects on a weekly basis. Here, she graded activities and depth of autonomy according to language levels, in line with generic principles of ELT and Gilly Salmon's (2000) theories on scaffolding students in blended learning environments. Thus, whereas her forum for a Sociology class included such titles as *'Breaching experiment'*, *'Class, poverty and welfare'* or *'Reading for research homework'*, the work with lower level classes focused more on students themselves and their interests. Thus topics such as *'Favourite books'* featured alongside *'Exam information'* and *'Presentation Schedule.'*

It was around this point in the study that Kelly then started her explorations with Camtasia, as discussed in previous chapters. As stated previously, this eventually reached *'a dead end'*, but had sparked a major cognitive development in terms of embedding and reawakening knowledge, where required. Towards the end of the study, she was still actively using the VLE outside of lessons, with students *'submitting their own work, through submitting assignments, and hopefully participating in the forum on there, which is for discussion'* as well as *'for storing PowerPoints and work so that the students can access it for self-study and for revision.'* Such usage of Moodle suggested continuance rather than change, whereas more obvious changes occurred in other areas of practice, to be discussed later.

ii. Matthew's usage of Moodle and a broader blend

In the introductory focus group session, Matthew stated that *'we're at the very beginning of a really exciting period of change in terms of integrating those technologies into the classroom because they're being used by the students anyway in their everyday lives through social networking.'* As a result of this changing dynamic in society he identified a need to use *'interactive learning environments'* such as Moodle. By the time of the second focus group session, having gone through a couple of workshops, he had become much more fluent in VLE usage, stating *'I've been uploading audio files of class seminars that we've had, so they've done individual long turns which I've been recording and putting them on Moodle for them to transcribe, which has been really useful and that's the most recent change.'*

This suggested that his practice had been reshaped as a consequence of new technological knowledge, of Moodle, and technological pedagogical knowledge, through his use of this resource to shape teaching and learning. Having spoken about the need for interactivity in FG1, he had now found a way of facilitating this through technology, as evidenced in the next section of dialogue. Here, he discussed what he had done in the past, and how this had been adapted to assume a new self-access dimension for students.

He defined this as being *'in terms of the more interactive element of using the class audio, taking the audio from class and getting them to listen back, that's something I've done in the past, but this gives them the chance to do it in their own time rather than in the class.'* Previously, his usage of audio involved *'bringing in recordings and listening as a group in the class'* but now *'students can listen to their own work individually and stop it where they need to, outside of class time.'* This seemed to be a clear espousal of developments in practice, caused by Moodle, as a teaching instrument, and a change in the division of workload to put greater emphasis on self-access. Though the traditional emphasis on listening and note-taking remained, students had greater control over their own learning. This was exemplified in giving them audio recordings of the actual lectures *'so that they can go back home, listen to it … listen very carefully and stop where they want to.'*

In the second focus group session, Matthew described technology as *'the great equaliser'* but suggested that the institutional VLE found itself *'competing with existing networking potential.'* He supposed that it would be great if the students used Moodle *'in the same way as they used Facebook to interact … rather than going onto Facebook and other social networking sites to interact in their own language.'* Reminiscent of the work of Jones & Lea (2008), he asked whether students prefer demarcation to crossover, suggesting that Moodle was symbolic of *'school and Facebook isn't school so it's whether or not you can make those boundaries a bit more fluid.'* This again resonated with Kear's (2011, p. 41) emphasis on the blurring of boundaries between social and academic spaces, and appeared to be a tension that Matthew actively sought to address. Eventually, he did achieve some degree of resolution through the forum on Moodle, which he defined as *'a really good way, an excellent way of improving fluency and accuracy'*, and *'hopefully something that they care about as well so it should be motivating.'*

However, by a later stage of the study, his usage of the VLE had evolved even further, and with it a suggestion of subtle change in his sense of EAP as a subject, and his role as a teacher. In the final focus group session, he stated that *'with Moodle I'm putting more and more, I'm using it more and more each term so there's more and more structure to it.'* Reflecting back on what he used to do, he suggested that *'at the beginning I was just putting stuff up there for students'* and *'it was an easy way for them to get access to materials'*, which echoes Mason's (1998, p.3) commentary on how teachers often use a VLE for little more than 'content + support', rather than more interactive forms of usage. Later on, he seemed to be going through Mason's 'pedagogical evolution' (1998, p. 3), as he spoke of *'an increasing interaction now, an increased kind of giving them the opportunity to upload their assignments.'* However, there was not a solitary variable or single knowledge base shaping these actions. Rather, he cited a range of factors centred upon the students such as facilitating authentic situations, to *'engage them with extended material and so on'*, to have more virtual interaction outside of class, and, on a pragmatic level, reducing *'hard copy'* and *'actual printing.'* Further to this, he touched upon ideas that again echoed the BALEAP competencies (2008) in suggesting that *'at the beginning of term there's more scaffolding'*, while towards the end students are placed *'in more of an authentic situation.'*

Like Kelly, Matthew did not rely on Moodle alone. He too had experimented with Camtasia, at the time of the aforementioned Bank Holidays, and by the end of the programme had begun to develop a growing interest in iPads. Unlike in Harry's case, for Matthew this appeared to have been shaped by a desire to explore these as one tool amongst many, rather than as a centrepoint of his practice. Thus, when asked about developments by the end of the programme in his final interview, he responded *'definitely, I would say that the use of Moodle has changed as have various other things I've integrated in terms of technology.'* He then went on to outline the work that he was doing with iPads and podcasts, in terms of dealing with emergent language and real-world interactions. Through this combination of 'school' technologies he had found *'a way of breaching or broaching that gap between the outside and inside worlds'*, and finally managed to *'transgress'* the challenges once posed by other forms of social media. Using the VLE as a base for giving structure to his classes, he was then able to reconfigure other technologies, such as podcasts, for the 'customized pedagogic purpose' (Koehler & Mishra, 2009, p. 66) of helping students to bridge the gap between the classroom, the outside world, and their future studies.

iii. Harry's usage of Moodle and a broader blend

Developments in Harry's practice differed from the others due to him coming from an EAP background, rather than ELT, in the first instance. Added to this, he arrived slightly later and missed the foundations of the opening workshop. This meant that, in the first focus group session, he admitted that *'I have no idea about how to use Moodle by the way so anything on that will be really useful for me. At this stage it's just a word for me.'* However, it soon became apparent that he possessed a 'working' knowledge of technology, alongside a deeper understanding of how it can be used from a practical perspective (Koehler & Mishra, 2009, p. 64). This was evidenced in his references to the resources that he had used in different teaching contexts. These included usage of video and the internet in IELTS listening classes, corpora for building vocabulary, and a combination of resources for the purposes of teaching and correcting writing. *'Access to technology'* made this *'a whole lot easier'* in such areas as *'redrafting'*, and having *'access to things like Google documents and shared documents.'* Additionally, computers and interactive whiteboards could be used for demonstration purposes, and it *'makes editing students' writing really interesting because you can get down to doing things like annotations, and they can see what they need to do in redrafting an essay.'* Interestingly too, in the same section of dialogue, he suggested that this process of electronic adaptation, which clearly takes place in a public/group setting, rather than a private/individual setting, has replaced the once ubiquitous *'red pen'*. Thus, from the very start, it appeared that Harry possessed a clear sense of how and why he was using technology for specific aspects of teaching EAP. As pointed out previously, he did suggest that *'EAP is all about writing essays, and those essays are written on computer'*, which is an assertion that I shall return to at a further stage of this study.

By the time of the second focus group session, Moodle was notably no longer *'just a word'*, and appeared to have become a regular part of Harry's practice. He stated that, although *'the whole system's quite new for me'*, he had been *'putting course materials up, like presentations I've done and links, like posting links to useful websites.'* Aside from this, he claimed to be *'using the forum to allow my students to set up tutorial meetings so that they can just post a time that is convenient for them within a time that is convenient for me.'* Through doing this, he was enacting newly acquired technological knowledge from the introductory workshops, and also changing the division of labour within the learning process. Strikingly, he had ambitions to build on this further, and increase his knowledge of how Moodle could be used from a practical perspective. He suggested that *'it would be nice on the forum to just set a discussion question and almost have a debate; something written and everybody has to reply to keep it going.'* There was, though, a sense of this being more of an aspiration than an action, at present, because he stated that *'I've done that before but haven't seen how you can do that with Moodle; maybe with the wikis.'* This suggests that he had previously enacted such a method of learning and teaching with different unspecified instruments. The second key point is that he was talking about wikis, which were also studied in the workshops, and comparing these to the VLE, which suggested an increase in technological knowledge. Still, though, at this stage, there was a sense of remaining unconvinced by tools such as Moodle or wikis, because they don't have *'that satisfying thing which really addictive technology has, something like Facebook or Twitter have, which keeps you going back to do it.'*

This desire to motivate students with more 'addictive' technologies eventually gave rise to encouraging the language centre to make mobile technologies an established part of activity, through purchasing a set of iPads for students, for specific use on an International Diploma course. Subsequently, his interest in Moodle *'tapered off as well actually in certain respects'* whilst he got the iPad programme up and running. However, he did return to the use of Moodle at a later stage of the study, when he found more effective ways of integrating the VLE and the iPads. He managed to do this through the use of an app that incidentally would only work with an upgrade of Moodle, which he eventually was given funding for, and again caused change in the language centre's system of activity, not just for himself, but for all users of the VLE.

iv. Rosemary's usage of Moodle and a broader blend

Exploration characterised Rosemary's efforts with Moodle from the outset in her quest for in-depth understanding of the resource. In early focus group sessions, she talked about the role that collaboration had played in this, stating that *'I have been lucky in that I have had a couple of teachers, Sebastian and Emily who were helping me.'* Through this collaboration, she learned about *'databases and stuff which you can use'*, but pointed out that teachers need *'time to get into gear'* and *'we don't have much time'*, which echoes concerns voiced by McGrath et al (2011) and Gilbert (2013). However, the potential benefits for students motivated her to use Moodle because it was *'good for quizzes and things, certainly in terms of testing my students I've found because it marks it for you as well.'*

Despite the relative ease with which Rosemary integrated Moodle into her practice, usage of other technologies did not come so naturally early on. She talked about the *'slow and cumbersome'* aspects of interactive whiteboards, and touched on ideas that have appeared in the work of Lam (2000), where teachers avoid using innovations, 'not because of technophobia, but because they were not convinced of the educational value of technology' (Attia, 2011). In Rosemary's case, she shared Patricia's concern with not wanting *'to be shown up in front of everyone else'* by admitting to a lack of technological knowledge in public view. Possibly, she concentrated her efforts on Moodle because she had created a safe terrain for in-depth exploration and helped build a sense of community around the VLE. Whereas Harry became a broker of instruments (iPads), Rosemary helped to broker a community of practice that outlived the duration of the teacher education workshops, and even the parameters of this research study.

This is not to say that Rosemary's enactment of blended learning was limited to usage of Moodle alone. From an early stage, she talked about other tools that she had experimented with, including '*Camtasia and Prezi.*' However, in the second focus group session, she pointed out that some of these resources '*looked amazing and great but again as Derek said we don't have the time at the minute and you need that time, initially you need that time to sit down and look at it and work it out.*' Again, in a discussion generated by Frank regarding using Camtasia as a feedback tool, she accepted that this '*is great in theory but with time constraints and the workload we've got at the minute it makes it difficult.*' Even though she felt that '*the benefit to the students is amazing*', she went on to say that '*there isn't time outside of teaching*' to explore the full range of resources that could be utilised.

Significantly, Rosemary was working on a different course to the other main cases: a Foundation English programme where much of the work could be described as relentless cycle. This shows how broader sociocultural variables also affect teachers' choices as regards uptake and usage of technology, and the way they implement a blend in their teaching. Time, as McGrath et al point out, is required for preparing teachers to 'infuse technology into the learning experiences of their students' (2011, p. 2). This might help explain Rosemary's loyalty to Moodle, though a VLE also lends itself to collaboration in a way that other technologies may not. Again, the importance of collaboration, not just for herself but for colleagues, comes across in the assertion that '*I've noticed as well how the subject teachers and the English teachers are looking at each other's Moodle pages and trying to sort of work together.*' This helped her because '*if you work it out yourself you can often spend longer than you would asking somebody else the questions.*'

Even at the point of the individual interviews, Rosemary felt that '*with regards to using technology, time constraints still apply, getting worse not better.*' Despite this, she had '*been doing some experimentation with technologies*', particularly the use of Spotify to bring music into the classroom. Interestingly, by this stage, she still felt that she was '*moving in the right direction*' with the VLE, even though most others in the workplace would have viewed her as something of an expert user and broker of activity when it came to usage of Moodle. Rosemary herself, though, is perhaps showing consciousness of the fact that development occurs in the form of a continuum (Richards, 1998), and that teaching is best viewed as 'a continuous process of becoming' and one which 'can never be finished' (Mann, 2005, p. 105).

Ultimately, though, the main advantages of Moodle that she highlighted were the ways in which it '*can benefit students outside of the classroom.*' Interestingly, this was not just in terms of *'the materials'*, stored at a 'content + support' level of Mason's (1998) developmental framework. Instead, *'you've got the quizzes that you can set up, the forums where students can interact, and rather than just the lesson ending you can continue on with the students.'* Rosemary's efforts inside and outside the classroom focused on *'student centred, student focused lessons'*, seeking depth rather than breadth in usage of technologies. Finally, in an interesting divergence from the work of Argyris & Schön (1974), her 'actual practice' is much stronger than her 'espoused practice.' This is evidenced by the humble way in which she attributed her development to collaboration with others, but many of those others saw her as leader and instigator of the work-place community that sprang up around the VLE.

Reshaping the blend in EAP teaching

Blended learning had been a constant presence in the work of all four teachers despite their differing perspectives and practices in the classroom. Moodle, especially, became an established, accepted, and embedded part of each person's practice. For some, the VLE became a foundation for moving gradually towards the introduction of new technologies into the blend. This had echoes of Mason's (1998) trajectory of development, with technology starting out as a repository for content and changing, over time, to become a mix of various 'event-based activities', as described by Valiathan (2002, p. 1). Such activities included Harry's use of iPads, or Matthew's *Guardian* podcasts, which eventually evolved into students creating their own podcasts. This suggested more than just a reshaping of technological usage. Technologies such as the iPads served as a filter for new forms of communicative and academic practices, radically reshaping both pedagogy and content.

Despite this, there was considerable divergence in teachers' perspectives when considering the 'blend' from a TPACK perspective: the synergy of pedagogy, technology, and content. The last of these caused the greatest divergence. Matthew, for example, talked about his *'ideal classroom situation'* being one where the teacher is crafting language around the activities that students themselves are creating. This suggested more of an EGAP than ESAP focus, as in Blue's (1998) categorisations, where the emphasis is on generic skills rather than subject-specific tasks. Such an approach, though, was largely shaped by sociocultural variables such as course of study, and students' language levels. Harry, on a subject-specific course, could prioritise understanding the language of Business and Economics. Rosemary, working with students of a low language level on a generic programme, concentrated her efforts on academic skills, and the acquisition of a more basic vocabulary.

Kelly, on the other hand, had the greatest opportunity to work with high-level students (from Humanities & Law), and thus had more interest in formulating or simulating the types of discussion found in actual disciplines. She described her favoured practice as involving an integration of *'the communicative aspect'* with *'real academic texts'* used by students. This involved *'working together'* and *'negotiating meaning'*, to reach a level of understanding that echoed Shulman's (1986, p. 9) call for a move beyond straightforward 'facts or concepts of a domain' to 'understanding the structures of the subject matter' in both substantive and syntactic terms. To facilitate such understanding, Kelly prioritised the use of texts in class. Content thus moved to the centre of classroom activity, as students engaged in deconstructing generic texts, and rebuilding them in the structures and syntax of specific disciplines. In doing this, Kelly echoed key aspects of BALEAP's (2008) competencies, and provided an excellent example of why technology is not the sole key component of blended learning. Content too plays a large part in the methodology, as do other sociocultural variables.

Rosemary's enactment of the blend and her reasons for choosing a blend in her teaching also differed in the sense of bringing affective factors (Arnold, 1999; Tomlinson, 2012) into the equation to a greater extent. Though very active in facilitating a blend of classroom-based instruction and usage of the VLE, the guiding principles for her approach were those of traditional English Language teaching, such as motivation and eminent need for interaction. Her work seemed to be guided by a powerful sense of learning being socially constructed regardless of the context. In her interview discussions, she stressed the importance of collaboration and group working, whether for her Foundation students or colleagues in teacher education workshops. This approach appears to support a view that the blend of activity cannot be detached from the broader sociocultural context, and teachers' personal philosophies about teaching and learning.

9.4 – Lessons learned at this stage

Teachers' usage of blended learning approaches served as a useful lens for observing developments not just at an individual level but also in the broader sphere of activity. Traditionally, the methodology has been seen as one that is built around technology, but in actuality the blend that is enacted, regardless of the tools chosen, resonates with the fundamental values of TPACK. This is because it is impossible to separate out pedagogy, technology, and content. Through the use of Moodle, for example, all of the teachers selected particular content according to what they wanted to teach in an EAP context, and made choices about the ways in which this blended into their classroom practice. The choices they made then served to cast further light upon their teaching philosophy, and their understandings of EAP in both practice and theory.

In the beginning, the institutional VLE served as a well-intentioned dumping ground of material as described in stage one of Mason's (1998) framework, and played out in large swathes of higher education even in this digital age. By the end, this had been transformed to a vehicle for learning that was still largely driven by the teachers, but now open to partnership and collaboration. Through this partnership, Moodle became an indivisible part of life in the language centre to the extent that even when newer resources such as podcasts and iPads were introduced, they interbred with this staple platform. Thus, in the language centre, the marriage of new technologies to 'old teaching' (Ham, 2010) proved to be a successful one not just in practical terms, but also in the way that teachers' personal philosophies shaped usage of blended learning, and vice versa. Ultimately, the VLE served as a tool for helping teachers overcome challenges they spoke of in the early focus group sessions, and put into practice ideals they could only aspire to back then.

CHAPTER 10

Understanding Espoused and Actual Practice

10.1 – Contextualisation

Teachers' perceptions of changes in their practice

Towards the end of the teacher education programme, participants voiced new perspectives on practice, not just in terms of using technology. Rather than concentrating on tools, they showed a heightened understanding of ways that knowledge informs practice and understanding or beliefs about teaching. As seen in previous chapters, there had been a greater shift towards autonomy on the part of the teachers, and on becoming more reflective practitioners, which feeds into much of the guidance from teacher education literature, including the work of Mann (2005). The role of knowledge in this process further helped establish a bridge between teacher education literature and the twin frameworks of PCK and TPACK. However, as also highlighted at an earlier stage, such knowledge structures can be 'difficult to tease out in practice' (Koehler & Mishra, 2009, p. 66).

Practice and knowledge in Harry's case

In the final series of interviews, Harry stated that he was now able to enact *'a finesse version'* of what he had been able to do a couple of years before, citing availability of resource as the primary driver for change in his practice. He stated that *'I think my classroom approach has been reasonably consistent, though I've had access to more resources than before.'* As such, he added *'the way that I teach has refined, but the resources I've been able to use to implement*

How to cite this book chapter:
Breen, P. 2018. *Developing Educators for The Digital Age: A Framework for Capturing Knowledge in Action.* Pp. 143–157. London: University of Westminster Press.
DOI: https://doi.org/10.16997/book13.j. License: CC-BY-NC-ND 4.0

that approach have been better.' This emphasis on resource resonates with recent inclusions of sociocultural elements linked together in an outer ring of 'context influence on TPACK knowledge' (TPACK, 2012). This outer ring of variables, particularly resource, had served to push inwards on the core knowledge components and alter these too, in different ways. Technology, which had been a lifelong interest for Harry, and his existing base of ELT pedagogy developed through education and experience, stayed more consistent than the third of the integral knowledge components.

Essentially, Harry's understanding of content, towards the end of the study, had shifted from an emphasis on simple facts or knowledge from the disciplines of Business and Economics, to a form of knowledge 'that embodies the aspects of content most germane to its teachability' (Shulman, 1986, p. 9). In embracing this new notion of content knowledge, and choosing to transform subject matter through his iPad project, he was also finding a stronger sense of 'equilibrium' amongst the component parts of Koehler & Mishra's (2009, p. 7) knowledge base for 'effective teaching.' This was evidenced in two final observations described later in this chapter and the next, and also in his final interview where he had moved away from a sense that EAP was *all about writing essays'*, as espoused in the opening focus group session. On the whole, by the end of the programme, he seemed to feel that his TPK had stayed the same, but towards the end of the interviews he made greater reference to the importance of '*content'* in his classroom instruction. From analysing such references throughout the interviews, it was also possible to track changes in his perception of '*content'*, which moved from subject matter alone, to a greater sense of synergy with pedagogy and technology. By doing so, he strengthened the opportunity for development of TPACK and what Hofer & Swan (2008, p. 181) define as 'excellence in teaching.'

Practice and knowledge in Matthew's case

Matthew's knowledge base had shifted too, though not so much in terms of content. His final commentary on changes in practice involved a declaration that increasingly he had been able to *'integrate what I used to do … interactive, workshoppy approaches, all of those approaches to learning, with a much more systematic way of improving the students' English.'* Providing the example of a writing class, he suggested that *'I've been able to create a much more structured approach whilst keeping those integral elements of interaction and so on.'* This in turn created a situation where he felt *'happier now in my teaching than I was at any previous time, because I've been able to marry those two things up so that one isn't bigger than the other.'*

When probed about reasons for this development, Matthew cited some aspects of the workshops that had fed into his teaching, but mainly gave credit to *'the staffroom based interaction which has been really good for sharing ideas, like having the iPads there and to have others to just bounce ideas off has been really useful.'* However, in terms of developing a knowledge base for his teaching, pedagogy and technology had come to the fore, creating TPK, with the role of content much harder to define since much of his work, even with the iPads, focused on language production. This, then, could be seen as a return to the knowledge base that he had started out with, having organised music and drama workshops in the past. These, combined with underlying principles of English Language teaching, appeared to drive his practice in the classroom, once he overcame a phobia of technology's *'bear pits'*, and used resources to guide, rather than inhibit, activities. The fact that he had gone back to what he knew best (workshops and ELT principles) again augments the notion of knowledge developing in a spiral. Once Matthew had acquired increased technological understanding, he was better able to return to what he already knew best, and shape innovative practices around this, with greater confidence in his existing knowledge base.

Practice and knowledge in Rosemary's case

Rosemary too talked about finding comfort in her existing knowledge base, but this came across as more of a protective measure to ensure that she provided the basics of EAP, in the face of institutional constraints. She spoke of changes in her practice largely being driven by student needs, and went on to situate technologies slightly outside her natural comfort zone. She suggested that if she was *'not aware of what technology would work'* in particular situations and *'didn't have time to figure that out'*, she would use a more familiar mix of techniques in the classroom. She didn't *'see the point in just using technology for the teacher'*, and stressed the importance of affective factors in the EAP classroom, drawing upon principles from the generic world of English Language teaching. Though she made no specific reference to particular theorists in either focus group sessions or individual interviews, her actions inside and outside the classroom suggested a belief in motivation as a means of overcoming language learners' anxieties. This is supported in the ELT literature through Steven Krashen's (1982) research on the Affective Filter Hypothesis, and the work of Zoltan Dörnyei (1991; 2001), and forms a significant part of the English Language teaching knowledge base, which then seems to be transferred to the knowledge base of EAP practitioners who have come through the general English teaching route.

Thus, it was partially because of her background in more general language teaching that Rosemary claimed to focus her efforts in the EAP classroom upon issues such as confidence, motivation, and dynamics, because she argued that the absence of these factors created difficulties when teaching skills in such areas as academic writing to students of lower language levels. As such, like Harry, Rosemary appeared to touch on the outer ring of TPACK, and the Vygotskian perspective of not separating cognitive and affective factors, but of seeing them as interdependent (Manning & Payne, 1993, p. 362). However, as stated previously in this work, context plays as much of a part as a teacher's background, and Rosemary's work was also shaped by having a group of learners who needed motivation and encouragement.

Such an emphasis on affective factors also came through in Rosemary's espoused usage of Moodle, where she used the VLE to expand study time beyond the content of the classroom. By facilitating activities outside of class, she was providing a possible trigger for development of autonomy and greater self-direction on the part of students. However, even though she talked at length about Moodle in her final interview, she did not necessarily see this as a manifestation of her enhanced technological knowledge. Perhaps because she used this outside of classroom teaching *'mainly for self-study'*, she did not always give herself the required credit for the 'innovation' (Mann, 2005) that this entailed. This suggested that Rosemary's actual practice differed from espoused practice, because her usage of the VLE implied deeper technological and pedagogical knowledge than she self-acknowledged. As such, she provided an example of why it was important to triangulate interview data not just with observations in the classroom, but also with analysis of materials created for the benefit of students. Naturally, this had even more significance in a study where blended learning played such a vital role.

Practice and knowledge in Kelly's case

Unlike Rosemary, Kelly did not express any continuing desire for training in individual technologies. As outlined in Chapter 8, she felt that she had reached a point of embedding knowledge so as to facilitate *'resurfacing'* at a time of her own choosing. As a consequence of embedding this understanding of technology, she was demonstrating an increased synergy between categories of knowledge, enacting what Kirk (2012) terms 'knowledge-in-action' through activities that drew on different aspects of a TPACK knowledge base. In doing this, she echoed one of Harry's lines about *'finding a way of teaching'* rather than just experimenting with technologies, in asserting that for her technology is not *'the saviour of learning'* but simply a tool through which teachers mediate the objectives of their lessons. Like Harry and Matthew, she saw one of technology's greatest benefits as being *'empowering students'* and giving them *'control over their own learning.'* This, she claimed, was something she tried to put into practice in her teaching.

Again as with Harry, having acquired a better synergy of TK with other elements of knowledge, Kelly seemed better equipped to then make strategic choices about when to use particular technologies, based around an emphasis on the subject matter, as proposed by Shulman (1986, p. 9). However, unlike Matthew and Harry, there is a sense that by the end of the education programme, Kelly did not see herself as having been on a linear continuum or trajectory of developing technology-related knowledge. Rather, she voiced a perspective of knowledge similar to Manning & Payne's (1993) Vygotskian framework, in which she reflected back on the content element of her EAP teaching, so as to find the right balance of this alongside the technology. In doing so, she ended the programme still asking questions of her own pedagogy (Mishra & Koehler, 2006, p. 103), in order to build upon and further activate the 'schema of knowledge' (Piaget, 1970) underpinning her practice.

One practical example of this came in her belief that she now had '*more of an idea of English for Academic Purposes and the different kind of skills that students need*', which she went on to define as going beyond '*lexical ability.*' Interestingly, she felt that she had developed as a teacher in having more awareness of emphasising academic context, and '*how to plan lessons that will not only give students the knowledge or the language, or even subject theory.*' Though these are important, she also aspired to provide information that '*supports them as somebody who's going to go on and do very well at university, and who will be okay on their own at the end of the course.*'

This, she asserted, was very different from '*previously, or before working here, when I might have been quite short term in my teaching range … very kind of short term learning for learning's sake*', as when working on General English or IELTS and Cambridge exam classes. Now she felt that her approach to teaching was '*much more serious*' because '*literally people's lives are at stake depending on whether they pass or fail the course.*' Thus, Kelly clearly felt that she had developed over the course of her time in the language centre, and that her teaching practices had changed. Significantly, once again, although such changes entailed the main components of TPACK, they also seemed to incorporate that outer ring of contextual influence too.

10.2 – Theoretical foundations

Reiterating challenges to evaluating knowledge in action

Any form of self-reported data has the potential to compromise a study's overall trustworthiness, and 'muddy relationships among variables' (Gonyea, 2005, p. 82). Historically, this has been recognised in the teacher education literature, where many leading voices have drawn attention to a possible mismatch between teachers' cognitions and their practices in the classroom (Attia, 2011). Argyris & Schön (1974) first defined this as differences between espoused theories and theories-in-use, whilst Donaghue (2003) amended the latter to 'theory in action' (p. 345). Very often these differences are not the fault of the teacher alone because contextual factors sometimes account for 'incongruence' and 'inconsistencies' (Attia, 2011, pp. 52–53).

Harry's first observed lesson, teaching a group of Foundation students in a cramped classroom, served as an example of such a mismatch. Though his actions differed from his aspirations in focus group sessions, he later claimed that he felt constrained by the context. As such, he made pedagogic decisions based on actual circumstances and student needs, rather than seeking the interactivity spoken of during focus group sessions. Kelly, on the other hand, proved more fluent in the use of technologies than she had given herself credit for. Taking these two examples, Argyris & Schön's (1974) advice seems salient, in that 'we cannot learn what someone's theory-in-use is simply by asking him', and that 'we must construct his theory-in-use from observations of his behavior' (pp. 6–7). This, though, does not mean that the observer rides roughshod over the thoughts and feelings of the teacher being observed. Rather, as in those first vignettes, the job of the observer-researcher is to be a reporter, not a judge.

Furthermore, the goal of observation in case study research is not to deconstruct teachers' practices by highlighting inconsistencies or incongruence. Instead, Attia (2011, p. 75) suggests that observations should facilitate 'detailed descriptions of events' so as to yield rich accounts which 'shed light on different context-specific features (Simons, 2009).' Such accounts, above all else, should capture 'the nitty-gritty reality of everyday life' (Silverman, 2005, p. 171), and not embellish the finished story in any way, by trying to fit the data around desired outcomes, for example. One way of avoiding this and reducing subjectivity is to conduct interviews after the observations, using stimulated recall where necessary, to get a sense of participants' feelings, and see if researchers' interpretations are correct. Thus, as in the first examples of practice, I spoke to the teachers before and after the observations now presented as a second series of vignettes; once again in echoes of Motteram & Sharma (2009) and Slaouti et al (2013).

10.3 – Practical considerations

Second vignette of Harry's practice

After the workshops, and amidst the individual interviews, I observed Harry teaching a group of students on the International Diploma programme. Once again the class was composed of various nationalities, and both sexes, with approximately 50% of students being Chinese. Since these students had progressed beyond Foundation level, they were in an IELTS range of at least 5.5 to 6.0. As before, the lesson unfolded in a standard classroom equipped with a desktop computer and IWB, but Harry had adapted the system by connecting his iPad to the board. Added to the change of instruments, content differed too. This time around, the focus was on a combination of essay writing and subject-specific work in the area of Economics.

The lesson got underway at 12.35 with students shuffled around to create mixed nationality pairs, as has long been common practice in English Language classrooms (Harmer, 1991). Upon completion of this, Harry displayed the class

Moodle page containing a homework task. This related to Porter's five forces model (Sloman & Wride, 2009), and could be accessed through an embedded YouTube link. Students had to access this before coming to the session, and as such it served as a 'flipped classroom' (Sams & Bergmann, 2012), where students do core work in advance of classes, rather than during their classes (Tucker, 2012). Furthermore, by drawing upon a theoretical framework of critical importance within Business and Economics, a deeper sense of discipline-specificity existed than in the lesson before. Now, he was touching upon an essential part of Shulman's original vision for content knowledge that transcends simple facts or language from a discipline, and 'embodies' content 'germane' to a subject's 'teachability' (1986, p. 9).

Once Harry had pitched the tempo of his session with the Moodle task, he asked the class to use their iPads to access a document on Dropbox, looking at a case study in the subject area of Economics to 'refresh' their memories. After opening this document, students were assigned one of two roles in a paired activity: reading or mind-mapping. Firstly, the 'readers' were instructed to open up their Economics textbooks (Sloman & Wride, 2009) at pages 70 & 71. Then the 'mind-mappers' opened or downloaded a free version of a tool named SimpleMind+. In pairs, the students mapped definitions of key terms, as Harry monitored the task until it was saturated and then elicited responses at whole-group level, using the technologies for display purposes.

Here, 'social' tools were being used in school to get a grasp of subject-specific knowledge in an English Language classroom that had been 'flipped' from the outset. Relating this to earlier discussions on school versus social media in the second focus group session, perhaps he had finally found a way of loosening the boundaries, and touching upon *'the satisfying thing'* offered by technologies used outside of the classroom. Yet it would be false to suggest that this was a lesson limited to technologies alone. Harry had also managed to successfully integrate other more traditional instruments into his teaching. As stated in his post-lesson interview, he was using *'students' textbooks themselves a lot more'* and that these were not just *'their English textbooks'*, as with Oshima & Hogue (2007) in the first vignette. The students' *'Business textbooks'* had become a more regular part of his teaching blend and this was *'something that has come from training sessions that we've done here.'*

Second vignette of Kelly's practice

As in her first vignette, I observed Kelly teaching a Graduate Diploma class. This time around, she had adapted a lesson from the *Oxford English for Academic Purposes Upper-Intermediate* textbook (de Chazal et al, 2012). Thus, it was a writing class based around a presentation of the target language leading up to less guided practice activities in which students generated examples of such language. Once again, the lesson was taught in a standard room, equipped with computer and IWB. The class was small: seven Pre-Masters students, consequently possessing higher-end IELTS scores, with a mix of genders and nationalities.

Kelly started the lesson with students being shown examples of the target language on the interactive whiteboard before doing an exercise in which they had to find similar examples in a worksheet designed with Microsoft Word. The focus of the lesson was *'Analysis & understanding of concluding paragraphs'*, as a form of preparation for students' own forthcoming research projects, not for EAP assessment, but in their specialist areas of study. Thus, the examples of the target language were provided in the form of authentic concluding paragraphs from the specific disciplines that students were going to progress into upon completion of this course. By using such materials and having students work with these independently, Kelly was drawing upon the increasing discipline-specificity expected of EAP practitioners. Echoing suggestions particularly found in the work of Hyland (2003; 2006), and Ding & Bruce (2017), she was using her expertise to present particular types of writing genres to students, and then have them unpack the language within these texts so as to not just get a sense of the linguistic construction but also a broader perspective on the ways that ideas are presented according to specific disciplinary conventions. Further to this, as with Hyland (2003), the focus did not seem to be on providing 'a recipe theory of genre' or a structural 'straightjacket' but on getting the students to understand the disciplinary conventions so that later they could produce their own work.

When students had completed the first exercise on their own they then compared answers with their partners before Kelly elicited responses at whole-group level. While doing this, she wrote up the answers on the interactive whiteboard and used its highlighting features to demonstrate how sentences are constructed and how the different parts interconnect with one another, so as to facilitate sentences coming together at paragraph level. Using the technology in this way was a more visual experience for students and it allowed elicitation to flow more freely than with use of a traditional whiteboard/teacher talk approach. Interestingly, in Kelly's elicitation stage, she was very careful to involve all students and to address their individual needs, to pause for pair work and reinforcement where necessary, and to concept check that all students were following the gist of what was happening in the lesson. This was significant because of her consistent emphasis on student needs and interactivity during the focus group sessions. Another way in which she facilitated this was to use material from a real-world context that directly related to the experience of these specific students. Thus, one of the texts related to factors that improve exam results, within which there was a section on the impact of small classes on student performance. This material was authentic, appropriate, and engaging, acting as a supplement to the central instrument of the Oxford EAP textbook, which provided the base from which to integrate other materials.

By bringing in authentic materials with a disciplinary dimension, and then concentrating on the texts at this stage of the lesson, Kelly was demonstrating further competency in line with the criteria laid out by Shulman (1986), and, through the way in which she was teaching it, prioritising PCK over TCK and TPK, when evaluated through Koehler & Mishra's (2009) definitions. However, when she returned to the use of technologies, TPK again came into play. This happened in the next activity, which was to look at a range of academic sources and find examples of cause and effect language, as she wrote up the choice of essay topics on the IWB. This work on the IWB then generated a brainstorming session where the technology was used to advance student learning and understanding of specific subject matter, as in Koehler & Mishra's (ibid, p. 66) depiction of TPK.

This was the point at which I left the lesson, having witnessed movement towards less guided production of language. Students, at this stage, appeared to have a solid grasp of the target language and how to use that in the context of incorporating sources into a piece of academic writing. Kelly had also adapted her role from direct instruction at the outset to becoming more of a facilitator as the lesson progressed, scaffolding the students towards understanding, as stipulated in BALEAP (2008, p. 7). As in her first vignette, technology played a normal and unobtrusive role in Kelly's classroom, where most of the focus was on the type of work described in BALEAP's (ibid) references to 'text processing and text production', and the language of 'academic discourse' in terms of 'grammar and syntax at the level of phrase, clause, and sentence' (p. 5). This lesson, on the whole, created a strong sense of Kelly becoming a more self-directed teacher, and of moving towards a more natural combination of language work and subject-specificity. Her practice now featured greater reliance on authentic texts (content) than on usage of technologies, which she could dip in and out of at will.

Second vignette of Matthew's practice

Although Matthew had shown an interest in a range of technologies such as podcasts throughout the study, he had started to experiment with iPads to a greater extent by the time of his final observed lesson. Once again, he was teaching on the English for University Study programme, with the focus being on listening and note-taking this time around. There were eleven students in the room, which was equipped with a standard IWB and computer. However, some students had their own personal laptops and iPads, but unlike in Harry's second vignette, where every student had equal access to an iPad, there was 'less than a class set' (Bennett, 2012) for Matthew's students. Matthew himself had possession of an iPad, which he mostly used as an electronic version of the teacher's traditional pen and paper, employed in monitoring and used for noting corrections. Though the instrument had changed, the ELT pedagogy remained the same: eliciting, listening, and correcting students' language. The class started with contextualisation of the session, which was based on the topic of *'lecture styles'*, which he described as being *'reading, conversational, and interactive'*. To get a sense of how these worked in practice, students would listen to a lecture relating to *'phobias'*, which Matthew described through use of images on screen to stimulate discussion. Alongside this backdrop of images, he used an online stopwatch to give students a sense of time and structure in the warm-up discussions.

From the start, Matthew emphasised a sense of partnership in producing language. Following standard ELT procedures, he arranged students into pairs and groups, depending on tasks, and constantly monitored their work, with the iPad at hand, acting as an electronic form of the traditional pen and notepad. Sometimes, during this monitoring, he wrote down errors for correction at whole group level, at a later stage. Other times, he corrected aspects of language individually, using the iPad as a demonstration tool. Here, different to his conceptualisation of *'bear-pits'* in the focus group sessions, the technology was a mobile presence that enabled him to avoid transmission-style teaching. Practising what he espoused, he employed a conversational and interactive lecturing approach, rather than chalk-and-talk.

Students were engaged and on-task, learning vocabulary that they required for the generic lecture on phobias, at the heart of the lesson. Interestingly, when it came to this lecture, from the textbook, Matthew chose to read it rather than use the audio resource, for what he claimed to be reasons of *'authenticity.'* Whether that was the correct decision or not for these students, again he appeared to be drawing upon his TPK base by choosing when, or when not to, apply technology to particular teaching situations. Relating this to the first vignette of practice, and others not described here, there were clear developments in terms of his actions, knowledge, and the specific professional practice of using technology in his EAP teaching. He was able to customise a particular technology (iPad) to fit the purpose of his lesson, and to use that technology 'not for its own sake, but for the sake of advancing student learning and understanding' (Koehler & Mishra, 2009, p. 66), which suggests an increased sense of TPK. The fact that he chose to use the iPad in a restricted way does not suggest lack of TK, but an ability to balance the affordances of the technology with the needs and pedagogic strategies of the lesson. It was being used in a natural, unobtrusive way, as proposed by Bax (2003), and McGrath et al (2011), as just another tool of teaching, with the production of language seeming to be the main object of learning.

On the whole, then, the lesson seemed more of an example of Blue's (1998, p. 48) EGAP teaching, than ESAP, and indeed bore many hallmarks of standard Communicative Language teaching. This, though, was not down to any lack of understanding about accepted differences between academic and general English Language teaching. Matthew's post-lesson interview suggested that he had a particular 'pedagogic creed' (Dewey, 1897) and sense of practice shaped by a combination of student needs, specific context, and his understanding of EAP as a subject. This was a sense of EAP as *a stepping stone between several different levels*, including *cultural aspects* and *academic context*, with no mention given to disciplinary preparation. Matthew's perception of the EAP teacher, in his specific context, was of a facilitator of language and skills. In his *ideal classroom situation*, the teacher's role was one of *crafting language* in collaboration with the students so that they were taking charge of their own learning to a greater extent. This, on the whole, suggests that by the end of the study Matthew had reached a point where he assumed a greater sense of confidence in going back to his existing knowledge base. Therein, from a combination of principles found in ELT and drama workshops, he reshaped his understanding of what the act of EAP teaching involved. This was very different in some ways to those who advocate a 'leap into TEAP' (Kirk, 2012), but equally valid in its own right. However, this was not a case of difference between espoused and actual practice because in his teaching he did what he aspired to in his interviews.

Second vignette of Rosemary's practice

During the final interviews, Rosemary alluded to continuing efforts to integrate new technologies with traditional English Language teaching principles. This included reference to prioritising affective factors, and using Moodle as a tool for scaffolding and supporting learners. On the whole, she felt that her work with the VLE was *becoming more integrated and heading in the right direction*, to the extent that *it's kind of a given we use that every week.* Describing her actual usage, she referred to quizzes, wikis, and forums, pointing out that she utilised these for interactivity, rather than using the VLE for simple storage of PowerPoints and Word documents. By taking this approach, she sought to *motivate students* and *benefit* them *outside of the classroom*, which seemed to reflect her general teaching philosophy and sense of EAP as a subject. She defined her role in quite a traditional English Language teaching sense as being one of *making sure that students understand* and having *student centred, student focused lessons*.

Since Moodle served as a bedrock for Rosemary's classes, this allowed for evaluating her practice through a slightly different lens. Rather than observing her classroom instruction, I opted for analysis of learning materials she provided for students through the VLE. Such analysis had been conducted for each of the four teachers as a means of secondary triangulation in analysing their espoused and actual practices. However, in this case, Moodle acted as more of a fulcrum for class activities – before, after, and during sessions – bringing to life advanced stages of Mason's (1998) model.

Drawing upon a dynamic and engaging personality, Rosemary's teaching has dramatic and affective qualities, difficult to replicate in an online domain. If the classroom serves as live theatre, Moodle can seem a pre-recorded show. There is no main protagonist to sweep through the curtains on lazy afternoons, capture students' attention, and stimulate discussion. Thus, all teachers face challenges in motivating students to use 'school' technologies (Jones & Lea, 2008). Salmon (2000) has suggested drawing upon a slow process of online socialisation as a means of overcoming the hurdles faced during 'e-moderation', and Rosemary used similar tactics in her battle to motivate students. In the first instance, she had personalised the page, creating a dedicated space for each class, possibly blurring the boundaries of academic and social spaces as advocated by Kear (2011, p. 41).

Displaying the high level of organisational skills expected of students in the academic context, Rosemary had laid everything out in week-by-week blocks. These incorporated materials used in class, generic EAP advice in areas such as referencing, and a range of self-study materials, which included optional homework exercises. The addition of these provided an interesting glimpse into Rosemary's development as an EAP teacher because, in her dialogue, I got a sense of her practice being shaped by traditional ELT principles. However, in light of materials presented on the VLE, it appeared that her sense of EAP went beyond just *making sure that students understand*, and actually grounded them in skills required for the academic context. She did, though, keep things *student centred and student focused* by also providing or reiterating important information to students through Moodle's announcement function, and by trying to stimulate discussions in a *'News Forum.'*

In the *'News Forum'*, students had to instigate or react to discussions on topics of popular contemporary interest in the media, which echoed Matthew's work on interacting with *'the real world outside of the classroom.'* Some of the discussions on the forum also related to subjects that could be seen as having direct relevance to the specific areas of study that the students were hoping to progress to after completing the Foundation programme. By trying to burst the bubble of classroom detachment from the real world, Rosemary was not just helping students understand 'academic contexts' (BALEAP, 2008, p. 4) but also the broader sociocultural environment beyond academia. She was also fostering a sense of autonomy not just at an individual level, but at a point of 'independence and interdependence' (ibid, p. 10), which lends itself to critical thinking and many of the other skills associated with scaffolding students towards comfort in a higher educational environment. Thus again, EAP methodologies and values came across more strongly in Rosemary's actual practice than in her espoused practice. When speaking in the focus group sessions and individual interviews, she appeared to draw more heavily upon a knowledge base shaped by traditional ELT principles. As stated earlier, she also failed to give herself the full credit that her work deserved at times.

On the whole, the analysis of Rosemary's Moodle materials provided an interesting glimpse into the blend that she enacted in her practice. They also showed an effective synergy between technology and pedagogy (TPK). Just as in Matthew's case, Rosemary's lessons focused largely on the form and function of language, as evidenced by headings given to materials placed on her VLE's weekly blocks. These included '*Parts of Speech – PowerPoint*', and a Microsoft Excel document detailing '*Phrasal Verbs*', but as the term developed, emphasis shifted from language to skills, scaffolding students towards such lessons as '*Editing and Proofreading Homework*.' Still, though, this type of ELT/EAP work, focusing on elements of language and skills alone, lacks the disciplinary focus required for TCK, and ultimately TPACK, but neither of these had been claimed in Rosemary's espoused practice.

Added to this, it would have been impossible on the Foundation programme to replicate the work that Kelly conducted with her higher-level Law and Humanities students. Having observed Rosemary's class several times, I could confidently assert that there was no way students of an IELTS level in the 4.5 to 5.5 region could ever hope to successfully dismantle a block of authentic text into its component parts and then look beyond the language to understand how ideas are presented in specific disciplines. Again, this supports the idea that the context of actual classrooms shapes what EAP practitioners do, to as large an extent as theory or resource. Going back to my reference to the teaching of music, in Chapter 3, it is pointless asking students to deconstruct a Mozart symphony and recreate that in their own style if they can't even understand the rudiments of musical composition. Rosemary thus focused on what students needed, and as such supported the idea of EAP being a subject that has to be grounded in context and reality.

10.4 – Lessons learned at this stage

As the lights began to fade on this study of teacher development, the second series of vignettes illuminated aspects of both practice and philosophy. Firstly, the observations revealed key aspects of the different journeys made by each teacher over the course of this study. Secondly, by 'peeling back the layers' (Creswell, 2009, p. 183) of each teacher's theories in action, it was possible to establish links between knowledge, beliefs, and other sociocultural variables. Though the goal was not to search for instances of TPACK, this framework also provided a lens through which to capture the portrait of developments. Those developments differed according to the individual and the courses they were teaching, but all shared common ground in their increased TPK. The issue of content knowledge, though, remained problematic, and perhaps that has much to do with EAP, as a subject, lacking any firm definition of this. Even now, there is no singular definition of 'content' in the EAP context.

This has meant that EAP practitioners, as seen in the vignettes, tend to shape their practice around the needs of students in a specific situation, which is a particular strength of English Language teaching. Other disciplines have much to learn from this type of pedagogy, which seems to be paradoxically strengthened by its lack of specific content, such as might be found in Chemistry, Criminology, or Media classes. Even Harry's integration of Economics and EAP, facilitated by the iPad project, was a form of Content-Based Instruction not designed to drill deep into 'the substantive and the syntactic structures' of the discipline, as Shulman (1986, p. 9) envisioned. Kelly voiced ambitions of exposing her classes to underlying theories in the Social Sciences, and achieved this, to some extent, with *'higher-level students'*, as she described them, participating in debates and discussions on the Moodle forum. Rosemary and Matthew sought to cultivate similar discussions, and again to bring the real world into the classroom which, like a succinct definition of content, sometimes seems to be lacking in EAP.

At first impression, then, Matthew and Rosemary's concentration on language rather than discipline specificity might be falsely interpreted as lack of EAP knowledge, and a situating of their practice in the comfort zone of English Language teaching. Such a scenario would feed into a commonly held view of EAP being the highest form of evolution in a language teacher's continuum. However, this narrow view often leads to good teachers abandoning solid ELT principles at the EAP classroom door, as pointed out by Alexander at al (2008, p. 5). In this study, though, after going through a programme of education, teachers found renewed confidence in returning to their ELT knowledge base, and using this as a foundation for shaping their practice in the EAP classroom. Another valuable lesson generated through this chapter has been the development of a framework for analysing teachers' practices. Though it has historically been difficult to reconcile such areas as knowledge, beliefs, and practice, others have attempted to do so using interviews and observations. In this study, the introduction of a third element into the equation has made for a better synthesis between espoused views or values and actual practice. That third element of analysing learning materials offered a straightforward but original dimension to the age-old issue of capturing knowledge-in-action. This then gave rise to a model of teacher development as shown in Figure 7 in Chapter 12, where the importance of such a model is discussed further.

However, to close this chapter, it is important to offer a defence of approaches to EAP instruction which prioritise language-related issues that might seem more suited to general English teaching. My argument is that such teaching is always going to be necessary in a corporate model of higher educational provision where quantity of students outweighs concerns about quality, and where contemporary visa regulations prioritise IELTS equivalence over all other signs of a student's readiness or ability to complete degree-level study in the United Kingdom. Under the neoliberal model discussed by Hadley (2014) and Ding & Bruce (2017), EAP is being increasingly forced into more of a 'butler stance' (Raimes, 1991, p. 243), catering to a large extent for international students whose language competency has not reached a level deemed satisfactory for direct entry onto university courses. This means that just as EAP is reaching new heights in terms of its theoretical foundations, its practices are still being shaped by very basic remedial work with language.

That, of course, is not a new finding because, as discussed at different stages of this work, EAP has often been a chameleon discipline in terms of both its overall identity and its subject content, as discussed in Bell's (2016) study of practitioners, pedagogies and professionalism. The EAP experts who are given voice in Bell's work differ in opinion amongst themselves and inevitably differ from the teachers in this study who have to work with students at the lower end of the IELTS spectrum on an everyday basis. Though Matthew and Rosemary made efforts to give their students an awareness of language as social practice, as in the work of Pennycook (1997) and Bhatia (2004), those students also needed something far more basic, shaped to a large extent by the sociopolitical demands placed on today's international students in UK higher education. For these students, needing a particular set of scores for progression to degree courses, language proficiency serves as the ticket for entrance to the social practices of higher education. By providing that basic language proficiency, it can be argued that Matthew and Rosemary are making their students every bit as *empowered* as Kelly's, for example, when she is concentrating on giving students *control of their own learning.* Every EAP teaching situation is different, but each is strengthened by teachers putting into practice the values they espouse, even if such practices challenge prevailing ideas about what the subject is supposed to entail.

CHAPTER 11

Teachers, Development and the Centre

11.1 – Contextualisation

By the time this study finished, a great deal had happened in the life of the language centre. Beneath the spiralling loops of Anish Kapoor's *ArcelorMittal Orbit*, the Queen Elizabeth Olympic Park assumed its final form for the Games of the XXX Olympiad, known in everyday terms as London 2012. That 'finished' form, of course, would later shift again for usage in the years after summer's glorious victories had faded into memory. London, like the educators in its midst, keeps changing, moving, mutating, moulding itself around the needs of the moment, endlessly travelling down a continuum of development. Just as teachers develop their practice around an intersection of new knowledge and past experience, planners would return to this Olympic summer venue, in the seasons after, reshaping it around fresh sporting, tourism and residential needs. That the continuum of development does not stop at one fixed point in time is as true of London's infrastructure as it is of the teachers in this story. However, in line with principles of case study research, it is important to firstly capture a sense of development at a fixed point in time – the end of the teacher education programme – before looking at outcomes from a more longitudinal perspective, as in the closing stages of this chapter.

In the cases of all four teachers in this study, there had been a number of significant developments in actions and knowledge on the use of technologies in the classroom both during and after the teacher education programme. Essentially, these developments led to technology becoming more embedded in their teaching, both inside and outside of the classroom. This entailed a gradual movement from tentative exploration at the outset, particularly in the cases of Matthew and Kelly, to an almost fluent usage of a range of technologies. Significantly too, even when not fully fluent in the affordances of new tools, the teachers appeared more comfortable with using 'aspects' of a resource – as seen in Kelly's usage of Camtasia, This was a significant movement from the

---

How to cite this book chapter:
Breen, P. 2018. *Developing Educators for The Digital Age: A Framework for Capturing Knowledge in Action*. Pp. 159–168. London: University of Westminster Press.
DOI: https://doi.org/10.16997/book13.k. License: CC-BY-NC-ND 4.0

opening stages of the study, where teachers seemed daunted and turned off by new technologies, rather than seduced by the allure of the language centre's high-tech classrooms.

By the end of the study, all four teachers had embraced particular tools with the passion of a new romance. The fact of each teacher using specific tools tailored to the needs of particular learning situations, as espoused by Mishra & Koehler (2006), further suggests that teachers' understanding of what is required in terms of content may also influence their choice of tools used to mediate the object and outcomes of their teaching. This was perhaps most apparent in Harry's integration of iPads into the language centre's system of activity so as to facilitate better 'content' understanding on the International Diploma programme, although Matthew's use of podcasts, Moodle, and iPads was suggestive of the same, as were Kelly's choices regarding usage of Camtasia, and Rosemary's consistent work with Moodle.

Referring back to Mishra & Koehler's (2006) analysis, it appears that an increase in the components of TPACK can have a demonstrable impact on professional practice, and on the broader activity of the workplace. TPACK, as a whole, does not have to be enacted at any one time or on a recurring basis in order for its influence to be apparent. Indeed, as the literature suggests, it is a difficult construct to 'tease out' in practice (Koehler & Mishra, 2009, p. 66), even with classroom observations, where tenets might come into view but not the whole construct. However, this study has shown that synergy between any of its constituent parts (TK, PK, CK, TPK, TCK, and PCK) can also serve as the basis for what Mishra & Koehler (2006) term expert teaching. Practical instances and enactments from each tenet of the TPACK framework can be easily unthreaded from the overall tapestry of vignettes.

Yet, as Lee Shulman has argued in his more contemporary work (2012), one of the most crucial areas of expertise in the classroom is the ability to make subject matter comprehensible to students. All four teachers in this study worked hard to achieve this, in sourcing, adapting, and delivering material for their lessons, such as in the examples of Matthew and Kelly's grading of language according to student levels, through interactions on the VLE or other more authentic, interactive forums. Rosemary also made use of Moodle forums whilst Harry sent his students out into the real-world business context of such places as Old Spitalfields Market.

Change, though, was not limited to usage of resources evolving over time. The most significant change came about through the placement of pedagogy at the forefront of teachers' practices. This in turn led to new approaches for delivering content, where technologies served as vehicles, rather than being the mainstay of teaching in themselves. There are valuable lessons within that across disciplines, whether teaching Law, Business, Humanities, or Science. Indeed, the last of these subjects provides a powerful instance of what this concept of technology as a vehicle means in practice.

When teachers use a microscope in a Science class, they are generally not doing so for the purposes of teaching about the instrument, even if it is essential to understand how to use such a piece of equipment. Generally, teachers use microscopy to give students a visual understanding of such scientific fundamentals as the structure of cells and organisms. To achieve this, there is a need to understand the technology, but such understanding is best achieved not by focusing on each individual tool in the Science classroom, whether a Bunsen Burner or a set of test tubes. Instead, the aspiring scientist must have an underlying and embedded set of values that guides their actions in the laboratory.

Though EAP is different to Science, by the end of this study, all four teachers appeared to be guided in their work by an underlying and embedded set of values regarding technology, pedagogy, and content. They may already have had fundamental elements of these at the outset, particularly pedagogy, since that is relatively well-developed on most teacher preparation courses. However, over time, they found a better synergy of these three components, and simultaneously deepened their understanding of EAP as a subject. That understanding may not always have fallen in line with BALEAP's (2008) framework, as in Matthew's case, but it did fall in line with Vygotskian perspectives on becoming more self-directed, as in the work of Manning & Payne (1993). That self-direction was not limited to developing fluency in technologies, but also incorporated gaining the confidence to effectively say 'this is the way I teach, and I do it for a reason.' Though no teacher said those precise words, they act as a fair summary of an ethos espoused at the time of the final individual interviews.

11.2 – Relating the study to the literature

Changing sense of teachers' practice

Historically, the literature on teacher education and cognition has found common agreement in the idea that development occurs as a result of teachers taking greater mental charge of their own practice, as suggested by Mann (2005, p. 108). Mishra & Koehler (2006, p. 1063) theorise that such a point comes about when teachers start asking questions of their own pedagogy, and the content they are delivering in the classroom. Such questioning and reflection on practice creates opportunities for professional growth, as suggested throughout the literature on the development of knowledge for teaching. Such a claim is supported by this study as a whole, wherein there have been clear and significant changes in the practice of all four teachers, and their understanding of what practice entails.

Even in Harry's case, coming to the programme with existing confidence in using technologies in the classroom, a greater emphasis on subject specificity eventually featured in his practice. Added to this, he reconfigured particular instruments to fit a customised pedagogic purpose in the EAP classroom, as advocated by Koehler & Mishra (2009, p. 66). Changes for Kelly, Matthew and Rosemary, on the other hand, were easier to trace as a result of the way in which their technological knowledge was more limited at the outset. However, once this was developed, TPK became a feature of their practice very quickly, leading on to instances of TCK and PCK in Kelly's case. The range of instruments used in the classroom, and outside, also suggested a shift in practice, as well as the ability to dip in and out of technology's usage, as best envisioned by Kelly who spoke of the *'snowballing'* of knowledge during focus groups, and its subsequent embedding, and *'resurfacing'* by the time of individual interviews. This captures a succinct sense of how knowledge can indeed take the form of a spiral, once a solid base or infrastructure is in place. However, unless teachers take mental charge of this 'cognitive space' (Mann, 2005, p. 108), they will always see themselves as needing fresh training for every new tool they encounter in the classroom.

Despite differing levels of self-direction, pedagogy remained central to the teachers' practices from start to 'finish', with a great deal of faith and emphasis placed upon traditional English Language teaching principles. These included the pre-eminence of affective factors, as in Rosemary's work with blended learning approaches. Harry also made a valuable assertion towards the end of the study regarding his belief that *'you can't just experiment with technology, you need to have the way of teaching to go with it.'* Though he may also have held similar views at the outset, this statement captures a sense of the 'pedagogic creed' (Dewey, 1897) and philosophy cultivated within the language centre on both an individual and communal basis. Each teacher's practice, to a greater extent than before, was shaped by a stronger sense of a more personalised, but goal-focused, *'way of teaching'* with technology. Furthermore, this was not limited to any single choice of instrument, even in Harry's adoption of iPads and Rosemary's faithfulness to Moodle, with both incorporating other tools, or none, into their practice when required. Even though I have associated teachers with particular resources, the idea is not to pigeonhole them into any sense of dogma as regards the technologies they use in their lessons. Rather, the point is that at one particular juncture on their developmental continuum, they had a tendency to use certain resources in their classrooms. Their choice of resources prior to that may have been different and so too their choices afterwards, such as in Harry's situation of later progressing on to a role as a designer of lessons and materials, first in the same or associated workplace, and then with a different organisation.

Embedding of technology within activity

Through much of the literature on TPACK, CALL, and blended learning, there is a sense that for technology to find an effective synergy with pedagogy, it has to become a natural part of everyday practice (Warschauer, 1996; Bax, 2003;

Mishra & Koehler, 2006; McGrath et al, 2011; Motteram, 2013). In this study, the embedding of technology reshaped the practice of all four teachers not just in the classroom but in work conducted outside of class as well. Moodle served as the best example of this, and was becoming embedded in teaching from as early as the second focus group session. Indeed, by that stage, Rosemary, as a broker and advocate of VLE usage, had introduced the practice of designing quizzes for revision purposes, not just in an EAP context, but across the disciplinary spectrum. By the end of the study, all four teachers had found a way of using and integrating a range of technologies into their practice, 'not for its own sake, but for the sake of advancing student learning and understanding' (Koehler & Mishra, 2009, p. 66).

The usage of tools being determined by student needs became a significant feature, even if this had already been part of the teachers' underlying philosophies, courtesy of having a shared ELT knowledge base shaped by standard training and educational procedures in this field. Each teacher found particular tools that worked at a given time, or in a specific situation.

In Kelly's case this had meant using Camtasia in a time of particular need, before reaching 'a dead end', whilst using various aspects of Moodle throughout. Within this usage of Moodle, she also reshaped the communicative aspect of her teaching, so that it shifted from a focus on conversational activities in the classroom, to written discussions outside of class.

Matthew also used Moodle quite extensively, and through podcasts, and some usage of iPads, brought new tools into the language centre's system of activity. Harry, though, was the one who brought about the greatest transformation in the language centre, in terms of resources and instruments used to 'mediate the object of activity' (Murphy & Rodriguez-Manzanares, 2008, p. 443). These new instruments that he brought into the language centre's activity system changed the practices of other teachers too, and also reconfigured the original purpose for which the iPads were intended (Koehler & Mishra, 2009; Motteram, 2013). Added to this, Harry's use of iPads as a vehicle for what he perceived to be 'CLIL', and Matthew's usage of them for crafting students' language, showed how particular tools can also be configured for different purposes within the same systems of activity, as was again the case with Kelly's suggestion of different ways of using Camtasia, and Rosemary's introduction of quizzes or wikis on Moodle.

Different understandings of content

Several voices in the literature have raised the complexity of defining content not just in English Language classrooms, but in a range of contexts (Freeman, 2002; Mishra & Koehler, 2006; Ball et al, 2008; McGrath et al, 2011; Çelik & Simpson, 2013). Again, this study has shown differing interpretations of content knowledge, and how that is organised in the minds of teachers, which feeds into Shulman's (1986) and Koehler & Mishra's (2009) defining of PCK. Harry envisioned himself as enacting CLIL, whilst Matthew's talk and actions suggested a focus on ELT/CLT practices in the EAP classroom, which went slightly against the grain of BALEAP's (2008, p. 8) recommendations on this. Rosemary too focused primarily on the language needs of students at the outset of her courses, but then scaffolded them gradually towards a greater emphasis on academic skills and contexts. However, Kelly's integration of content and language was perhaps most reflective of BALEAP's expectations regarding discipline-specific work in EAP classrooms, as exemplified in the work of Dudley-Evans & St. John (2009), Sloan & Porter (2010), Alexander et al (2011), Gilbert (2013), Macallister & Kirk (2013), and Bell (2016).

In Kelly's case, such an approach was possible because of her familiarity with the disciplinary pathway that her students were engaged in, and by their levels of English. Matthew's English for University Study class, as described in his vignettes of practice, had far less fluency and similar types of content integration might therefore not have been possible. Thus, he chose to focus on language as 'content.' This, in part, was also shaped by his understanding of the object of EAP teaching, as giving students the generic language and skills they need to undertake future degree studies. This was the same approach adopted by Rosemary, with students of a similar level to Matthew's, but with a more pressing need to scaffold them towards the academic context they would be entering directly after their course. Matthew and Rosemary's emphasis on language differed notably from Harry's, who perceived the objective of his lessons as being the teaching of concepts and lexicon from a specific set of subjects, with no apparent emphasis on the more substantive aspects of discourse in these subjects, as found in Kelly's work.

On the whole, then, regarding the four teachers' differing understandings of content, there is clear evidence that EAP classes are predominantly shaped by an environment of 'these students in this situation and this set of concerns' (Burns, 1999, p. 3). This makes EAP markedly different to many other subjects within higher education, but at the same time shows why pedagogically the field of Academic English teaching can claim to be at the forefront of *student centred, student focused lessons'*, as defined by Rosemary. Furthermore, in terms of establishing a relationship between the classroom and the real world, EAP is again ahead of many other subjects. Hence, its practitioners appear to have found it easier to make that leap into teaching with technologies, and in drawing upon the affordances of social media and authentic resources, as seen in Matthew's work, for example. EAP, through not having a fixed body of subject knowledge, has considerable flexibility to act as a bridge between other disciplines and the world outside academia. Whilst the four teachers had different beliefs or needs when it came to content, they all sought a meaningful relationship between their teaching and the real world, which perhaps owes more to ELT than EAP. That again serves as a challenge to the possible fallacy of seeing EAP as being higher up the evolutionary ladder of a language teacher's career.

Whilst true in terms of economics and required qualifications, it is important not to forget the indispensable contribution of the knowledge base and key pedagogic principles established in ELT contexts. Such principles are ultimately as important to EAP 'content' as the relationship with academic disciplines.

Increased sharing of practice in the workplace

One of the strongest features of this study was the increased sharing of practice in the workplace over time. Indeed, Matthew described this as having more of an impact on his own development than the actual workshops, whilst there was a sense that not only Kelly's understanding of technology was *'snowballing'* but also her sharing of knowledge, exchange of ideas, and collaboration with colleagues. Rosemary, too, consistently emphasised the role that collaboration played in her experimentation with Moodle, and her growing confidence in integrating technologies into the Foundation programme. Like Rosemary, Harry served as a broker of activity, in becoming the main instigator of introducing others to iPads and educating them in their usage. Some features of this suggested the development of a community of practice within the workplace (Wenger, 1998; Wenger & Snyder, 2000; Wenger et al, 2002), but it could equally be seen as a specific feature of practice brought about by the acquisition of new knowledge. Finally, the fact of running workshops in the first place as a stimulus for development supports Wenger & Snyder's (2000) work on 'cultivated' communities of practice, and also the Vygotskian belief that knowledge has to be 'activated' or triggered in some way (Wilson & Berne, 1999, p. 194).

11.3 – Practical developments at close of study

Summary of cross-case developments

Over the course of this research journey, each teacher demonstrated an increased understanding of the impact of technology on the practices and purposes of the EAP classroom, albeit with differing senses of relationships between technology, pedagogy, and content. The goal of the study, though, was never to unearth explicit instances of TPACK, which can be difficult to locate and could also be seen as a contradiction to the idea of teaching as a professional continuum, rather than a search for an end point of development. Instead, the focus was on evaluating developments in the practice of each teacher, and finding a way of capturing their knowledge-in-action so as to make the story accessible and trustworthy for a wider audience. That means of capturing knowledge-in-action has also been depicted in diagrammatic format in Figure 7, as detailed in Chapter 12. This emphasis on evaluating development, alongside activating it in the first instance, is what makes this study unique and gives it broader resonance beyond the EAP context.

Through the teachers' dialogue and their vignettes of practice, it has been possible to see how they have developed both as people and as professionals, for it is impossible to separate the two. If not true of all subjects, that certainly seems to be the case in English Language teaching, and the specific domain of EAP also seems more impoverished of character when teachers leave their real-world personas at the classroom door, alongside traditional ELT principles, as suggested by Alexander et al (2008, p. 5). Each teacher's practice and personal development within this study has been enriched by aspects of who they are as people – Harry's lifelong love of technology and instruments, whether for musical or learning purposes; Kelly's passion for Psychology and Sociology; Matthew's creativity; and Rosemary's powerful desire to build and be a part of teams or communities. Each of the teachers, over the course of the study, changed in some way, becoming self-directed to a greater extent, and adopting technologies of choice – personalised vehicles of their pedagogy akin to Batmobile, TARDIS, or Millennium Falcon.

Yet, in line with the idea of teaching as 'a continuous process of becoming' which 'can never be finished' (Mann, 2005, p. 105), it is important not just to stop the story at the point where the case study concluded. This is why, in closing, it seems beneficial to offer a final vignette of overall developments.

Closing vignette: longer term developments

London, as the setting for the language centre at the heart of this study, provides a spectacular backdrop for any story, with a series of landmarks mapped out across its riverside, stretching from east to west. Imagine then, this closing vignette through the eyes of someone looking out across such a view, scanning terrain that stretches from Stratford to Liverpool Street. Therein, a story of development spirals like the steps of a mezzanine or a steely sculpture rising above the Olympic Stadium. That story continued long after this research study for both the teachers and their place of work. For some, that became a former place of work as they moved to pastures new, generally progressing well on the continuum of professional development.

Matthew and Kelly remained longest at the language centre, with many of the other main players departing within a similar time period, a couple of years after the Olympic Games had faded to memory. Rosemary became a Programme Director for another public-private partnership organisation in London, rising gradually to the level of Programme Convener for Business Management degrees. Harry carried on his love affair with new technologies, becoming a learner designer and media developer for educational media and publishing companies. These roles entailed increased usage of adaptive learning platforms, software by Adobe, and other development products, alongside continuing connection with such resources as Moodle. I too moved on, completing my PhD before ending up working as a Senior Lecturer in English for Academic Purposes at the University of Westminster, continuing to play an active role in researching technology and teacher education.

This does not mean that Kelly and Matthew did not experience a similar journey in their professional lives. Though both stayed in the language centre several years after Harry, Rosemary, and I had left, they became more significant actors in its activity system. Over time, they assumed leadership roles on their respective programmes, becoming coordinators, and continuing to build on their foundations of integrating technologies with their teaching. Emily, by the time of the next Olympic Games in 2016, had taken over my former role and was now the Director of English Language Programmes. Alongside Emily as the main broker of activity, Matthew and Kelly continued to build on usage of VLEs, as the language centre moved towards the adoption of the Box cloud storage facility as the main repository of teaching materials. Just as with Harry's subsequent work, the passing of time brought a shift towards usage of more mobile resources situated at the cutting edge of technology. It could be argued, though it would be difficult to prove, that the workshops and original philosophy of the language centre had facilitated this ability to adopt to the circumstances of the time, and the speed at which technologies change.

What does seem clear in looking back over the study from a distance is that the original workshops activated a culture of teachers working together to activate developments in their practice as a community. Each of the four main cases in this study had benefitted from exchanging ideas with others, especially in the early stages of the project. Emily and Rosemary, in particular, fostered a culture of working together around the VLE, which still exists in the language centre today, long after the original seeding of this practice. Evidence for that comes about through being granted access to the contemporary VLE, where many of the same practices exist as in days past, such as more experienced teachers mentoring their newer colleagues. I then sought verification of this by speaking to some of today's new teachers and, although they cannot provide a definitive historical linkage, they spoke of a culture instantly recognisable as one fostered right from the outset.

It could be argued that without the initial workshops, the language centre today would be a very different place. The lives of the teachers might be different too because those workshops gave them greater confidence in themselves, their beliefs, and their pedagogy, helping them to get over the hurdle of hardware inhibiting their practice. Having orienteered their way around technological obstacles, in some cases they then became more comfortable dipping or spiralling in and out of their existing ELT knowledge base. Therein, 'humanware' has always been emphasised over hardware or software (Warschauer & Meskill, 2000, p. 315). Perhaps there is truth in T. S. Eliot's famous assertion that 'the end of all our exploring will be to arrive where we started and know the place for the first time' (1943, pp. 143–144).

However, in looking back on the overall picture, it is important to stress that the workshops alone did not create all of these developments, and that a broader series of sociocultural variables has played its part in this story. Perhaps, over time, this group of teachers would have developed in the same way without the spark, cultivation, or activation of the synergy they eventually found between pedagogic knowledge and other fundamental TPACK tenets. What is striking, though, is that each teacher has developed significantly in their career, not just in this language centre but in their new workplaces too.

11.4 – Lessons learned at this stage

To close the chapter and provide a sense of how far teachers travelled on this journey of development, I am going to present a very brief final vignette of Harry's practice in the academic year after the Olympic Games, which have served as a motif throughout this story. Ironically, and not intentionally, this post-study observation had been scheduled to take place in the classroom featured in the first vignette, where things had become messy because of limited space. However, this time around the situation was very different; hence why I have chosen to include this as a closing vignette. Though the location remained the same, Harry had altered the boundaries by shepherding the students into break-out areas in the corridor beyond, working in small groups as he drifted amongst them. They were rebranding London as a tourist destination in the aftermath of the 2012 Olympics and using a set of iPads for different purposes: as a research device, as a presentation design tool, and as a recording facility. Differently to the first lesson I observed, where so much of the activity had been teacher-led and textbook-driven, here the students were taking charge of their own learning in a less constrained space, pedagogically, physically, and even psychologically. Effectively, they were creating the core materials for use in the class and Harry, having already introduced research and presentation skills at the beginning of the lesson, was now a facilitator, sitting in the background, letting the lesson take shape around the technology, the content, and the learning outcomes. As such, I was witnessing a rebranding of his theories in action (Argyris & Schön,1974), every bit as much as the rebranding of London in the post-Olympic world, and the post-workshop environment of the language centre.

CHAPTER 12

Conclusion

12.1 – Contextualisation

Overview of knowledge generated

The focus of this study has been to explore developments that occurred in terms of actions and knowledge during and after a teacher education programme on the use of technologies in the classroom, and how these developments have shaped or reshaped the specific professional practice of integrating technologies into traditional teaching methods. The developments have been significant, and my main contribution to existing literature has been an increased understanding of ways to explore the knowledge base of teaching. Through gaining a better understanding of such a base, it has then been possible to stimulate existing knowledge, and activate new knowledge. This happened at the point of synergy between three key elements in the lives of today's teachers: pedagogy, content, and usage of technologies.

The study has helped to build on the work of Lee Shulman from the 1980s onwards, and on the work that took place both before and after his formulation of the Pedagogical Content Knowledge framework. This includes notable predecessors who shaped his work, such as Bloom (1956) and Schwab (1972), right up to Mishra & Koehler's (2006) evolution of TPACK. The fact that all these theorists were concerned with education in general rather than one specific subject means that the findings actually lend themselves to a much broader exploration of teaching with technologies than purely in an EAP context. That said, the study has been unique in the sense of being set in such a context, and using EAP as a 'subject.' This is because discussions around teacher knowledge usually take place within more established disciplines.

By positioning a story of teacher education and development in the context of a language centre, I hope to support a growing standpoint that EAP and ELT should be treated as disciplines in their own right, rather than serving a

How to cite this book chapter:
Breen, P. 2018. *Developing Educators for The Digital Age: A Framework for Capturing Knowledge in Action*. Pp. 169–180. London: University of Westminster Press. DOI: https://doi.org/10.16997/book13.l. License: CC-BY-NC-ND 4.0

purpose akin to a mobile First Aid service for other specialisms. For the subject to be accorded the seriousness it deserves, there is a need for more rigorous teacher education. EAP teachers are still commonly seen as the St John Ambulance at the side of higher education's playing field – stretcher-bearers providing the academic skills that regular lecturers have no desire to teach. Often, such attitudes can cause EAP practitioners and departments to retreat into their own shells, excelling in their work, but showcasing this in self-referential bubbles detached from the disciplinary mainstream. Partially, that stems from their lack of access to a world outside the margins, and a general lack of understanding about who EAP teachers are, and what they actually do. Despite all its efforts over the past half century to find a settled home within academia, even now the subject struggles to shake off its remedial associations, as described by Hyland & Hamp-Lyons (2002, p. 6).

Studies such as this can therefore showcase the tremendous creativity, innovation, motivation, pedagogic aptitude, and sociocultural awareness that exists amongst EAP practitioners. As seen in the dialogue and vignettes in this study, today's EAP teachers are striving to make their subject not just a transit point between language fluency and academia, but also a bridge to real-world interaction. Of course, the more generalised field of ELT has often been ahead of the game in its adoption of creative pedagogies and technologies, as evidenced by its early advocacy of blended learning methodologies, for example, and today's teachers, working in a digital context, seem just as innovative as those from the earlier 'CALL generation'.

Perhaps too, where ELT has been ahead of the game is in its prioritisation of pedagogy over content, and the positive effect this has on performance in the classroom. That, of course, can be negated by lack of emphasis on content, or a struggle to define the precise content of language-based classes, but increasingly there is a better understanding of the subject matter that needs to be incorporated into EAP classes. That is undeniably largely shaped by contextual variables, and a historic feature of EAP has been the ability to survive as an 'eclectic and pragmatic discipline' (Hamp-Lyons, 2011, p. 89). Now, though, it seems that EAP is coming of age, and its practitioners, such as those in this study, have much to contribute in the broader domain of higher education, especially in providing 'exemplar cases' (Kuhn, 1987) of 'excellence in teaching' (Hofer & Swan, 2008, p. 181).

12.2 – Theoretical contributions

Mapping out shared terrain in ELT and EAP pedagogy

Clearly this study has sought to make a specific contribution to the subjects of English Language Teaching and English for Academic Purposes. Regardless of whether or not one accepts that there is a subject distinction between them, the study has helped address one of the key issues discussed by those such as Kirk (2012) and Çelik & Simpson (2013), who seek to define and locate the content aspect of TPACK more precisely within EAP and ELT respectively. In this study, the same questions linger, at times, with regard to the precise role that content plays, but its contribution in this area can be to suggest future ways of addressing this recurring issue. Through delivering this teacher education programme, and analysing surrounding developments, there is evidence to support the view that in two out of the four cases (Harry & Kelly), there was a shift in thinking as regards the role played by 'content'.

However, in Rosemary and Matthew's cases, the interaction of technology with traditional ELT pedagogy played a greater part in their practice than any incorporation of subject content, because of the language level of learners on their courses. By taking this approach, they exhibited a different form of self-direction, putting their students and other contextual factors first in their teaching. Paradoxically, though, rather than rejecting the content aspect of TPACK, they may actually be meeting Shulman's (1986) call to prioritise the representation of specific content in such a way as to make it comprehensible to students. Most strikingly, however, as in Rosemary's emphasis on affective factors and Matthew's desire for creativity, these cases present a challenge to EAP's tendency to divorce itself from all aspects of its ELT past. Matthew's case also challenges the idea that once exposed to EAP knowledge, 'English' teachers embark on a one-way journey or transition to the academic context.

In his case, we see a teacher absorbing such knowledge and then choosing to use that education to enhance his work with language for communicative purposes, rather than seeking a move towards a more academic context. Another question raised by Matthew's actions and preferences is whether or not teachers see as much possibility for creativity in EAP as in ELT. If not, then why not, in an age when disciplines across the spectrum are seeking more creative ways of presenting subject matter to students? My belief, from seeing such work as that conducted by Harry, is that there should be plenty of scope for EAP to incorporate more aspects of creativity, innovation, and interactivity into the presentation of its subject matter in this digital age. There also does not have to be such a schism between the different fields of English Language teaching, or any sense of hierarchy in what people teach.

Developing a framework for capturing knowledge in action

As far back as 1987, Lee Shulman advocated the creation of a periodic table of teacher knowledge, of which he claimed only to have identified the rudimentary elements (Ball et al, 2008, p. 397). Some in the literature, such as Ball et al (ibid), have argued that such a table is impossible because of disciplinary differences, and this might be compounded further in the EAP context by lack of agreement on a disciplinary definition (Bell, 2016). However, Mishra &

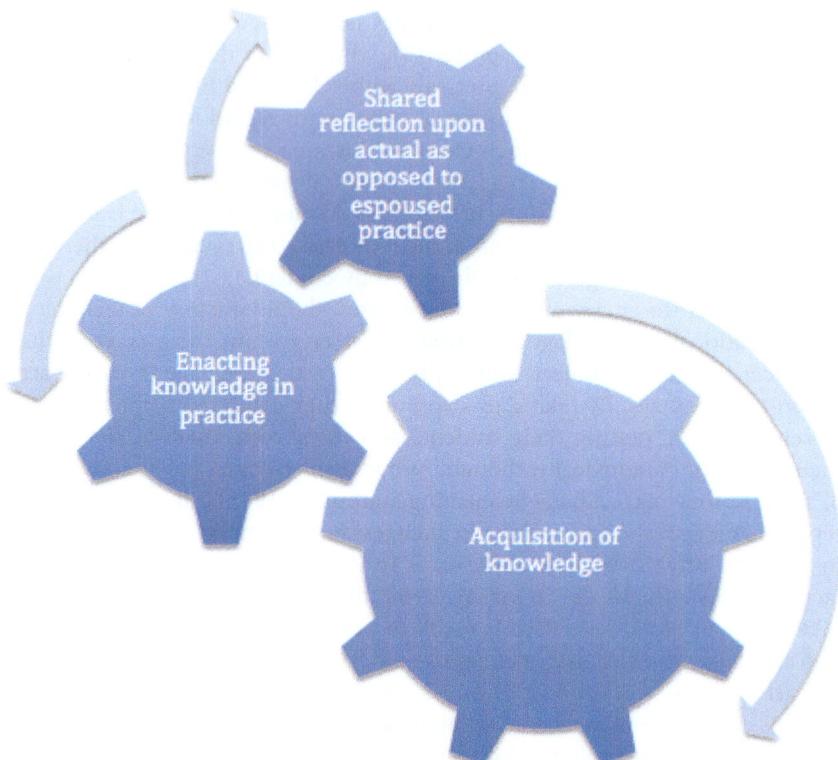

Figure 6: The development of knowledge in a reflective cycle.

Koehler's (2006) formulation of TPACK is one possible means of transcending such differences within and across disciplines, since it came into being to serve as an update on Shulman's (1986) PCK model, according to the demands of the more interdisciplinary digital age.

Whilst TPACK makes no claim to being the definitive framework of teacher knowledge, it has provided the fundamental prism through which I have sought to capture a sense of what Kirk (2012) has described as 'knowledge in action' in the EAP classroom. Historically, capturing an accurate sense of teacher knowledge has been deemed problematic for a number of reasons, such as those described in the works of Argyris & Schön (1974), Borg (2003), Donaghue (2003), Mishra & Koehler (2006), and Ball et al (2008). However, through a combination of the TPACK conceptual framework and the research methods used in this study, I have been able to capture a sense of how teacher knowledge is enacted in practice, which has been greatly assisted by having technology and pedagogy as a focus for exploration. Through focusing on the integration of technologies with more traditional pedagogy, I have evaluated an area of teaching that is very much centred upon activity, which is again in line with ideas from TPACK, teacher cognition, and teacher education literature. A diagrammatic representation of how that knowledge developed is provided in Figure 6 opposite, where I have depicted the reflective cycle in a series of three interconnected cogwheels which have no particular order of hierarchy. These three cogwheels turn and feed into one another, regardless of which one is taken to be the starting point, in a continuous cycle of reflection. **Shared reflection upon actual practice** takes place on an everyday basis, as does **enacting knowledge in practice**, but with the **acquisition of knowledge** there is an inevitable change to both reflection and action. That acquisition can come before or during the cycle in which, as in Richards' (1998) concept of a language teacher's developmental continuum, there is no endpoint.

Within this depiction, knowledge is seen as developing in the form of a kind of spiral, wherein constant reflection and assessment of actual practice is used as a means of evaluating espoused practices. The shared reflection is carried out through a combination of observations, discussions in groups or individually, and an evaluation of learning materials not for the purposes of appraisal but for the enhancement of knowledge. The idea is that when new knowledge has been acquired and embedded in the practices of the teacher, the spiralling process occurs when they use this new knowledge to reflect back on previous practices, and synthesise old and new.

Role of technological knowledge in activating this cycle

By its very nature, the act of teachers using technology serves as something concrete through which to observe actions and instances of practice, and then to compare these to what had been espoused in the focus groups and individual interviews. Traditionally, challenges have arisen in weighing up espoused practices against actual practice, as first highlighted in the work of Argyris & Schön (1974). Focusing on something as practical as technology established foundations for surmounting this historical obstacle, with further bolstering coming in the form of an analytical framework adapted from an ISTE Classroom Observation Tool, shown as Appendix 2. Usage of technologies in teaching could be seen and recorded on such an instrument, and then mapped to both macro themes and micro references in the dialogue from interviews and focus group sessions. Furthermore, because this was done longitudinally, differences could be noted and these differences linked to knowledge gained through teacher education workshops in line with other variables such as sharing of ideas in the workplace, and access to resources.

Technology too had the affordance of providing accessible repositories of learning materials that could serve as a further means of triangulation, and the mapping out of espoused practices against actual practices. The VLE also served as a form of social history, not just of individuals but of the workplace, further strengthening evaluation of how the research journey and the stories of teachers' development had unfolded over time. That was assisted to a large extent by having such a deep knowledge of the research setting, as a consequence of the study being conducted from an insider's perspective.

This study, then, has made a significant contribution to teacher education because of that historical struggle to capture instances of knowledge being enacted in practice. Though I would not claim to have identified unique elements of teacher knowledge, I have established a strong framework through which this can be evaluated, and shared a research study, and journey, that has been unique. I would even argue that the particularity of the research setting is such that it perhaps meets the definition of the Greek term *'kairos'*, which Sheard (1993) describes as being about much more than simply the right moment or opportune time. Rather, it is a particular set of circumstances coming together to create an end result that may well not have been replicated in the event of any one element being withdrawn.

This particular setting was unique in bringing together a group of teachers to a new language centre at a time when the rapid emergence of learning technologies was creating a distinctive tension. As such, perhaps the context as much as the technology helped to shape the developments and findings in the study, lending further support to the use of its particular, tailored theoretical framework. Above all, though, the interplay of variables (methods, context, conceptual lens) has facilitated a significant contribution to capturing a sense of the knowledge base required for teaching in the digital age.

Depicting the framework used for evaluation

Over the past few decades, there has been an increasing demand for qualitative research to use its 'moral mandate' for social research that actually addresses problems in the real world (Lincoln & Denzin, 2003, p. 3). This is closely allied to calls for a revolution in the presentation of ideas formulated through such research (ibid, p. 7) and an increasing emphasis on these having 'real-world' relevance, in a way that once upon a time may have been seen as the preserve of scientists in other fields of enquiry (ibid, p. 301). Therefore, even though it is difficult to narrow down the range of methods used in understanding the development of knowledge and action in this study, there is a practical need to offer something concrete in terms of final output. As such, I have developed a framework that is intended to serve as a guideline for others who might want to attempt a similar study, or for teacher educators seeking a means of evaluating their own development programmes. This is not intended to be any kind of definitive guide because that was never the purpose of the research study and this publication, or indeed the expected outcome of any qualitative investigation. Rather, this is a framework that has emerged from one instance of a teacher development programme that worked well in this situation and may work well in others.

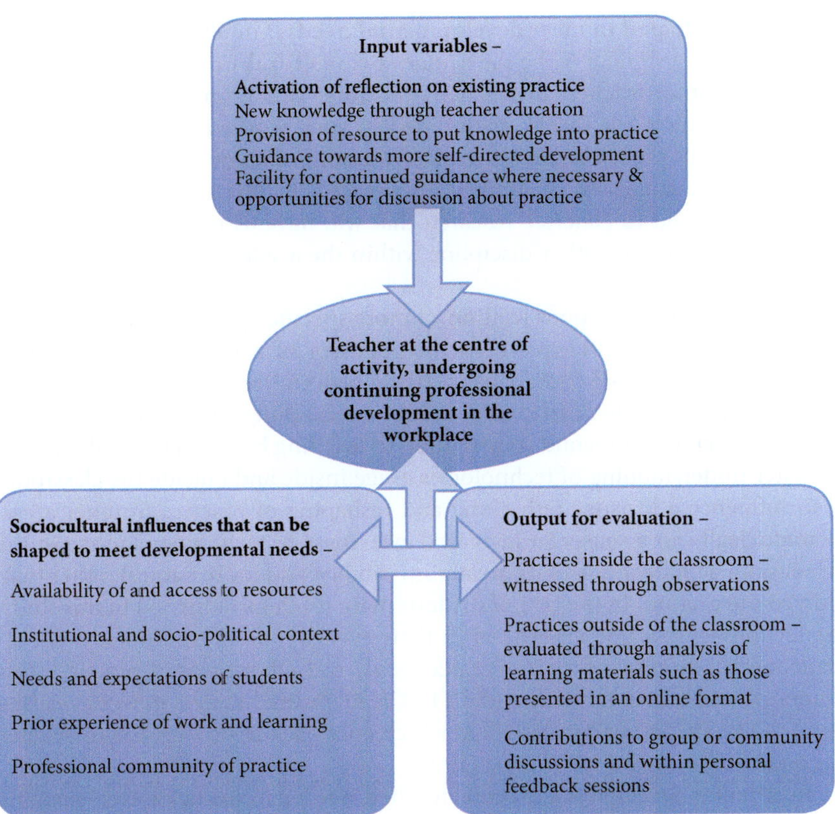

Figure 7: Framework to develop and evaluate knowledge in action.

Application of this framework to other contexts

As suggested in the overview of this chapter, my contribution in terms of understanding and capturing teacher knowledge is not limited to the context of EAP, but rather serves to illustrate how studies conducted in the field of academic language teaching can help inform other disciplines. The model in Figure 7 is one that can be applied to any context where teachers are undergoing continuing professional development in the workplace. This is particularly true of any context that realises the value of teacher development, and the importance of placing teachers at the centre of higher education's activity systems. Furthermore, within this framework none of the principle categories are restricted in belonging to an EAP context alone. On the contrary, these categories are applicable, relevant and transferable across all disciplinary and even institutional contexts. Every developmental situation requires **input variables** alongside some form of **output for evaluation**, and **sociocultural influences**

that can be shaped to meet developmental needs. Simultaneously, of course, there are always going to be particular **sociocultural influences** beyond the control of either teachers or teacher educators. This is an accepted truth not just in education but in life, as outlined in such works as Wenger's seminal study of claims processors in his work on Communities of Practice (1998), and Engeström's adaptations of Activity Theory (1999; 2001). Thus, an EAP context can be used to generate research that will have as much of a real-world impact as that of any other discipline within the academy, from Accountancy to Zoology.

Rather than being a 'poor relation' of more specific subjects in higher education (Hamp-Lyons, 2011, p. 91) or the purveyor of a 'butler stance' (Raimes, 1991, p. 243), an EAP context has actually proven itself to be a fertile source of knowledge for other disciplines and the overarching educational domain in which it operates. A second contribution to teaching has been to highlight how a better understanding of technology's usage inside and outside the classroom can influence a broader rethinking and reshaping of practice in other areas. Paradoxically, in a sense, an increased awareness of technology's usage in the classroom actually leads to its greater invisibility, and more natural rather than forced integration. In the case of the four main teachers discussed in this study, as technology became embedded in their everyday work, there was a simultaneous questioning of their own pedagogy, and other areas of practice. This supports views held not just in the TPACK literature but also in work relating to Activity Theory, particularly that which goes back to its Vygotskian origins, as outlined by Manning & Payne (1993).

In order for development to occur, teachers needed to go back and re-examine old practices in light of new knowledge, such as Kelly's act of reshaping communicative activities or Rosemary designing a series of quizzes following acquisition of deepened understanding of Moodle's affordances. Thus, it was not only teachers' knowledge and practice that were being reshaped, but also the role of tools themselves within the broader system of activity. Some of these tools, such as Harry's iPads and Matthew's podcasts, were later reconfigured for new and 'customized pedagogic purposes', as suggested by Koehler & Mishra (2009, p. 66). Much of this took place through teachers developing a heightened sense of self-direction, as proposed by Mann (2005).

Since this is very much a part of what is needed in today's teaching context, not just in EAP per se but in the increasingly digitised terrain of higher education (Hamp- Lyons, 2011), this study can thus serve as an example, and even an exemplar (Kuhn, 1987), of what happens when teachers are directed towards a questioning of their own pedagogy, and guided in usage and integration of new technologies into their teaching. Thus, even though those such as Ball et al (2008) might argue that different disciplines require differing representations of content, the shift towards questioning of personal pedagogies benefits teachers across subject areas.

Of course, the use of technologies in Mathematics is going to be different to an EAP context, but the quest for synergy in elements of knowledge is the same. As in Shulman's more contemporary line of thought (Garritz, 2013), the emphasis is not so much on micro aspects of content but on macro. Thus the instances of TPACK in EAP, as described by Kirk (2012), involve the same underlying principles of representing content as those found in contemporary examples of the model being put into practice in other everyday situations beyond the teaching of Academic English in higher education. These include the work of a group of Australian teachers who are running a Science project known as *'Possum Magic'*, in which children monitor the lives of possums in Queensland on real-time classroom computers, instead of learning about them in books (Armstrong, 2014). Use of technology for innovative practices, of course, is nothing new and has been happening for decades but it is the representation of content that makes something an enactment of TPACK, regardless of the micro features of the subject matter.

12.3 – Summary of practical developments and benefits

Benefits of the study for the research setting and the discipline

Since this research was originally shaped by needs arising in the workplace, it is important that there was a contribution to the language centre, and the lives of the teachers who work(ed) there. Without betraying the values of this study, with its emphasis on allowing the voices of the teachers to come to the fore, I believe that there has been a significant contribution to their practice. Clearly, as can be tracked over time, there have been major developments in the way that they use technologies in the classroom, and also their understanding of EAP as a subject, and EAP teaching as a profession. Their actions as a result of the workshops, whether directly or as a possible by-product of collaboration and exploration, as in Harry's iPad project, have also had a significant impact on shaping and reshaping the broader activity system of the language centre in which they worked.

Added to this, I would hope that those teachers whose stories did not feature in the final analysis and report have also developed along the way, because even though these participants may be 'background cases' (Seawright & Gerring, 2008, p. 294) in terms of their role in this book, the developments that occurred in their practice over the course of the study are of equal importance. Furthermore, the stories of the teachers who took part in this research study should provide strong evidence that it is unfair to label those who work for private providers of EAP courses as somehow being less qualified or contributing to existential damage to the profession. Indeed, those within EAP who treat the staff of private providers as such are simply mirroring the very attitudes we have to come to despise when directed at us from others further up the perceived hierarchy of academic disciplines. To paraphrase a not so celebrated politician of recent times, we are all in this together in terms of the battle to have EAP recognised as a serious discipline, regardless of our workplace. EAP will always occupy a position on the margins of academia until we find a way of getting across the message that we have much to contribute to the broader world of higher education beyond our own hermetically sealed environments.

Practical guidance for teacher educators in other disciplines

Although the teachers in this study were working in a particular subject area, there are lessons for teacher educators not just in EAP and ELT, as argued before, but in the context of teacher education as a whole. The lessons learned from this study go far beyond the boundaries of English Language teaching, and can be applied across any number of courses and situations. The need for synergy of technology, pedagogy, and content is as relevant for primary school educators as for EAP teachers, or for postgraduate trainees undertaking a certificate in Further Education. Some aspects of context and many aspects of activity are going to be different in each situation, but the underlying principles, going back to the work of Shulman (1986), seem to be consistent.

Therefore, the first lesson for teacher educators is that drawing on TPACK in teacher education opens up a filter for teachers to question other areas of their practice and pedagogy, and develop these as a consequence. The second is that creating a sense of community in the workplace, whether organic or 'cultivated', as suggested by Wenger & Snyder (2000), can lead to increased forms of collaboration, exploration, and more self-directed practices. However, in line with Vygotskian perspectives on teacher education, there is still a need to activate knowledge at the outset (Manning & Payne, 1993). A further lesson is that technology has opened up tremendous potential for linking together knowledge and actions, in such a way that it is now more possible to observe knowledge in action. Technology can serve as a means of putting knowledge into practice, and of providing foundations and examples of ways in which teachers can develop. Furthermore, an emphasis on knowledge in action allows teachers to have that development evaluated in a practical manner that can be either qualitative, as in this study, or quantitative, as in possible future studies. Finally, a study such as this could be easily replicated in other contexts, though naturally the individual stories will be very different.

12.4 – Closing thoughts and lessons learned from this study

Reflecting back on Robert Yin's (2009, p. 29) likening of any research journey to that of Christopher Columbus setting out to find the new world, this study has mapped out new terrain in terms of teacher knowledge. There have been few studies that have used a theoretical framework of this nature and none, as far as I am aware, within the field of EAP, wherein there is perhaps a lack of doctoral studies in the first instance. My study has made contributions to knowledge, methodological understandings, and professional development, not just for EAP but teaching as a whole. As such, I hope that in the longer term, others may judge it to have served as one of those exemplar cases demanded by Shulman (1986) and Kuhn (1987), to provide valuable sources of information on the knowledge base of teaching.

Above all, though, this has been a human story, not just of the four main cases (*Harry, Kelly, Matthew, and Rosemary*), but all nine participants in the focus groups. Special mention should also go to all those who participated in the teacher education workshops, and the later 'generations' of teachers who joined the workplace community of practice. Perhaps the main contribution on a professional level is the notion that for teachers to progress on the developmental continuum, there has to be an embedding of knowledge and a strengthened sense of self-direction in their practice. Such a stance originates in Vygotskian perspectives on how we develop as human beings, and fits in very well with the ethos of academia and EAP, but to date has not played a major part in preparing teachers for the higher educational context.

Ideally, as we move towards ever greater incorporation of new technologies in our classrooms and an increasing emphasis on the student experience, teachers should be offered bottom-up, rather than top-down, opportunities for partnership in shaping the course of their own professional development. Too often, the voices of teachers are not given enough attention in determining their needs and ultimately the needs of students. This can mean that the existing knowledge base of practice and experience that teachers bring to the classroom is often overlooked at the expense of keeping up to date with new 'fashions and fads' that are today's hot topics and in danger of going cold tomorrow (Alvesson & Sandberg, 2013, p. 20).

The TPACK framework clearly shows that technological knowledge is not based upon understanding the affordances of the latest gadgets to enter the techno-corporate matrix. Rather, it is about understanding how to integrate resources into teaching so that they become as naturalised and unobtrusive as the periodic table on the walls of Science classrooms. We have come far from Shulman's (1986; 1987) rudimentary outline of teacher knowledge but, even though gaps still remain, there is a growing sense that development occurs not just by filling in the blank squares with new knowledge. Instead, such development comes about through drawing upon existing knowledge and practice, and by envisioning this developmental continuum as a spiral (Manning & Payne, 1993). Support for this stance comes in the developments in the practice of the four teachers who formed the essence of this study, through the ways in which they found synergy not just in the components of TPACK but also in synthesising this new knowledge with past experience and their personal philosophies.

Looking back, then, on the full landscape of this research journey, there has been a significant contribution to the fields of teacher education and teacher knowledge. Above all, it has served as an example of what can be achieved if strong foundations for development are established from the outset. That was done, in the first instance, through needs analysis and a carefully layered 'intra-muscular approach' (Breen, 2013) to teacher development. On the basis of such foundations, educational workshops constituted the next phase, alongside ana-lytical and observational frameworks used to synthesise developments in the teachers' practice and knowledge. Through this parallel process of education and analysis, the importance of pedagogy and personalised, student centred ways of teaching came to the fore, reinforcing long-held values and principles of English Language Teaching. Ultimately, then, as has been the case since the earliest days of computers blended into the world of classroom instruction, EAP has much to offer in the lessons it can provide for all those seeking to develop educators for this digital age.

APPENDICES

Appendix 1 – BALEAP Competency Statements

Summary of BALEAP Competency Statement (2008, p. 3)

Summary of competency statements

Academic practice	an EAP teacher will –
Academic contexts	have a reasonable knowledge of the organizational, educational and communicative policies, practices, values and conventions of universities.
Disciplinary differences	be able to recognize and explore disciplinary differences and how they influence the way knowledge is expanded and communicated.
Academic discourse	have a high level of systemic language knowledge including knowledge of discourse analysis.
Personal learning, development and autonomy	recognize the importance of applying to his or her own practice the standards expected of students and other academic staff.
EAP students	**an EAP teacher will understand –**
Student needs	the requirements of the target context that students wish to enter as well as the needs of students in relation to their prior learning experiences and how these might influence their current educational expectations.
Student critical thinking	the role of critical thinking in academic contexts and will employ tasks, processes and interactions that require students to demonstrate critical thinking skills.
Student autonomy	the importance of student autonomy in academic contexts and will employ tasks, processes and interactions that require students to work effectively in groups or independently as appropriate.
Curriculum development	**an EAP teacher will understand –**
Syllabus and programme development	the main types of language syllabus and will be able to transform a syllabus into a programme that addresses students' needs in the academic context within which the EAP course is located.
Text processing and text production	approaches to text classification and discourse analysis and will be able to organize courses, units and tasks around whole texts or text segments in ways that develop students' processing and production of spoken and written texts.
Programme implementation	**an EAP teacher will be –**
Teaching practices	familiar with the methods, practices and techniques of communicative language teaching and be able to locate these within an academic context and relate them to teaching the language and skills required by academic tasks and processes.
Assessment practices	able to assess academic language and skills tasks using formative and summative assessment.

Appendix 2 – ISTE Observation Tool

Original ISTE Classroom Observation Tool (ICOT)

1. Setting:		
Date:	Observation Start Time/End Time:	# Students:

2. Room Description and Student Characteristics

3. Student Groupings (check all observed during the period)	
Individual student work	Small groups
Student pairs	Whole class
Other (please comment):	

4. Teacher roles (check all observed during the period)	
Lecturing	Interactive direction
Discussion	Facilitating/coaching
Modeling	Other (please comment):

5. Learning activities (check all observed during the period)	
Creating presentations	Test taking
Research	Information analysis
Writing	Simulations
Drill and practice	Hands-on skill training
Other (please comment):	

6. How essential was technology to the teaching and learning activities?	
Not needed; other approaches would be better.	Somewhat useful; other approaches would be as effective.
Useful; other approaches would not be as effective.	Essential; the lesson could not be done without it.
Other (please comment):	

7. Technologies used by teacher (check all observed during the period):

Blog	Calculator CD-ROM	Database Data Projector Desktop Computer Digital Camera Document Camera Drill/Practice	E-mail
Graphics	Interactive Whiteboard	Laptop Computer Library Database	Mobile Learning Device
Netbook	Outliner	Podcast Presentation	Response System (Clicker)
Science Probe Simulation Spreadsheet	Tablet Computer	Video Camera Videoconferencing	Web Authoring Web Browser Web 2.0 Tool Wiki Wireless Slate Word Processing

Other (please comment):

8. Technologies used by students (check all observed during the period):

Blog	Calculator CD-ROM	Database Data Projector Desktop Computer Digital Camera Document Camera Drill/Practice	E-mail
Graphics	Interactive Whiteboard	Laptop Computer Library Database	Mobile Learning Device
Netbook	Outliner	Podcast Presentation	Response System (Clicker)
Science Probe Simulation Spreadsheet	Tablet Computer	Video Camera Videoconferencing	Web Authoring Web Browser Web 2.0 Tool Wiki Wireless Slate Word Processing

Other (please comment):

9. Oregon Technology Standards (choose all standards that apply):

ET.1 Creativity and Innovation: Students demonstrate creative thinking and problem solving skills to develop innovative products and processes using (digital) technology.

ET.2 Communication and Collaboration: Students use digital media and environments to communicate and work collaboratively, across the global community, to support individual learning and contribute to the learning of others. ET.3 Research and Information Fluency: Students select and apply digital tools to gather, evaluate, validate, and use information.

ET.4 Critical Thinking, Problem Solving and Decision Making: Students use critical thinking skills to plan and conduct research, manage projects, solve problems, and make informed decisions using appropriate digital tools and resources. ET.5 Digital Citizenship: Students understand human, cultural, and societal issues related to digital technology and practice legal, ethical, and responsible behavior.

ET.6 Technology Operations and Concepts: Students utilize technology concepts and tools to learn.

Comments:

10. Three-Minute Chart

During each 3-minute period, was technology *in use* by students and/or teachers, and was the time spent with technology used *for teaching and learning* (as opposed to recreation or routine tasks, such as boot-up and log on)?

Technology is:	00-03	03-06	06-09	09-12	12-15	15-18	18-21	21-24	24-27	27-30	30-33	33-36	36-39	39-42	42-45	45-48	48-51	51-54
Used by students																		
Used for learning																		
Used by teacher																		
Used for learning																		

11. Estimated Time Technology Used (if 3-minute chart is not used)

Total minutes technology used by students: Minutes students used for learning:
Total minutes technology used by teacher: Minutes teachers used for learning:

12. Any other comments?

Source: The International Society for Technology in Education (ISTE) – https://www.iste.org. Last Accessed 10-07-2014 at http://iste.org/icot. Currently available at: www.iste.org/docs/excel-files/icot.xlsm?sfvrsn=2

Notes

1. Acronym for 'Teaching English as a Second or Other Language'
2. In this work I prefer the term 'teacher education' for epistemological reasons, but in the case of this course that I studied the preferred term was 'teacher training.'
3. Again, the actual term used by teachers themselves rather than that which fits in best with my epistemological position.
4. Technology should be used 'not for its own sake, but for the sake of advancing student learning and understanding' (2009, p. 66).

References

Aitken, J. 1998. *The Capable Teacher, 2* (Summer 1998). Accessed in BALEAP Competency Framework for Teachers of EAP.

Alexander, O., S. Argent, and J. Spencer. 2008. *EAP Essentials: A Teacher's Guide to Principles and Practice.* Reading: Garnet Publishing.

Alexander, O. 2010. 'The Leap into TEAP: The role of the BALEAP competency framework in the professional development of new EAP teachers'. In *Joint Conference IATEFL English for Specific Purposes SIG Bilkent University.* (29).

Alexander, O., D. Sloan, & E. Porter. 2011. 'Not just some random English class: Raising the profile of in-sessional provision through the CEM model'. In *BALEAP Conference, April 2011,* (pp. 10–12).

Alvesson, M., and J. Sandberg. 2013. *Constructing Research Questions: Doing Interesting Research.* London: Sage Publications.

Allwright, D. and J. Hanks. 2009. *The Developing Language Learner.* Basingstoke: Palgrave Macmillan.

Angeli, C., and N. Valanides. 2008. 'TPCK in pre-service teacher education: Preparing primary education students to teach with technology'. In *Annual Meeting of the American Educational Research Association New York City.*

ArcelorMittal. 2010. *ArcelorMittal Orbit Brochure.* Last accessed at http://arcelor mittalsa.com/Portals/0/Orbit%20Brochure.pdf 17 April 217.

Argyris, C., and D. A. Schön. 1974. *Theory in Practice: Increasing Professional Effectiveness.* San Francisco: Jossey-Bass.

Arksey, H., and P. Knight. 1999. *Interviewing for Social Scientists*. London: Sage Publications.

Armstrong, B. 2014. 'Possum magic: Embedding technology in deep learning'. Brooke Armstrong blog, 2 September 2014. Accessed at https://brookearm strongblog.wordpress.com, 18 November 2014.

Arnold, J. 1999. *Affect in Language Learning*. Cambridge: Cambridge University Press.

Atkinson, P. and M. Hammersley. 1994. 'Ethnography and participant observation'. In: *Handbook of Qualitative Research*, edited by N. Denzin and Y. Lincoln. London: Sage Publications, pp. 248–259.

Attia, M. 2011. *Teacher Cognition and the Use of Technology in Teaching Arabic to Speakers of Other Languages*. (PhD). Manchester: The University of Manchester.

Attia, M. 2014. 'The role of early learning experience in shaping teacher cognition and technology use'. In *Cases on Teacher Identity, Diversity, and Cognition in Higher Education* (pp. 1–21). Hershey, PA: IGI Global.

Bailey, K.M., A. Curtis and D. Nunan. 2001. *Pursuing Professional Development: The Self as Source*. Boston: Heinle & Heinle.

BALEAP. 2008. *Competency framework for teachers of English for academic purposes*. Accessed at: http://www.baleap.org.uk/projects/eap-teacher-competencies 1 October 2013.

Ball, D. L., M. H. Thames, and G. Phelps. 2008. Content knowledge for teaching what makes it special? *Journal of Teacher Education* 59(5): 389–407. DOI: https://doi.org/10.1177/0022487108324554.

Barlow, M., and H. J. Robertson. 1994. *Class Warfare: The Assault on Canada's Schools*. Toronto: Key Porter Books.

Bartunek, J., and M. R. Louis. 1996. *Insider/Outsider Team Research*. Thousand Oaks, CA: Sage Publications.

Bax, S. 2003. 'CALL—past, present and future'. *System 31(1)*: 13–28. DOI: https://doi.org/10.1016/S0346–251X(02)00071–4.

Baxter, P., and S. Jack. 2008. 'Qualitative case study methodology: Study design and implementation for novice researchers'. *The Qualitative Report* 13(4), 544–59.

Beatty, K. 2003. *Teaching and Researching: Computer-Assisted Language Learning*. Harlow: Pearson Education.

Becker, H. J. 2000. 'Findings from the teaching, learning, and computing survey: Is Larry Cuban right?' *Education Policy Analysis Archives* 8, p. 51. DOI: https://doi.org/10.14507/epaa.v8n51.2000.

Beetham, H. and R. Sharpe. 2007. *Rethinking Pedagogy for a Digital Age: Designing and Delivering E-Learning*. Abingdon: Routledge.

Bell, Douglas E. 2016. *Practitioners, Pedagogies and Professionalism in English for Academic Purposes (EAP): The Development of a Contested Field*. PhD thesis. Nottingham: University of Nottingham.

Beloff, M. 1970. *The Plateglass Universities*. Cranbury, NJ: Fairleigh Dickinson University Press.

Benesch, S. 2001. *Critical English for Academic Purposes: Theory, Politics, and Practice*. Mahwah, NJ: Lawrence Erlbaum Associates.

Bennett, K. R. 2012. 'Less than a class set'. *Learning and Leading with Technology* 39(4), 22–25.

Bhatia, V. K. 2004. *Worlds of Written Discourse: A Genre-Based View*. London: Bloomsbury.

Bird, C. M. 2005. 'How I stopped dreading and learned to love transcription'. *Qualitative Inquiry* 11(2): 226–248. DOI: https://doi.org/10.1177/1077800404273413.

Blanchard, K. H. 2004. *Leadership Smarts*. Colorado Springs, CO: David C. Cook Publishers.

Blin, F. 2004. 'CALL and the development of learner autonomy: Towards an activity theoretical perspective'. *reCALL* 16(2): 377–395. DOI: https://doi.org/10.1017/S0958344004000928.

Bloom, B. S. 1956. *Taxonomy of Educational Objectives: Vol. 1: Cognitive Domain*. New York: McKay.

Blue, G. 1988. 'Individualising academic writing tuition'. In P. Robinson (Ed.), *Academic Writing: Process and Product* (pp. 95–99). ELT Documents 129. Available at https://www.teachingenglish.org.uk/sites/teacheng/files/ELT-14-screen_0.pdf

Bogdan, R. C., and S. K. Biklen. 1982. *Qualitative Research for Education: An Introduction to Theory and Methods*. Boston: Allyn & Bacon.

Borg, S. 1998. 'Teachers' pedagogical systems and grammar teaching: A qualitative study'. *Tesol Quarterly* 32(1): 9–38.

Borg, S. 2003. 'Teacher cognition in language teaching: A review of research on what language teachers think, know, believe, and do'. *Language teaching* 36(2): 81–109. DOI: https://doi.org/10.1017/S0261444803001903.

Borg, S. 2006. *Teacher Cognition and Language Education: Research and Practice*. London: Continuum.

Borko, H., J. Whitcomb, and D. Liston, D. 2009. 'Wicked problems and other thoughts on issues of technology and teacher learning'. *Journal of Teacher Education* 60(1): 3–7. DOI: https://doi.org/10.1177/0022487108328488.

Branzburg, J. 2008. The whiteboard revolution. *Technology & Learning* 28(9), 44: 46–7.

Breen, P. 2007. 'Lessons from an international e-learning project'. *The International Review of Research in Open and Distance Learning* 8(3). DOI: https://doi.org/10.19173/irrodl.v8i3.411.

Breen, P. 2013. 'An intramuscular approach to teacher development in the field of transnational higher education.' In *Handbook of Research on Transnational Higher Education Management*, edited by S. Mukerji and P. Tripathi. Hershey, PA: IGI Global.

Breen, P. 2014. *The Charlton Men*. London: Thames River Press.

Brinton, D. M., M. A. Snow, and M. B. Wesche. 1989. *Content-Based Second Language Instruction* (p. vii). New York: Newbury House.

British Sociological Research Association. 2002. *Statement of Ethical Practice*. Last accessed 14-07-2014 at – http://www.britsoc.co.uk/about/equality/statement-of-ethical-practice.aspx

Brockett, R.G., and R. Hiemstra. 1991. *Self-Direction in Learning: Perspectives in Theory, Research, and Practice*. Routledge: London, UK.

Brooks-Harris, J. E., and S. R. Stock-Ward. 1999. *Workshops: Designing and Facilitating Experiential Learning*. Thousand Oaks, CA: Sage Publications.

Bruner, J. 1985. 'Vygotsky: A historical and conceptual perspective'. In *Culture, Communication, and Cognition: Vygotskian Perspectives*, edited by J. V. Wertsch: pp.21–34. Cambridge: Cambridge University Press.

Burns, A. 1999. *Collaborative Action Research for English language Teachers*. Cambridge: Cambridge University Press.

Butler, M. 2007. 'Profiteer or prophet?' *English Language Gazette* 332.

Cafasso, J. 2015. 'What are intramuscular injections?' Article on *Health Line* website. Accessed at http://www.healthline.com/health/intramuscular-injection#intramuscular-injections1 16-04-2017.

Calderhead, J. 1981. 'Stimulated recall: A method for research on teaching'. *British Journal of Educational Psychology* 51(2): 211–17. DOI: https://doi.org/10.1111/j.2044–8279.1981.tb02474.x.

Çelik, S. and A. J. Simpson. 2013. 'The Many Faces of TPACK: Perspectives and Approaches'. In *English Language Teacher Education*, edited by E. Baran. The Wikimedia Foundation: Wikibooks / Wikimedia.

Chapelle, C. A. 2010. 'The spread of computer-assisted language learning'. *Language Teaching* 43(1): 66–74. DOI: https://doi.org/10.1017/S0261444 809005850.

De Chazal, E., S. McCarter, and L. Rogers. 2012. *Oxford EAP: A Course in English for Academic Purposes. [Student's Book]. Upper-intermediate/B2*. Oxford: Oxford University Press.

Clark, C. M., and P. L. Peterson. 1986. 'Teachers' thought processes'. In *Handbook of Research on Teaching*, edited by M. C. Wittrock, 3rd ed., pp. 255–96. New York: Macmillan.

Clark, R. E. 1983. 'Reconsidering research on learning from media'. *Review of Educational Research* 53(4): 445–59. DOI: https://doi.org/10.3102/003465430530044445.

Coffey, A., and P. Atkinson. 1996. *Making Sense of Qualitative Data: Complementary Research Strategies*. Thousand Oaks, CA: Sage Publications.

Coghlan, D. 2001. 'Insider action research projects: Implications for practising managers', *Management Learning* 32: 49–60. DOI: https://doi.org/10.1177/135050760132004.

Coghlan, D., and T. Brannick. 2009. *Doing Action Research in Your Own Organization*. London: Sage Publications.

Cohen, L. 1976. *Educational Research in Classrooms and Schools: A Manual of Materials and Methods*. London: Harper and Row.

Cohen, L., Manion, L., & Morrison, K. (2013). *Research Methods in Education*. New York. Routledge

Cole, J., and H. Foster. 2007 *Using Moodle: Teaching With the Popular Open Source Course Management System*. Sebastopol, CA: O'Reilly Media, Inc.

Crandall, J. J. 2000. Language teacher education. *Annual Review of Applied Linguistics* 20: 34–55. DOI: https://doi.org/10.1017/S0267190500200032.

Creswell, J. W., and D. L. Miller. 2000. 'Determining validity in qualitative inquiry'. *Theory Into Practice* 39(3): 124–30. DOI: https://doi.org/10.1207/s15430421tip3903_2.

Creswell, J. 2009. *Research Design: Qualitative, Quantitative, and Mixed Methods Approaches*. London: Sage Publications.

Crookes, G., and P. M. Chandler. 2001. 'Introducing action research into the education of postsecondary foreign language teachers'. *Foreign Language Annals* 34(2): 131–140. DOI: https://doi.org/10.1111/j.1944–9720.2001.tb02818.x.

Cuban, L. 2003. *Oversold and Underused: Computers in the Classroom*. Cambridge, MA: Harvard University Press.

Cummins, J. 2000. 'Academic language learning, transformative pedagogy, and information technology: Towards a critical balance'. *TESOL Quarterly* 34(3): 537–48. DOI: https://doi.org/10.2307/3587742.

Darling-Hammond L., and N. Richardson. 2009. 'Teacher learning: What matters?' *Educational Leadership* 66(5): 46–53.

Denzin, N. K., and Y. Lincoln. 2000. *Qualitative Research*. CA: Thousand Oaks.

Dewey, J., and A. W. Small. 1897. *My Pedagogic Creed* (No. 25). New York, NY: E. L. Kellogg & Company.

Diaz-Maggioli, G. 2004. *Teacher-Centered Professional Development*. Alexandria, VA: ASCD.

Dickenson, P. 2014. 'Redesigning teacher education programs to meet the needs of today's second career pre-service teachers', pp. 61–86 in *Cases on Teacher Identity, Diversity, and Cognition in Higher Education*, edited by Breen, P. (2014). Hershey, PA: IGI Global.

Ding, A., and I. Bruce. 2017. 'Overview of the book: The status of EAP and the identity of the practitioner'. In *The English for Academic Purposes Practitioner*: pp. 1–12. London: Palgrave Macmillan.

Donaghue, H. 2003. 'An instrument to elicit teachers' beliefs and assumptions'. *ELT Journal* 57(4): 344–51. DOI: https://doi.org/doi.org/10.1093/elt/57.4.344.

Dörnyei, Z., and S. Thurrell. 1991. 'Strategic competence and how to teach it'. *ELT Journal* 45(1): 16–23. DOI: https://doi.org/10.1093/elt/45.1.16.

Dörnyei, Z. 2001. *Motivational Strategies in the Language Classroom*. Cambridge: Cambridge University Press.

Dudley-Evans, T., and M. J. St. John. 2009. *Developments in English for Specific Purposes*. Cambridge: Cambridge University Press.

Economic and Social Research Council. 2005. *Research Ethics Framework (REF)*. Swindon: ESRC Publications.

Edge, J. 2003. 'Teacher development (MSc TESOL Module)'. Birmingham: Aston University.

Edge, J. 2005. 'Build it and they will come: Realising values in ESOL teacher education'. In *Second Language Teacher Education: International Perspectives*, edited by D. J. Tedick: pp. 181–198. Mahwah, NJ: Lawrence Erlbaum.

Edwards, B. 2002. 'Deep insider research'. *Qualitative Research Journal* 2(1): 71–84.

Elbaz, F. 1991. 'Research on teacher's knowledge: The evolution of a discourse'. *J. Curriculum Studies* 23(1): 1–19. DOI: https://doi.org/10.1080/0022027910230101.

Eliot, T. S. 1944 [1943]. 'Little Gidding'. In *Four Quartets* (pp. 144–145). London: Faber & Faber.

Ellis, C., and L. Berger. 2003. 'Their story/my story/our story'. In *Inside Interviewing: New Lenses, New Concerns*, edited by J. A. Holstein and J. F. Gubrium: 467–93. Thousand Oaks, CA: Sage Publications.

Ellis, R. 1986. 'Activities and procedures for teacher training'. *ELT Journal* 40(2): 91–99. DOI: https://doi.org/10.1093/elt/40.2.91

Ellis, R. 1997. 'SLA and language pedagogy'. *Studies in Second language acquisition* 19(01), pp.69–92.

Engeström, Y. 1999. 'Activity theory and individual and social transformation'. In Y. Engeström, R. Miettinen & R-L. Punamäki-Gitai (eds.) *Perspectives on Activity Theory*: pp.19–38. Cambridge: Cambridge University Press.

Engeström, Y. 2001. 'Expansive learning at work: Toward an activity theoretical reconceptualization'. *Journal of Education and Work* 14(1): 133–56. DOI: https://doi.org/10.1080/13639080020028747.

Eshet-Alkalai, Y. 2004. 'Digital literacy: A conceptual framework for survival skills in the digital era'. *Journal of Educational Multimedia and Hypermedia* 13(1): 93–106.

Fenwick, T., and R. Edwards. 2010. *Actor-Network Theory in Education*. Abingdon: Routledge.

Freeman, D. 1983. *Margaret Mead and the Heretic: The Making and Unmaking of an Anthropological Myth*. New York: Penguin.

Freeman, D. 1996. 'Redefining the relationship between research and what teachers know'. In *Voices from the Language Classroom: Qualitative Research on Language Education*, edited by K. M. Bailey & D. Nunan: pp. 88–115. New York: Cambridge University Press

Freeman, D. 2002. 'The hidden side of the work: Teacher knowledge and learning'. *Language teaching* 35: 1–13. DOI: https://doi.org/10.1017/S0261444801001720.

Garton, S., and K. Richards. 2007. 'Is distance education for teachers second best?' *The Teacher Trainer* 21(3): 5–8.

Garrett, N. 1991. 'Technology in the service of language learning: Trends and issues'. *The Modern Language Journal*, 75(1): 74–101.

Garritz, A. 2013. 'PCK for dummies'. *Educación Química* 24/2: 462–65

Garrison, D. R. 1988. 'Andragogy, learner-centredness and the educational transaction at a distance'. *Journal of Distance Education* 3(2): 123–7.

Gibbons, M., and P. Norman. 1987. 'An integrated model for sustained staff development'. In *Staff Development for School Improvement: A Focus on the Teacher*, edited by M. F. Wideen & I. Andrews: pp. 103–110. London: Falmer Press.

Gilbert, J. 2013. 'English for academic purposes'. In *Innovations in Learning Technologies for English Language Teaching*, edited by G. Motteram. London: British Council.

Glaser, B., and A. Strauss. 1967. *The Discovery of Grounded Theory*. London: Weidenfield & Nicolson.

Glassner, B., and J. Loughlin. 1987. *Drugs in Adolescent Worlds: Burnouts to Straights*. Basingstoke: Macmillan.

Glesne, C., and A. Peshkin. 1992. *Becoming Qualitative Researchers: An Introduction:* p. 6. White Plains, NY: Longman.

Gonyea, R. M. 2005. 'Self-reported data in institutional research: Review and recommendations'. *New Directions for Institutional Research* 127: 73. DOI: https://doi.org/10.1002/ir.156.

Goodwyn, A. 1997. *Developing English Teachers: The Role of Mentorship in a Reflective Profession*. Buckingham: Open University Press.

Greene, J. C. and V. J. Caracelli. 1997. 'Defining and describing the paradigm issues in mixed-method evaluation'. In *Advances in Mixed-Method Evaluation: The Challenges and Benefits of Integrating Diverse Paradigms*, edited by J. C. Greene, and V. J. Caracelli: pp. 5–18. San Francisco: Jossey-Bass.

Hadley, G. 2014. *English For Academic Purposes in Neoliberal Universities: A Critical Grounded Theory*. Cham: Springer.

Hall, J. 2010. 'Mind boggling artwork that will tower over London'. *The Independent* 31 March. Available at http://www.independent.co.uk/arts-entertainment/architecture/mind-boggling-artwork-that-will-tower-over-london-1932413.html

Ham, V. 2010. 'Technology as Trojan horse'. In *Researching IT in Education: Theory, Practice, and Future Directions*, edited by A. McDougall, J. Murnane, A. Jones, and N. Reynolds, pp. 25–38. New York, NY: Routledge

Hammersley, M. and P. Atkinson. 1983. *Ethnography: Principles in Practice*. London: Tavistock.

Hammersley, M. 1993. 'On the teacher as researcher'. In *Educational Research: Volume One; Current Issues*, edited by M. Hammersley. London, Paul Chapman Publishing Limited/The Open University.

Hammersley, M. and A. Traianou. 2012. *Ethics in Qualitative Research: Controversies and Contexts*. London: Sage Publications.

Hamp-Lyons, L. 2011 'English for academic purposes'. In *Handbook of Research In Second Language Teaching And Learning (Volume 2)*, edited by E. Hinkel, pp. 89–105. New York: Routledge.

Harmer, J. 1991. *The Practice of English Language Teaching*. Harlow: Longman.

Harris, J. B. 2008. 'TPACK in inservice education: Assisting experienced teachers' planned improvisations'. In *Handbook of Technological Pedagogical Content Knowledge for Educators*, edited by AACTE Committee on Innovation and Technology. pp. 251–71. New York: Routledge.

Harris, J., P. Mishra, and M. Koehler. 2009. 'Teachers' technological pedagogical content knowledge and learning activity types: Curriculum-based technology integration reframed'. *Journal of Research on Technology in Education* 41(4). DOI: https://doi.org/10.1080/15391523.2009.10782536.

Hargreaves, A., and E. Tucker. 1991. 'Teaching and guilt: Exploring the feelings of teaching'. *Teaching and Teacher Education* 7(5): 491–505. DOI: https://doi.org/10.1016/0742–051X(91)90044-P.

Hawkins, B. S. R. 1990. *The Management of Staff Development in A Contracting Education Service* (Ph.D. thesis) Birmingham, Birmingham Polytechnic.

Hitchcock, G., and D. Hughes. 1995. *Research and The Teacher: A Qualitative Introduction to School-Based Research*. London: Routledge.

Hockey, J. 1993. 'Research methods researching peers and familiar settings'. *Research Papers in Education* 8 (2): 199–225. DOI: https://doi.org/10.1080/0267152930080205.

Hofer, M., and K. O. Swan. 2008. 'Technological pedagogical content knowledge in action: A case study of a middle school digital documentary project'. *Journal of Research on Technology in Education* 41(2): 179–200. DOI: https://doi.org/10.1080/15391523.2008.10782528.

Holstein, J. A., and J. F. Gubrium. 1997. 'Active Interviewing'. In: Silverman, D. (Ed.). *Qualitative Research: Theory, method and practice*. London: Sage Publications.

Holstein, J., and J. F. Gubrium. 2003. *Inside Interviewing: New Lenses, New Concerns*. Thousand Oaks, CA: Sage Publications.

Hung, D.W., and D. T. Chen. 2001. 'Situated cognition, Vygotskian thought and learning from the communities of practice perspective: Implications for the design of web-based e-learning'. *Educational Media International, 38*(1): 3–12. DOI: https://doi.org/10.1080/09523980121818.

Hutchinson, T. and A. Waters. 1987. *English for Specific Purposes*. Cambridge: Cambridge University Press.

Hyland, K. 2003. 'Genre-based pedagogies: A social response to process'. *Journal of Second Language Writing* 12: 17–29. DOI: https://doi.org/10.1016/S1060–3743(02)00124–8.

Hyland, K. 2006. *English For Academic Purposes: An Advanced Resource Book*. London: Routledge.

Hyland, K., and L. Hamp-Lyons. 2002. 'EAP: issues and directions'. *Journal of English for Academic Purposes* 1(1): 1–12. DOI: https://doi.org/10.1016/S1475–1585(02)00002–4.

Jackson, P. 1968. *Life in Classrooms*. New York: Holt, Rinehart & Winston.

Jarvis, H. A. 2009. 'Computers in EAP: Change, issues and challenges'. *Modern English Teacher* 8(2): 51–54.

Jarvis, H., and M. Achilleos. 2013. 'From Computer Assisted Language Learning (CALL) to Mobile Assisted Language Use (MALU)'. *Tesl-Ej*, 16(4): 1–18.

Jenkins, J. 2013. *English as a Lingua Franca in the International University: The Politics of Academic English Language Policy*. Abingdon: Routledge.

Joffe, H., and L. Yardley. 2003. 'Content and thematic analysis'. In *Research Methods for Clinical and Health Psychology*, edited by D. F. Marks and L. Yardley, pp. 56–69. London Sage Publications:

Johns, T. F. 1981. 'Some problems of a world-wide profession'. In *The ESP Teacher: Role, Development and Prospects. ELT Documents: 112, edited by* J. McDonough and T. French. London: British Council

Johnson, N. F., D. C. MacDonald, and T. F. Brabazon. 2008. 'Rage against the machine? Symbolic violence in elearning supported tertiary education'. *ELearning* 5(3): 275–283. DOI: https://doi.org/10.2304/elea.2008.5.3.275.

Jones, S., and M. R. Lea. 2008. 'Digital literacies in the lives of undergraduate students: Exploring personal and curricular spheres of practice'. *Electronic Journal of E-learning* 6(3).

Jordan, R. R. 2002. 'The growth of EAP in Britain'. *Journal of English for Academic Purposes* 1(1): 69–78. DOI: https://doi.org/10.1016/S1475–1585(02)00004–8.

Judson, E. 2006. 'How teachers integrate technology and their beliefs about learning: Is there a connection?' *Journal of Technology and Teacher Education*, 14(3): 581.

Kavanagh, P. 1967. 'The Parish and the Universe'. *Collected Prose*, pp.281–283. London: McGibbon and Kee.

Kear, K. 2011. *Online and Social Networking Communities: A Best Practices Guide for Educators*. New York: Routledge.

Kerstetter, K. 2012. 'Insider, outsider, or somewhere in between: The impact of researchers' identities on the community-based research process'. *Journal of Rural Social Sciences* 27(2): p.99.

Kimble, C., Grenier, C., and K. Goglio-Primard. 2010. 'Innovation and knowledge sharing across professional boundaries: Political interplay between boundary objects and brokers'. *International Journal of Information Management*, 30(5): 437–44. DOI: https://doi.org/10.1016/j.ijinfomgt.2010.02.002.

King, A. 1993. 'From sage on the stage to guide on the side'. *College Teaching* 41(1): 30–5.

Kirk, S. 2012. *'Building e-AP Awareness'*. Blog post on *The TEAPing Point* blog 9 December. Available at https://theteapingpoint.wordpress.com/2012/12/09/building-e-ap-awareness/

Klatt, B. 1999. *The Ultimate Training Workshop Handbook: A Comprehensive Guide to Leading Successful Workshops and Training Programs*. New York: McGraw Hill.

Knorr-Cetina, K. D. 1981. *The Micro-Sociological Challenge of Macro-Sociology: Towards A Reconstruction Of Social Theory And Methodology.* Boston: Routledge & Kegan Paul: pp. 1–47.

Koehler, M., and P. Mishra. 2009. 'What is technological pedagogical content knowledge (TPACK)?'. *Contemporary Issues in Technology and Teacher Education* 9(1): 60–70.

Kolb, D. A. 1984. *Experiential Learning: Experience as The Source of Learning And Development,* Upper Saddle River, NJ: Prentice Hall.

Korte, L. 2007. *Moodle Magic: Make It Happen.* FTC Publishing Inc.

Krashen, S. D. 1981. *Second Language Acquisition and Second Language Learning.* Oxford: Oxford University Press.

Krashen, S. D. 1982. *Principles and Practice in Second Language Acquisition.* Prentice-Hall: Englewood Cliffs.

Kuhn, T. 1987. 'What are Scientific Revolutions?' In *The Probabilistic Revolution,* edited by L. Krüger, L. Daston, and M. Heidelberger Cambridge, MA: MIT Press.

Kvale, S. 1996. *Interviews: An Introduction to Qualitative Research Interviewing.* London: Sage Publications.

Lam, Y. 2000. 'Technophilia vs. technophobia: A preliminary look at why second-language teachers do or do not use technology in their classrooms'. *Canadian Modern Language Review* 56(3): 390–420. DOI: https://doi.org/10.3138/cmlr.56.3.389.

Laurillard, D. 1993/2002. *Rethinking University Teaching: A Conversational Framework for the Effective Use of Learning Technologies.* New York: Routledge.

Lave, J. and E. Wenger. 1991. *Situated Learning: Legitimate Peripheral Participation.* New York: Cambridge University Press. DOI: https://doi.org/10.1080/03075071003664021.

Lea, M. R., and S. Jones. 2011. 'Digital literacies in higher education: Exploring textual and technological practice'. *Studies in Higher Education* 36(4): 377–93. DOI: https://doi.org/0.1080/03075071003664021.

Leedy, P. D., and J. E. Ormrod. 2005. *Practical Research: Planning and Design.* Upper Saddle River, NJ: Pearson Education.

Lewin, K. 1946. 'Action research and minority problems'. *Journal of Social Issues* 2(4): 34–46. DOI: https://doi.org/10.1111/j.1540–4560.1946.tb02295.x.

Lincoln, Y. S., and E. G. Guba. 1985. *Naturalistic Inquiry.* Newbury Park, CA: Sage Publications.

Lincoln, Y. S., and N. K. Denzin, eds. 2003. *Turning Points in Qualitative Research: Tying Knots in a Handkerchief.* Walnut Creek, CA: Rowman Altamira.

Little, D. 1991. *Learner Autonomy: Definitions, Issues and Problems, 4:* 33. Dublin: Authentik Language Learning.

Macallister, C. and S. Kirk. 2013. 'Plausibility, power and progress: Enhancing student language learning through professional collaboration'. Paper presented at AULC Conference, Durham University, 10 January.

McCormick, R. and P. Scrimshaw. 2001. 'Information and communications technology, knowledge, and pedagogy'. *Education, Communication and Information* 1(1): 37–57. DOI: https://doi.org/10.1080/14636310120048047

McGrath, J., G. Karabas, and J. Willis. 2011. 'From TPACK concept to TPACK practice: An analysis of the suitability and usefulness of the concept as a guide in the real world of teacher development'. *International Journal of Technology in Teaching and Learning* 7(1).

Maddux, C. D. and D. L. Johnson. 2011. 'Technology in education and the concept of cultural momentum'. *Computers in the Schools*, 28(1): 1–4. DOI: https://doi.org/10.1080/07380569.2011.553150.

Malone, S. 2003. 'Ethics at home: Informed consent in your own backyard'. *Qualitative Studies in Education* 16(6): 797–815. DOI: https://doi.org/10.10 80/0951839030100001632153.

Mann, S. J. 2005. 'The language teacher's development'. *Language teaching* 38(3): 103–18. DOI: https://doi.org/10.1017/S0261444805002867.

Manning, B. H., and B. D. Payne. 1993. 'A Vygotskian-based theory of teacher cognition: Toward the acquisition of mental reflection and self-regulation'. *Teaching and Teacher Education* 9(4): 361–71. DOI: https://doi.org/10.1016/0742–051X(93)90003-Y.

Marland, P. W. 1993. 'A review of the literature on implications of teacher thinking research for preservice teacher education'. *South Pacific Journal of Teacher Education* 21(1): 51–63. DOI: https://doi.org/10.1080/0311213930210107.

Marsh, D. 1994. *Bilingual Education and Content and Language Integrated Learning*. International Association for Cross-cultural Communication, Language Teaching in the Member States of the European Union (Lingua) Paris: University of Sorbonne.

Martin, P. 2014 'Teachers in transition: The road to EAP'. In *Cases on Teacher Identity, Diversity, and Cognition in Higher Education*, edited by P. Breen.. Hershey, PA: IGI Global.

Marx, R. W., P. C. Blumenfeld, J. S. Krajcik, and E. Soloway. 1998. New technologies for teacher professional development. *Teaching and Teacher Education* 14(1): 33–52.

Mason, J. 1996. *Qualitative Research*. London: Sage Publications.

Mason, R. 1998. 'Models of online courses'. *ALN magazine* 2(2): 1–10.

Mauthner, N. S., and A. Doucet. 2003. 'Reflexive accounts and accounts of reflexivity in qualitative data analysis'. *Sociology* 37(3): 413–431. DOI: https://doi.org/10.1177/00380385030373002.

Mayer, R. E. 2005. 'Cognitive theory of multimedia learning'. In *The Cambridge Handbook of Multimedia Learning*, edited by R. Meyer: pp. 31–48. New York: Cambridge University Press.

Mazur, E. 1997. 'Peer instruction: Getting students to think in class'. In *The Changing Role of Physics Departments in Modern Universities, AIP Conference Proceedings 399*.

Mead, M. 1936 [1928]. *Coming of Age in Samoa: A Psychological Study of Primitive Youth for Western Civilization*. New York: Blue Ribbon books.

Meltzer, J. 2010. *Five Research-Based Approaches to Teacher Development*. Public consultancy document accessed at: http://www.publicconsulting group.com/poland/en/resources/articles/Approaches to Teacher Development_ EN.pdf

Mercer, J. 2007. 'The challenges of insider research in educational institutions: Wielding a double-edged sword and resolving delicate dilemmas'. *Oxford Review of Education* 33(1): 1–17. DOI: https://doi.org/10.1080/03054980601094651.

Merriam Webster Dictionary. 2016. Accessed at https://www.merriam-webster.com on 30 November.

Merton, R. 1972. 'Insiders and outsiders: A chapter in the sociology of knowledge'. *American Journal of Sociology* 78(July): 9–47. DOI: https://doi.org/10.1086/225294.

Miles, M. B., and A. M. Huberman. 1994. *Qualitative Data Analysis: An Expanded Sourcebook*. Thousand Oaks, CA: Sage Publications.

Miller, J., and B. Glassner. 1997. 'The 'inside' and the 'outside': Finding realities in interviews'. In *Qualitative Research: Theory, Method and Practice*, edited by D. Silverman. London: Sage Publications.

Mishra, P., and M. Koehler. 2006. 'Technological pedagogical content knowledge: A framework for teacher knowledge'. *The Teachers College Record* 108(6): 1017–54

Mishra, P., and M. Koehler. 2012. 'TPACK model 2012 version'. Accessed at www.tpack.org.

Monahan, T. 2005. *Globalization, Technological Change and Public Education*. New York: Routledge.

Moore, B. 2007. 'Original sin and insider research'. *Action Research*, 5(1): 27- 39. DOI: https://doi.org/10.1177/1476750307072874.

Mortimer, B. 1997. 'Portraits of the Postmodern Person in 'Taxi Driver', 'Raging Bull', and 'The King of Comedy''. *Journal of Film and Video*: 28–38.

Motteram, G. 2004. 'Blended education and the transformation of teachers: A long-term case study in postgraduate UK higher education'. Paper presented at Network Learning Conference (2004).

Motteram, G., and P. Sharma. 2009. 'Blending learning in a web 2.0 world'. *International Journal of Emerging Technologies and Society* 7(2): 83–96.

Motteram G. 2013. 'Developing and extending our understanding of language learning and technology'. In *Innovations in Learning Technologies for English Language Teaching*, edited by G. Motteram: pp 175–91. London: British Council.

Munro, R. K. 2010. 'Setting a new course for research on information technology in education'. In *Researching IT in Education: Theory, Practice, and Future Directions*, edited by A. McDougall, J. Murnane, A. Jones, and N. Reynolds, pp.46–53. New York, NY: Routledge.

Murphy, E. and M. Rodriguez-Manzanares. 2008. 'Contradictions between the virtual and physical high school classroom: A third-generation Activity Theory perspective'. *British Journal of Educational Technology* 39(6): 1061–72. DOI: https://doi.org/10.1111/j.1467–8535.2007.00776.x.

Nidumolu, S.R., M. Subramani, and A. Aldrich. 2001. 'Situated learning and the situated knowledge web: Exploring the ground beneath knowledge management'. *Journal of Management Information Systems* 18(1): 115–150.

Nisbet, J., and J. Watt. 1984. 'Case study': In *Conducting Small-Scale Investigations in Educational Management*, edited by J. Bell, T. Bush, A. Fox, J. Goodey and S. Goulding: pp. 79–92. London: Harper & Row.

Njenga, J. K., and L. C. H. Fuerte. 2010. 'The myths about e-learning in higher education'. *British Journal of Educational Technology* 41(2): 191–212. DOI: https://doi.org/10.1111/j.1467–8535.2008.00910.x.

Oliver, M., and K. Trigwell. 2005. 'Can 'blended learning' be redeemed'. *E-learning*, 2(1): 17–26. DOI: https://doi.org/10.2304/elea.2005.2.1.17.

Onwuegbuzie, A. J., W. B. Dickinson, N. L. Leech, and A. G. Zoran. 2009. A qualitative framework for collecting and analyzing data in focus group research. *International Journal of Qualitative Methods* 8(3): 1–21. DOI: https://doi.org/10.1177/160940690900800301.

Oshima, A., and A. Hogue. 2007. *Introduction to Academic Writing*. Harlow: Longman.

Pajares, M. F. 1992. 'Teachers' beliefs and educational research: Cleaning up a messy construct'. *Review of Educational Research* 62(3): 307–32. DOI: https://doi.org/10.3102/00346543062003307.

Papert, S. 1987. 'Computer criticism vs. technocentric thinking'. *Educational Researcher* 16(1): 22–30. DOI: https://doi.org/10.3102/0013189X016001022.

Patton, M. 1990. *Qualitative Evaluation and Research Methods*, pp. 169–186. Beverly Hills, CA: Sage Publications.

Pennington, M.C. 1990. 'A professional development focus for the language teaching practicum.' In *Second Language Teacher Education*, edited by J. C. Richards and D. Nunan. pp.132–151. Cambridge: Cambridge University Press.

Pennycook, A. 1997. 'Vulgar pragmatism, critical pragmatism, and EAP'. *English for Specific Purposes* 16(4): 253–269. DOI: https://doi.org/10.1016/S0889–4906(97)00019–7.

Pennycook, A. 2017. *The Cultural Politics of English as an International Language*. Abingdon: Routledge.

Piaget, J. 1959. *The Language and Thought of the Child* (Vol. 5) Translated by M. and R. Gabain. London: Routledge and Kegan Paul.

Piaget, J. 1970. *Genetic Epistemology*. Trans. E. New York, Columbia University Press.

Pierson, M., and A. Borthwick. 2010. 'Framing the assessment of educational technology professional development in a culture of learning'. *Journal of Computing in Teacher Education* 26(4): 126–131. DOI: https://doi.org/10.1080/10402454.2010.10784645.

Pim, C. 2013. 'Emerging technologies, emerging minds: Digital innovations within the primary sector'. In *Innovations in Learning Technologies for English Language Teaching*, edited by G. Motteram, *pp. 175–91*. London: British Council.

Platt, J. 1981. 'On interviewing one's peers'. *The British Journal of Sociology*, 32(1): 75–91.

Poland, B. 1995. 'Transcription quality as an aspect of rigor in qualitative research'. *Qualitative Inquiry* 1(3): 290–310. DOI: https://doi.org/10.1177/107780049500100302.

Postman, N. 1992. *Technopoly: The Surrender of Culture to Technology*. New York: Vintage Books.

Prensky, M. 2001. 'Digital natives, digital immigrants part 1'. *On The Horizon* 9(5): 1–6. DOI: https://doi.org/10.1108/10748120110424816.

Raimes, A. 1991 'Instructional balance: From theory to practices in the theory of writing'. In *Georgetown University Round Table on Languages and Linguistics: Linguistics and Language Pedagogy: The State of the Art* edited by J. E. Alatis, pp. 238–249. Washington DC: Georgetown University Press.

Reason, P. and J. Rowan. eds. 1981. *Human Inquiry: A Sourcebook Of New Paradigm Research*. Chichester: John Wiley & Sons.

Richards, J. C. 2008. 'Second language teacher education today'. *RELC Journal* 39(2): 158–177. DOI: https://doi.org/10.1177/0033688208092182

Richards, J. C. and T. S. C. Farrell. (Eds.). 2005. *Professional Development for Language Teachers: Strategies for Teacher Learning*. New York: Cambridge University Press.

Richards, J. C. and T. S. Rodgers. 2014. *Approaches and Methods in Language Teaching*, 3rd edition. Cambridge: Cambridge University Press.

Richardson, S., and M. McMullan. 2007. 'Research ethics in the UK: What can sociology learn from health?' *Sociology* 41(6): 1115–32. DOI: https://doi.org/10.1177/0038038507082318.

Robb, T. 2004. 'Moodle: A virtual learning environment for the rest of us'. *TESL-EJ* 8(2): 1–8.

Roberts, C. 1997. 'Transcribing talk: Issues of representation'. *TESOL Quarterly* 31: 167–171.

Roberts, J. 1998. *Language Teacher Education*. London: Arnold.

Robson, C. 2002. *Real World Research*. Oxford: Blackwell Publishing.

Roehler, L. R., G. G. Duffy, B. A. Herrmann, M. Conley, and J. Johnson. 1988. 'Knowledge structures as evidence of the 'personal:' Bridging the gap from thought to practice'. *Journal of Curriculum Studies*, 20: 159–165. DOI: https://doi.org/10.1080/0022027880200206.

Rogers, J. 2000. 'Communities of Practice: A framework for fostering coherence in virtual learning communities'. *Educational Technology and Society* 3(3).

Romeo, G., and G. Russell. 2010. 'Why 'what works' is not enough for information technology in education research'. In *Researching IT in Education: Theory, Practice, and Future Directions*, edited by A. McDougall, J. Murnane, A. Jones, and N. Reynolds, p. 54 New York: Routledge.

Rubin L. 1978. *The In-Service Education of Teachers: Trends, Process and Prescriptions*. Boston, MA: Allyn and Bacon.

Salmon, G. 2000. *E-Moderating*. Kogan Page: London.

Samaras, A.P., and S. Gismondi. 1998. 'Scaffolds in the field: Vygotskian Interpretation in a Teacher Education Program'. *Teaching and Teacher Education*, 14(7): 715–733.

Sams, A., and J. Bergmann. 2012. *Flip Your Classroom: Reach Every Student in Every Class Every Day*. Alexandria, VA: International Society for Technology in Education.

Schwerdtfeger, P. 2011. 'In the year of chemistry: From Mendeleev to Albert Einstein–the periodic table of the elements and beyond'. *Chemistry in New Zealand*, April.

Schön, D. A. 1983. *The Reflective Practitioner: How Professionals Think in Action*. New York: Basic Books.

Schlager, M. S., and J. Fusco. 2003. 'Teacher professional development, technology, and communities of practice: Are we putting the cart before the horse?' *The Information Society* 19: 203–220. DOI: https://doi.org/10.1080/01972240309464.

Schwab, J. J. 1972. 'Structure of the disciplines: Meaning and significances'. In J. M. Rich (ed.), *Readings in the Philosophy of Education*. Wadsworth: California.

Scott, S. 1985. 'Working through the contradictions in researching postgraduate education'. In R. Burgess, (Ed). *Field Methods in the Study of Education*. Lewes: Falmer Press.

Seawright, J., and J. Gerring. 2008. 'Case selection techniques in case study research: A menu of qualitative and quantitative options'. *Political Research Quarterly* 61(2): 294–308. DOI: https://doi.org/10.1177/1065912907313077.

Seed, J. 1958. *The Jimmy Seed Story*. London: Phoenix Books.

Selwyn, N. 2010. *Schools and Schooling in the Digital Age: A Critical Analysis*. Abingdon: Routledge.

Shakespeare, W. 1998 [1606]. *The Tragedy of Macbeth*. (Ed.) Nicholas Brooke. Oxford: Oxford University Press.

Sheard, C. M. 1993. 'Kairos and Kenneth Burke's psychology of political and social communication'. *College English* 55: 291–310.

Shulman, L. 1986, 'Those who understand: Knowledge growth in teaching'. *Educational Researcher* 15(24): pp. 4–14. DOI: https://doi.org/10.3102/0013189X015002004.

Shulman, L. S. 1987. 'Knowledge and teaching: Foundations of the new reform'. *Harvard Educational* Review, 57(1): 1–23. DOI: https://doi.org/10.17763/haer.57.1.j463w79r56455411

Shulman, L. S. 2012. PCK Summit Keynote Speech. *PCK Summit 2012 – PCK Reflections After 25 Years*. Colorado Springs, USA 20–26 October. Proceedings accessed 25-07-14 at http://pcksummit.bscs.org

Silverman, D. 2005. *Doing Qualitative Research: A Practical Handbook*. London: Sage Publications.

Simmel, G. 1950. 'The Stranger'. In *The Sociology Of Georg Simmel*: pp 402–08. New York: Free Press.

Simons, H. 2009. *Case Study Research in Practice*. London: Sage Publications.

Slaouti, D., G. Motteram, and Z. Onat-Stelma. 2013. 'Technology and adult language teaching'. In Motteram, G. (ed.) *Innovations in Learning Technologies for English Language Teaching*. London: British Council.

Sloan, D., and E. Porter. 2010. 'Changing international student and business staff perceptions of in-sessional EAP: Using the CEM model'. *Journal of English for Academic Purposes* 9(3): 198–210. DOI: https://doi.org/10.1016/j.jeap.2010.03.001.

Sloman, J. and A. Wride. 2009. *Economics*. Harlow: Pearson

Soffer, O. and Y. Eshet-Alkalai. 2009. 'Back to the future: An historical perspective on the pendulum-like changes in literacy'. *Minds and Machines, 19*(1): 47–59. DOI: https://doi.org/10.1007/s11023–008-9119–1.

Sokol, M. 2011. 'Delta is equal to a masters, says regulator'. *EL Gazette*. Accessed at: http://mag.digitalpc.co.uk

Spires, H., E. Wiebe, C. Young, K. Hollebrands, and J. Lee. 2009. 'Toward a new learning ecology: Teaching and learning in one-to-one learning environments'. *Friday Institute White Paper Series*. NC State University: Raleigh, NC. Retrieved from http://www.fi.ncsu.edu/ podcast/white-paper-series/2009/04/22/toward- a-new-learning-ecology/

Spires, H. A., M. Zheng, and M. Pruden. 2012. 'New technologies, new horizons: Graduate student views on creating their technological pedagogical content knowledge (TPACK)'. In *Student Reactions To Learning With Technologies: Perceptions And Outcomes*, edited by K. Moyle and G. Wijngaards: pp. 23–41. Hershey, PA: IGI Global.

Spiro, R. J. and J. Jehng. 1990. 'Cognitive flexibility and hypertext: Theory and technology for the non-linear and multidimensional traversal of complex subject matter'. In *Cognition, Education, and Multimedia*, edited by D. Nix and R. Spiro: pp. 163–205. Hillsdale, NJ: Erlbaum.

Stake, R. E. 1995. *The Art of Case Study Research*. Thousand Oaks, CA: Sage.

Stenhouse, L. 1975. *An Introduction to Curriculum Research and Development* (Vol. 46). London: Heinemann.

Stevick, E. W. 1996. *Memory, Meaning and Method*. Boston, MA: Heinle & Heinle.

Stoll, C. 1996. *Silicon Snake Oil: Second Thoughts on the Information Highway*. New York: Anchor Books.

Strevens, P. 1974. 'Some basic principles of teacher training'. ELT Journal, 29(1): 19–27. DOI: https://doi.org/10.1093/elt/29.1.19.

Sykes, G. 1996. 'Reform of and as professional development'. *Phi Delta Kappan, 77*(7): 465–467.

Tapscott, D. 1998. *Growing up Digital: The Rise of the Net Generation*. New York: McGraw-Hill.

Taxi Driver. (Schrader, P., M. E. Phillips, M. Scorsese, and B. Herrmann). 1976. Gaumont Columbia Tristar Home Vidéo.

Teddlie, C., and A. Tashakkori (editors). 2009. *Foundations of Mixed Methods Research: Integrating Quantitative and Qualitative Approaches in the Social and Behavioral Sciences*. Thousand Oaks, CA: Sage Publications.

Thornbury, S. 2000. 'A dogma for EFL'. *IATEFL Issues*, 153(2).

Thorpe, M. 2002. 'Rethinking learner support: The challenge of collaborative online learning'. *Open Learning* 7(2): 105–20. DOI: https://doi.org/10.1080/02680510220146887a.

Tomlinson, B. 2003a. 'Humanising the coursebook'. *Anthology Series-Seameo Regional Language Centre*: 12–29.

Tomlinson, B. 2003b. 'Developing materials to develop yourself'. *Humanising Language Teaching* 5(4), July.

Tomlinson, B. 2012. 'Materials development for language learning and teaching'. *Language Teaching* 45(2): 143–179. DOI: https://doi.org/10.1017/S0261444811000528.

Trilling, B., and C. Fadel. 2009. *21st Century Skills: Learning for Life in Our Times*. San Francisco, CA: Jossey-Bass.

Tucker, B. 2012. 'The flipped classroom'. *Education Next* 12(1): 82–83.

Tuckman, B. W. 1965. 'Developmental sequence in small groups'. *Psychological Bulletin* 63(6): 384. DOI: https://doi.org/10.1037/h0022100.

Valiathan, P. 2002. *Blended Learning Models*. Retrieved originally July 2006 from: http://www.learningcircuits.org/2002/aug2002/valiathan.html

Velliaris, D. and C. Willis. 2014. 'Getting personal: An autoethnographic study of the professional identit(ies) of lecturers in an Australian pathway institution'. In *Cases on Teacher Identity, Diversity, and Cognition in Higher Education*, edited by P. Breen. Hershey, PA: IGI Global.

Von Trier, L., and T. Vinterberg. 2002. 'Dogme 95: The Vow of Chastity'. In *The European Cinema Reader*, edited by C. Fowler, p. 83. London: Routledge.

Vygotsky, L. S. 1978 [c.1934]. *Mind in Society: The Development of Higher Psychological Processes* (Trans. A. R. Luria, M. Lopez-Morillas and M. Cole [with J. V. Wertsch], Cambridge, Mass: Harvard University Press.

Wallace, M. J. 1991. *Training Foreign Language Teachers: A Reflective Approach*. Cambridge: Cambridge University Press.

Wallop, H. 2010. 'Royal Wedding: four bank holidays in 11 days'. *The Daily Telegraph*, 23 November. Available at http://www.telegraph.co.uk/news/uknews/royal-wedding/8154445/Royal-Wedding-four-bank-holidays-in-11-days.html

Ward, C., and S. Kushner-Benson. 2010. 'Developing new schemas for online teaching and learning: TPACK'. *MERLOT Journal of Online Learning and Teaching* 6(2).

Warschauer, M. 1996. 'Computer-assisted language learning: An introduction'. In *Multimedia Language Teaching*, edited by S. Fotos: pp.3–20.

Tokyo: Logos International. Available at https://www.ict4lt.org/en/warschauer.htm

Warschauer, M. 2000. 'T'he changing global economy and the future of English teaching'. *TESOL Quarterly* 34 (3): 531–555. DOI: https://doi.org/10.2307/3587741.

Warschauer, M. 2002. 'A developmental perspective on technology in language education'. *TESOL Quarterly* 36(3): 453–475. DOI: https://doi.org/10.2307/3588421.

Warschauer, M. 2003 'Demystifying the digital divide'. *Scientific American* 289(2).

Warschauer, M., and D. Healey. 1998 'Computers and language learning: An overview'. *Language Teaching* 31(2): 57–71. DOI: https://doi.org/10.1017/S0261444800012970.

Warschauer, M., and C. Meskill. 2000. 'Technology and second language teaching'. In Rosenthal, J. W. *Handbook of Undergraduate Second Language Education*, pp. 303–318. Mahwah, NJ: Lawrence Erlbuam.

Watson, J. 2012. 'An A-Z of technologies'. Opening keynote speech. BALEAP PIM 10 November, Avenue Campus, University of Southampton.

Watson-Gegeo, K. A. 1988. 'Ethnography in ESL: Defining the essentials'. *Tesol Quarterly 22*(4): 575–92. DOI: https://doi.org/10.2307/3587257.

Watson-Todd, R. 2003. *EAP or TEAP? Journal of English for Academic Purposes* 2(2): 147–56. DOI: https://doi.org/10.1016/S1475–1585(03)00014–6.

Wayne's World. 1992. Screenplay by Myers, M., Turner, B. and Turner, T. Directed by Penelope Spheeris. Paramount Pictures.

Wenger, E. 1998. *Communities of Practice: Learning, Meaning, And Identity*. Cambridge: Cambridge University Press.

Wenger, E. 2000. Communities of practice and social learning systems. *Organization* 7(2): pp.225–46. DOI: https://doi.org/10.1177/135050840072002.

Wenger, E. and W. Snyder. 2000 'Communities of practice: The organizational frontier'. *Harvard Business Review*. January-February: 139–145.

Wenger, E., R. McDermott, and W. M. Snyder. 2002. 'Seven principles for cultivating communities of practice'. In *Cultivating Communities of Practice: A Guide to Managing Knowledge*, 49–64. Boston: Harvard Business School Press.

White, C. 2003. *Language Learning in Distance Education*. Cambridge: Cambridge University Press.

Williams, C. L. 1996. 'Dealing with the data: Ethical issues in case study research'. In *Ethics and Representation in Qualitative Studies of Literacy*, edited by P. Mortensen and G. E. Kirsch, 40–57. Urbana, IL: National Council of Teachers of English.

Wilson, S. M. and J. Berne. 1999) 'Teacher learning and the acquisition of professional knowledge: An examination of research on contemporary professional development'. *Review of Research in Education* 24(1): 173–209.

Wiseman, J.P. and M. S. Aron. 1972. *Field Reports in Sociology*. London: Transworld Publishers.

Yin, R. K. 2009. *Case Study Research: Design and Methods* (Vol. 5). Los Angeles, CA: Sage.

Yinger, R.J. 1986. 'Examining thought in action: A theoretical and methodological critique of research on interactive teaching.' *Teaching and Teacher Education*, 2(3): 263–82. DOI: https://doi.org/10.1016/S0742–051X(86)80007–5.

Young, J. 2005. 'On insiders (emic) and outsiders (etic): Views of self, and othering.' *Systemic Practice and Action Research* 18(2), 151–62. DOI: https://doi.org/10.1007/s11213–005-4155–8.

Zhao, Y., KJ. Pugh, S. Sheldon, and J. Byers. 2002. 'Conditions for classroom technology innovations.' *The Teachers College Record* 104(3): 482–515.

Zimbardo, P. G. 1972. Stanford Prison Experiment: A Simulation Study of the Psychology of Imprisonment. Philip G. Zimbardo Incorporated.

Zuber-Skerritt, O. (Ed.). 1991. *Action Research for Change and Development* (Vol. 1). Aldershot: Avebury.

Printed and bound by CPI Group (UK) Ltd, Croydon, CR0 4YY

07/07/2026

14916228-0001